# ATLA MONOGRAPH SERIES

1. Ronald L. Grimes. *The Divine Imagination: William Blake's Major Prophetic Visions.* 1972.
2. George D. Kelsey. *Social Ethics among Southern Baptists, 1917–1969.* 1973.
3. Hilda Adam Kring. *The Harmonists: A Folk-Cultural Approach.* 1973.
4. J. Steven O'Malley. *Pilgrimage of Faith: The Legacy of the Otterbeins.* 1973.
5. Charles Edwin Jones. *Perfectionist Persuasion: The Holiness Movement and American Methodism, 1867–1936.* 1974.
6. Donald E. Byrne Jr. *No Foot of Land: Folklore of American Methodist Itinerants.* 1975.
7. Milton C. Sernett. *Black Religion and American Evangelicalism: White Protestants, Plantation Missions, and the Flowering of Negro Christianity, 1787–1865.* 1975.
8. Eva Fleischner. *Judaism in German Christian Theology Since 1945: Christianity and Israel Considered in Terms of Mission.* 1975.
9. Walter James Lowe. *Mystery & the Unconscious: A Study in the Thought of Paul Ricoeur.* 1977.
10. Norris Magnuson. *Salvation in the Slums: Evangelical Social Work, 1865–1920.* 1977.
11. William Sherman Minor. *Creativity in Henry Nelson Wieman.* 1977.
12. Thomas Virgil Peterson. *Ham and Japheth: The Mythic World of Whites in the Antebellum South.* 1978.
13. Randall K. Burkett. *Garveyism as a Religious Movement: The Institutionalization of a Black Civil Religion.* 1978.
14. Roger G. Betsworth. *The Radical Movement of the 1960s.* 1980.
15. Alice Cowan Cochran. *Miners, Merchants, and Missionaries: The Roles of Missionaries and Pioneer Churches in the Colorado Gold Rush and Its Aftermath, 1858–1870.* 1980.
16. Irene Lawrence. *Linguistics and Theology: The Significance of Noam Chomsky for Theological Construction.* 1980.
17. Richard E. Williams. *Called and Chosen: The Story of Mother Rebecca Jackson and the Philadelphia Shakers.* 1981.
18. Arthur C. Repp Sr. *Luther's Catechism Comes to America: Theological Effects on the Issues of the Small Catechism Prepared in or for America prior to 1850.* 1982.
19. Lewis V. Baldwin. *"Invisible" Strands in African Methodism.* 1983.
20. David W. Gill. *The Word of God in the Ethics of Jacques Ellul.* 1984.
21. Robert Booth Fowler. *Religion and Politics in America.* 1985.

22. Page Putnam Miller. *A Claim to New Roles*. 1985.
23. C. Howard Smith. *Scandinavian Hymnody from the Reformation to the Present*. 1987.
24. Bernard T. Adeney. *Just War, Political Realism, and Faith*. 1988.
25. Paul Wesley Chilcote. *John Wesley and the Women Preachers of Early Methodism*. 1991.
26. Samuel J. Rogal. *A General Introduction of Hymnody and Congregational Song*. 1991.
27. Howard A. Barnes. *Horace Bushnell and the Virtuous Republic*. 1991.
28. Sondra A. O'Neale. *Jupiter Hammon and the Biblical Beginnings of African-American Literature*. 1993.
29. Kathleen P. Deignan. *Christ Spirit: The Eschatology of Shaker Christianity*. 1992.
30. D. Elwood Dunn. *A History of the Episcopal Church in Liberia*. 1992.
31. Terrance L. Tiessen. *Irenaeus on the Salvation of the Unevangelized*. 1993.
32. James E. McGoldrick. *Baptist Successionism: A Crucial Question in Baptist History*. 1994.
33. Murray A. Rubinstein. *The Origins of the Anglo-American Missionary Enterprise in China, 1807–1840*. 1996.
34. Thomas M. Tanner. *What Ministers Know: A Qualitative Study of Pastors as Information Professionals*. 1994.
35. Jack A. Johnson-Hill. *I-Sight: The World of Rastafari: An Interpretive Sociological Account of Rastafarian Ethics*. 1995.
36. Richard James Severson. *Time, Death, and Eternity: Reflections on Augustine's "Confessions" in Light of Heidegger's "Being and Time."* 1995.
37. Robert F. Scholz. *Press toward the Mark: History of the United Lutheran Synod of New York and New England, 1830–1930*. 1995.
38. Sam Hamstra Jr. and Arie J. Griffioen. *Reformed Confessionalism in Nineteenth-Century America: Essays on the Thought of John Williamson Nevin*. 1996.
39. Robert A. Hecht. *An Unordinary Man: A Life of Father John LaFarge, S.J.* 1996.
40. Moses Moore. *Orishatukeh Faduma: Liberal Theology and Evangelical Pan-Africanism, 1857–1946*. 1996.
41. William Lawrence. *Sundays in New York: Pulpit Theology at the Crest of the Protestant Mainstream*. 1996.
42. Bruce M. Stephens. *The Prism of Time and Eternity: Images of Christ in American Protestant Thought from Jonathan Edwards to Horace Bushnell*. 1996.

43. Eleanor Bustin Mattes. *Myth for Moderns: Erwin Ramsdell Goodenough and Religious Studies in America, 1938–1955.* 1997.
44. Nathan D. Showalter. *The End of a Crusade: The Student Volunteer Movement for Foreign Missions and the Great War.* 1997.
45. Durrenda Onolehmemhen and Kebede Gessesse. *The Black Jews of Ethiopia: The Last Exodus.* 1998.
46. Thomas H. Olbricht and Hans Rollmann. *The Quest for Unity, Peace, and Purity in Thomas Campbell's* Declaration and Address, *Text and Studies.* 2000.
47. Douglas W. Geyer. *Fear, Anomaly, and Uncertainty in the Gospel of Mark.* 2002.
48. Ronald B. Flowers. *To Defend the Constitution: Religion, Conscientious Objection, Naturalization, and the Supreme Court.* 2002.
49. Julien R. Fielding. *Discovering World Religions at 24 Frames per Second.* 2009.
50. Joseph Dougherty. *From Altar-Throne to Table: The Campaign for Frequent Holy Communion in the Catholic Church.* 2010.

# From Altar-Throne to Table

## The Campaign for Frequent Holy Communion in the Catholic Church

Joseph Dougherty

*ATLA Monograph Series, No. 50*

THE SCARECROW PRESS, INC.
*Lanham, Maryland • Toronto • Plymouth, UK*
and
American Theological Library Association
2010

SCARECROW PRESS, INC.

Published in the United States of America
by Scarecrow Press, Inc.
A wholly owned subsidary of
The Rowman & Littlefield Publishing Group, Inc.
4501 Forbes Boulevard, Suite 200, Lanham, Maryland 20706
www.scarecrowpress.com

Estover Road, Plymouth PL6 7PY, United Kingdom

British Library Cataloguing in Publication Information Available

**Library of Congress Cataloging-in-Publication Data**

Dougherty, Joseph, 1953–
  From altar-throne to table : the campaign for frequent Holy Communion in the
Catholic Church / Joseph Dougherty.
     p. cm. — (ATLA monograph series ; no. 50)
  Includes bibliographical references.
  ISBN 978-0-8108-7164-9 (cloth : alk. paper) — ISBN 978-0-8108-7092-5 (ebook)
  1. Mass—Frequency of celebration. 2. Lord's Supper—Catholic Church. 3. Catholic
Church—Doctrines. I. Title.
  BX2236.6.D68 2010
  264'.02036—dc22                                                    2009044413

To the Brothers of the Christian Schools of the District of Baltimore
and its successor, the District of Eastern North America

*Live, Jesus, in our hearts forever!*

Did God mould up this Bread in Heaven, and bake,
Which from his Table came, and to thine goeth?
Doth he bespeake thee thus, This Soule Bread take.
Come eat thy fill of this thy Gods White Loafe?
Its Food too fine for Angells, yet come, take
And Eate thy fill. Its Heavens Sugar Cake.

—Edward Taylor

# Contents

Foreword                                                                    xi

Preface                                                                    xiii

Acknowledgments                                                           xix

Abbreviations                                                              xxi

Introduction                                                             xxiii

1   History of the Frequency of Holy Communion                             1

2   Prelude to Pope Pius X                                                 41

3   The Pope of Holy Communion                                            81

4   American Journals and Associations for Frequent Communion            111

5   Promotion of and Opposition to Frequent Communion                    139

6   Competition among Pieties                                            163

7   Theology, Liturgical and Systematic                                  195

Bibliography                                                             209

About the Author                                                         225

# Foreword

The ATLA Monograph Series has been in existence since 1972. Since the publication of the first volume in the series (*The Divine Imagination: William Blake's Major Prophetic Visions* by Ronald L. Grimes), the series has included a wide variety of topics in nearly every field of religious studies and theology. Most of the volumes have addressed specific issues in historical context, from biblical times to the contemporary world.

The current volume, Joseph Dougherty's book, *From Altar-Throne to Table: The Campaign for Frequent Holy Communion in the Catholic Church*, continues that tradition. From the very earliest days of the Christian Church there have been a variety of views about how frequently Christians should receive Communion. Dougherty's book surveys the history and the literature about the topic and describes the tensions that existed before and continued to exist after Pope Pius X's strong endorsement of daily communion being desirable for the faithful in his decree *Sacra Tridentina Synodus*.

Dougherty's thorough analysis of Communion frequency is a significant addition to the ATLA Monograph Series.

Dennis A. Norlin
Executive Director, American Theological Library Association

# Preface

This monograph began as an appropriately academic dissertation wrestling with two questions. The first was methodological: How would liturgical scholars investigate a tectonic change in the most important ritual of a Christian church if that change was not textual? For generations, historical liturgical study was perforce and fruitfully tied to ritual *texts*. The short answer to the first question is that we need to step outside the liturgical realm into the devotional, whose literary remains are available. The second was causative: Why did this particular change—frequent reception of Holy Communion—happen when and where it did? In fact, the faithful had been urged for well over a millennium to come to the table more often, but these exhortations were, with few exceptions, futile. The short answer is that the so-called restoration of frequent Holy Communion succeeded among English-speaking Roman Catholics in the United States largely because of extra-ecclesial factors, such as fraternalism (e.g., Masons, Elks, Shriners), assimilation of immigrants, and attitudes toward law in a democracy. Happily, the answer to the second question is found in a voluminous reading of the primary materials, which were developed largely for purposes of piety, of the campaign itself for frequent Holy Communion.[1]

The original plan of this study would have been limited to the campaign only in the United States. This case study of the success of the campaign in chapters 4, 5, and 6 depends largely upon the methodology pioneered in Ann Taves's *The Household of Faith: Roman Catholic Devotions in Mid-Nineteenth-Century America*. Her book depicts the creation of a Catholic subculture among English-speaking Americans in the nineteenth century. She achieves this perspective by deft analysis of a large body of popular devotional literature. The primary sources for my very restricted investigation thus logically were the periodicals of the Eucharistic movement (and hence of the campaign for frequent reception) in this country, the *Sentinel of the Blessed Sacrament* (*Ssac*) and *Emmanuel: Official Monthly of the Priests' Eucharistic League* (*EPUL*). Taves reminds us that "devotional literature tells us more about the beliefs of those who wrote and promoted it than about those for whom it was intended."[2] The fact is, however, that the campaign for frequent reception of Holy Communion did succeed here in America, and so the pious literature, mostly penned by the religious elite, must have played a role in reshaping the devotional lives and ritual practices of the faithful. These two magazines seem to have helped form Catholic religious practice that was official, clerically regulated, common among all immigrant Catholics (despite culture of origin), and essentially sacramental.

A case study solely of the American campaign for frequent Holy Communion proved infeasible because no historical context had been established and no theologically critical scholarship had treated the European origins of the campaign for more reception and more frequent reception. In an atmosphere of ultramontanism and of anti-intellectualism, especially after Pope Pius X's condemnations of Americanism and modernism, such a scholarly gap makes much sense.

Despite the great blossoming of the study of the liturgy since Vatican II, this book alone seeks to examine the campaign for frequent Holy Communion. Most American Catholics who are baby boomers or older express interest in the topic; most also correctly associate Pope Saint Pius X with frequent Communion. Younger Catholics are flabbergasted that Catholics for generations had received Holy Communion only annually. As this book demonstrates, Pius X's crucial decrees—*Sacra Tridentina Synodus* (*STS*, 1905) and its reinforcer, *Quam Singulari* (*QS*, 1910)—are the supreme accomplishments of the Eucharistic movement that arose in France and Belgium in the late nineteenth century. The apparent energies of this movement, coupled with the growing authoritarian style of the papacy, led to an emphatic papal declaration of the value of frequent Holy Communion and a radical simplification of the dispositions for the sacrament. Subsequently, writers such as Mother Mary Loyola, IVBM (d. 1930; a Sister of Loretto), and Father Joseph Kramp, SJ (d. 1940), articulated a liturgical theology that encouraged the laity to participate in the sacrifice of the altar *with* the priest—practically speaking, to receive Holy Communion during the Mass—and so anticipated the empowerment of the laity that became such a cherished outcome of the Second Vatican Council.

The matter of this book is largely historical and admittedly obscure. Not only do such celebrities as Cornelius Jansen and Saint Alphonsus Liguori appear, but also do some largely forgotten players such as Antonio de Molina

(d. 1612; *not* the Quietist Miguel de Molinos and *not* the economist Luis de Molina) and Jules Lintelo, SJ (d. 1917), the apostle of frequent Communion. Indeed, the proximate source of frequent Holy Communion among Roman Catholics is one Émilie Tamisier (d. 1910), a poor French laywoman whose vision of a new social order for France through devotion to the Eucharist gave rise to the Eucharistic movement. This movement engendered the campaign for frequent reception of the Body and Blood of Our Lord. Similarly, the case study of the campaign in the United States will summon such personages as John Francis O'Hara, CSC, of the University of Notre Dame (d. 1960; eventually cardinal archbishop of Philadelphia) and Camillus Paul Maes, bishop of Covington, Kentucky (d. 1915); from obscurity it will draw the founder of the Priest's Eucharistic League in the United States, Father Bede Maler, OSB (d. 1936), of Saint Meinrad's Archabbey in southern Indiana. Although the main purpose of this book is liturgical history, to do justice to the momentousness of the Catholics' return to the practice of frequent Holy Communion required elements of intellectual and social history, moral casuistry, biography, and cultural criticism. While the details may be daunting, the book confirms the theory that liturgical change, even completely nontextual change, starts at the margins.

Chapter 1 begins where a comprehensive history must, by perusing Communion frequency through the ages. In reality, this chapter traces the rapid decline of Communion and then the steady state of generally minimal recourse to the Eucharistic table.

Chapter 2 sets the stage for the undeniably pivotal figure, Pope Pius X. It examines Pope Leo XII's encyclical *Mirae Caritatis* (*MC*, 1902), which gives Leo some claim to the title "the pope of Holy Communion." It then probes the acrimonious and public dispute between two Belgian priests, François-Xavier Godts and Jules Lintelo, that occasioned the epochal *STS*. Here, the book becomes intellectual history, tracing the thoughts of the disputants and their forebears and champions. This body of literature is in French, and I am responsible for the translations. Finally, this chapter considers the heart of the question—the proper dispositions for reception of Holy Communion—and here the book intersects with moral theology.

Chapter 3 delves into the decree itself in its anticipations, its formulation, its interpretations, and its implementations. It also tries to reconstruct from very scant evidence the practical and reasonable opposition to the decree.

Chapter 4 then begins the historical narrative, in several chapters, of the critical moments of the campaign for frequent Communion among English-speaking Catholics in the United States. The geographic limitation of this section follows from the availability of both primary resources and excellent historical studies of American Catholicism. Because theology alone fails to explain this significant ritual modification, here is a social history of it.

The temporal limitation, from 1894 until 1926, makes sense for three reasons: While formulaic calls for greater frequency of Communion had sprung up in America and perhaps had prepared the way for the successful campaign of the twentieth century, *EPUL* was initiated at a meeting in March 1894, and it began publication with an issue in January 1895. The American Eucharistic movement began, then, in 1894.

Second, Communion piety was evidently beginning to supplant the Real Presence piety at the Twenty-Eighth International Eucharistic Congress at Chicago in 1926. Typical to the genre of Eucharistic congresses, and normal for any public extravaganza (such as fireworks), the most important event was the concluding exercise. Chicago's congress concluded with a procession and benediction at Mundelein Seminary, enhanced by a spectacular thundershower. But the congratulatory letter of Pope Pius XI to Cardinal Mundelein upon the conclusion of the congress specified that the million Communions deliberately generated by the congress, either locally in Chicago or in solidarity with it throughout the United States, were *the* highlight of the congress.[3] Third, that same year serves conventionally as the starting point for the American liturgical movement because of the founding of the periodical *Orate Fratres* by Virgil Michel.

In the United States, frequent Holy Communion is largely attributable to the campaign's official agents, the Priests' Eucharistic League (PEL) and the People's Eucharistic League (PPL). Chapter 4 depicts the publishing environment for their two magazines, the *Sentinel of the Blessed Sacrament* for the laity and *Emmanuel* for the clergy. This is necessary because they provide a convenient chronological record of the eucharistic leagues in the United States and the popular theology of the campaign. Then this chapter clarifies the terminology and institutional relationships of the PEL and the PPL, and also explains the original program of the PEL—namely, promoting a particular form of meditation, the Adoration, for use by the clergy.

Chapter 5 reveals four tactics of the campaign to promote frequent Holy Communion. These are, in brief, as follows: first, to trumpet the will of Rome regarding frequent Holy Communion; second, to sustain the lives of their own Eucharistic associations; third, to multiply clubs, unions, and bands that focus on frequent reception; fourth, to make frequent reception into a priority for groups that were otherwise concerned. The book also nods to the phenomenon of Communion breakfasts, which no doubt intended to and did contribute to popularizing receiving the sacrament among men; evidence for this phenomenon is regrettably meager. The chapter imagines explicit opposition to frequent Holy Communion and speculates on some cultural factors in the United States that may have slowed its implementation.

Chapter 6 examines the last and perhaps most interesting tactic to promote the seismic sacramental change: redirecting or "spinning" extant popular devotions such as those centered on Mary and the Sacred Heart into vehicles encouraging reception. It then concludes with a clear ranking of the benefits of popular devotions and sacramental practices, a ranking that demotes all particular ethnic devotions in favor of the unifying and clerically controlled reception of Holy Communion.

Chapter 7 focuses on the connection between frequent Holy Communion and the liturgical movement. It contrasts the then-standard apologetical definitions of the Eucharist with the practically sacramental and dynamic perspectives of a writer with his feet in both movements, Father Kramp. His essay treats when Communion should be received, and he pursues this ritual question to profound soteriological conclusions.

The modest but necessary goal of this monograph is identical to Philip Gleason's in his *Contending with Modernity: Catholic Higher Education in the Twentieth Century.* Gleason explains that the pioneering historian's task and service is to tell the story so that some "intelligible form" emerges. This form reveals a "developmental pattern that makes sense, draws the attention of other scholars to problematic features of the story, and invites further work to confirm or correct the interpretation offered here."[4] Because the phenomenon of more and more frequent Communions has been essentially ignored, I offer a preliminary investigation, and can hope that scholars will treat the same theme in other denominations, will analyze the Eucharistic Congresses for their ability to empower the laity, and so on. Unlike Gleason, who creates a fully realized picture of his topic, I am ambitious only to assemble part of the frame of this multidimensional puzzle.

## NOTES

1. *Campaign* in connection with the program of Pius X seems apt because it is the word that those who promoted frequent Communion used themselves, but the word has long been used in scholarship to describe similar movements. For example, L. Pérouas uses the French form of the word, *campagne,* to describe the promotion of monthly Communion in the diocese of La Rochelle at the turn of the eighteenth century. L. Pérouas, "La Pastorale liturgique au XVIIᵉ siècle," *Mélanges de science religieuse* 33 (1966): 42.

2. Ann Taves, *The Household of Faith: Roman Catholic Devotions in Mid-Nineteenth-Century America* (Notre Dame, Indiana: Notre Dame University Press, 1986), viii.

3. Quoted in Cornelius Francis Donovan, *The Story of the Twenty-Eighth International Eucharistic Congress Held at Chicago, Illinois, United States of America, from June 20–24, 1926* (Chicago: Eucharistic Congress Committee, 1927), 495.

4. Philip Gleason, *Contending with Modernity: Catholic Higher Education in the Twentieth Century* (New York: Oxford University Press, 1995), vii.

# Acknowledgments

A theological and devotional history, like a litany, begins by speaking many names in gratitude. Like the clement Church, however, it cannot name all for that would overwhelm the faithful.

I thank archivists and publishers for permission to use materials in their custody: Paul Bernier, SSS (Fathers of the Blessed Sacrament); Susan Brosnan (Knights of Columbus Supreme Archives); Wm. Kevin Cawley (University of Notre Dame, Indiana); Marietta Crahan, OSB (Benedictine Sisters of Perpetual Adoration); Cyprian Davis, OSB (Saint Meinrad Archabbey); Bernd Günther, SJ (German Province of the Society of Jesus); David Klingeman (Saints John's Abbey); and Hubert Ngueha (Catholic University of America Press).

The Benedictines, the Blessed Sacrament Fathers, the Priests of Holy Cross, the Dominicans, and the Brothers of the Christian Schools of Saint Mary's College High School, Berkeley, supported this work with their gracious and generous hospitality.

Surajit Bose, Kent Burreson, Mia Grogan, Gene Halus, Jim Lodwick, Craig Satterlee, and Walter Ray all helped me through the growing pains of this project. To the committee for the dissertation upon which this book is based—Michael Driscoll, Maxwell Johnson, John A. Melloh, SM, and Lawrence Cunningham—I owe special gratitude for their distinctive contributions and corrections. The late James F. White directed this research with patient confidence.

Supplemental research for this book was enabled by a generous grant from the Brother Damian Connelly Fund at La Salle University. I thank Mr. Jacques Moore for establishing this fund, and the provost of La Salle University, Richard A. Nigro, for his encouragement. La Salle University also allowed a sabbatical semester for the final preparation of the manuscript. The ultimate preparation of the manuscript was enthusiastically eased by the Brothers of the Christian Schools of La Salle College High School, Wyndmoor, Pennsylvania.

# Abbreviations

| | |
|---|---|
| *AM* | François-Xavier Godts, *L'apôtre moderne* |
| Bregenzer | Peter Bregenzer, "The Devotion to the Eucharistic Heart" |
| CEF | E. Dublanchy, "Communion eucharistique (fréquente)," *Dictionnaire de thèologie catholique* |
| Chinnici | Joseph Chinnici, "The Eucharist, Symbol of the Church" |
| *CS* | Eugene P. Willging and Herta Hatzfeld, *Catholic Serials of the Nineteenth Century in the United States: A Descriptive Bibliography and Union List* |
| DD | Casimir Gennari, "De la Communion fréquente et du décret 'Quemadmodum'" |
| Derély | J. M. Derély, "Les décrets eucharistiques du bienheureux Pie X," *Dictionnaire de spiritualité, ascètique et mystique, doctrine et histoire* |
| Dolan | Jay Dolan, *Catholic Revivalism: The American Experience, 1830-1900* |
| Duhr | Joseph Duhr, "Communion fréquente," *Dictionnaire de spiritualité, ascètique et mystique, doctrine et histoire* |
| *EH* | François-Xavier Godts, *Exagérations historiques* |
| *EPUL* | *Emmanuel: Official Monthly of the Priests' Eucharistic League* |
| Ferreres | Juan B[autista] Ferreres, *The Decree on Daily Communion: A Historical Sketch and Commentary* |
| Hardon | "Historical Antecedents of St. Pius X's Decree on Frequent Communion" |
| Knox | R[onald] A[rbuthnot] Knox, *Enthusiasm: A Chapter in the History of Religion, with Special Reference to the XVII and XVIII Centuries* |
| Lintelo | Jules Lintelo, *The Eucharistic Triduum* |

| | |
|---|---|
| *LP* | Jules Lintelo, *Lettres à un prêtre* |
| *MC* | *Mirae Caritatis* |
| MM | "The Priests' Communion League, Read at the Eucharistic Meeting of Metz" |
| *NCE* | *New Catholic Encyclopedia*, 1967 |
| PPL | People's Eucharistic League |
| PEL | Priests' Eucharistic League |
| Pope | Barbara Corrado Pope, "Immaculate and Powerful: The Marian Revival in the Nineteenth Century" |
| *QMM* | *Quemadmodum* |
| *QS* | *Quam Singulari* |
| *RL* | François-Xavier Godts, *Réponse aux lettres* |
| RPAT | Joseph Kramp, "A Religio-Psychological Attitude Toward the Eucharist" |
| Scannell | Thomas B. Scannell, "The History of Daily Communion" |
| *SOA* | Eamon Duffy, *The Stripping of the Altars: Traditional Religion in England, c. 1400–c.1580* |
| *SSac* | *Sentinel of the Blessed Sacrament* |
| *STS* | *Sacra Tridentina Synodus* |
| Taves | Ann Taves, *The Household of Faith: Roman Catholic Devotions in Mid-Nineteenth-Century America* |

# Introduction

This work of historical theology investigates a momentous change in the ritual actions of the Catholic liturgy. As Robert A. Taft, SJ, assesses it:

> The greatest and most successful liturgical reform in Catholic history is surely the movement for the restoration of frequent communion, sanctioned by Pius X in 1905. There are still pockets of resistance, and there are abuses, but nothing can detract from this great pastoral victory that has turned around fifteen centuries of devotional history in fifty years.[1]

This restoration has, however, surprisingly attracted scant attention from church historians and has been ignored by liturgical scholars, except periodically to celebrate it with a few glib remarks. This book seeks to detail the valorization of frequent, even daily, Holy Communion and to describe the tactics of the official campaign for frequent Communion in the United States of America in the first quarter of the twentieth century. For more than fifteen hundred years, Communion was received once a year. In fact, the decline of reception of Holy Communion seems, according to Taft, to be the cause of some changes in the texts of the Eucharistic liturgy, wherein, for example, a full psalm shrank to a mere antiphon.[2]

Most scholars agree that Communion reception has grown fairly constantly throughout the twentieth century.[3] Anecdotal evidence massively supports this conclusion. A prominent activist in the American liturgical movement, H. A. Reinhold, reported the following personal impressions on the frequency of Holy Communion since Pius X's *Sacra Tridentina Synodus (STS)*:[4]

> The number of individuals receiving Communion has risen since the day on which Pius X promulgated his famous Communion decrees. You see it at weekday Masses in our cities. You see evergrowing crowds thronging the altar

rails on first Fridays. You have a goodly number of regular communicants on
Sundays. Of course, not even the smuggest observer could say that we are any-
where near the ideal—Communion of all who participate in the Mass. But will
that ever be attained?[5]

Such testimonials could be multiplied ad infinitum. Similarly, innumerable
data-rich reports on the success of Communion campaigns in parishes, dioceses, and nations also attest to the efficacy of Pius's decrees. What a stark
contrast in ritual practice thus presents itself: The imaginary parish priest in
1890 at the early Sunday morning Mass would see a congregation of one
hundred and distribute Communion to three; one hundred years later, the
priest would see one hundred people in the congregation, with ninety-two
receiving Communion.

But oceans of propaganda for and mountains of testimonials in confirmation of a fundamental change in sacramental practice do not explain this
change. Deep resistance to *STS* was actually expected. This is why the pope
insisted upon its implementation heavy-handedly. The text specifically mandated both that all disputation about the frequency of Communion stop and
that the decree itself be translated into the vernacular and read aloud in all
religious houses during the octave of the feast of Corpus Christi. Frequent
Communion, once it was embraced and promulgated by Saint Pius X, was
never opposed in print. The secondary literature at best only hints at opposition. For example, without elaboration, the *New Catholic Encyclopedia*
biography of Pius X reported that his second major Eucharistic decree, *Quam
Singulari (QS)*, "demolished the apprehensive resistance" that met the pope's
efforts to increase the use of Communion.[6] Similarly, H. A. Reinhold referred
to the lack of public opposition from the clergy when he praised the efficacy
of Pius's agenda, saying that "the roadblock of unauthorized custom and
tradition was swept out of the way [by Pius X]. But as we know, even as
obedient a Church as the Catholic Church will take a long time to carry out
as sweeping a return as one deemed by the Pontiff."[7] The "long time" indicates Reinhold's awareness of the Church's natural inertia, which greets any
impulse for change in tradition and hallowed ritual performance.

On the other hand, many impressionistic and transparently propagandistic
accounts of the triumphs of campaigns for frequent Communion exist. Specific instances of the difficulties of implementing the decree often remain
buried.

It would be difficult to say exactly [how much resistance there was to the restoration of frequent communion], but from all indications there was much neglect.
For instance, Father Fidelis Busam, OSB, of St. Vincent Archabbey, complained

in a letter to [Virgil] Michel on December 14, 1926, that "there are not many pastors who observe the decree of Pius X on frequent and daily communion."[8]

Also, that so many of the papers at the meetings of the Priests' Eucharistic League detailed schemes for increasing the numbers of Communions itself points to the difficulties in changing a deeply ingrained and admittedly ancient ritual.

The evidence suggests, then, that Communion only gradually became frequent and habitual, that is, weekly, in the United States among the English-speaking, churchgoing laity. Indeed, an official American episcopal document, by clarifying the need for juridical worthiness to approach the Eucharistic table, suggests that the campaign has been too successful in that Holy Communion has become casual. In other words, "Happy Are Those Who Are Called to His Supper" (2006) reiterates the ancient teaching that only those in the state of grace may receive.[9] Anecdotal evidence indicates, however, that Communion has never become so frequent in more tradition-bound regions and cultures, where custom dictated the infrequency, and correlative paucity, of lay Communion.

For example, in the summer of 1995, Peter Jurcik, a priest ordained in 1993 for the diocese of Spisska, Slovakia, and now incardinated in the diocese of Allentown, Pennsylvania, explained to me that, in his home diocese, the first Friday of the month was still Communion day—so much so that hearing confessions occupied the bulk of the priest's Thursday. Rare indeed were the communicants at the Sunday Mass in his diocese, he added. Thus, among practicing and observant Catholics, at least in this Slovak diocese, *monthly* Communion seemed usual, and even this was a great advance over the practice of yesteryear. In the same vein, several pastors, experienced in both Mexican and Mexican American parishes, report that, unless and until priests and bishops vigorously promote frequent reception of Communion, it will remain rare in these cultures. Still, Holy Communion is generally regarded as much more frequent in the early twenty-first century throughout the world than it had been for the previous fifteen hundred years.

Has, in fact, frequent Communion has been restored? Essentially, the restoration pertains to the laity, and the term *frequent* describes a relative condition. Further, greater frequency of reception logically implies a perceptible and numerical increase in the numbers of Communion hosts distributed— thus more Communions. Because Pius X is indisputably pivotal in the alleged restoration, let him assess its success.

According to the precise terms of *STS*, the keystone of Pope Pius X's Eucharistic—and hence, liturgical—program, Holy Communion has not become sufficiently frequent because it is not yet received daily by the majority of the laity. The Sacred Congregation of the Council during Pius X's pontificate merely proscribed forbidding daily Communion:

> Frequent and daily Communion, as a practice most earnestly desired by Christ our Lord and by the Catholic Church, should be open to all the faithful, of whatever rank and condition of life; so that no one who is in the state of grace, and who approaches the holy table with a right and devout intention . . . can be prohibited therefrom.[10]

The Eucharistic decrees and actions that surround *STS*, however, left no doubt that the pope intended a positive campaign to encourage universal and daily recourse to the Lord's Table. The revolutionary "restoration" of frequent Holy Communion has been met, certainly, in the area of our focused investigation, among English-speaking citizens of the United States, where Communion is weekly among those who attend Sunday Mass. The more dramatic goal of daily Communion remains largely unattained. Furthermore, this book hopes to encourage investigations of Communion practices in other cultural spheres so that Pius's achievement can be properly evaluated.

The campaign for frequent reception of Holy Communion is clearly a product of the lay Eucharistic movement that began in France. Its arguable starting date is 1881, when the first international Eucharistic congress was held. The Eucharistic movement commands our attention also because it bolstered the liturgical movement. The latter has been studied profitably but monolithically. In fact, in attracting scholarly attention, the liturgical movement has completely overshadowed the Eucharistic movement. The latter aided the liturgical movement by arguing for frequent Communion from the texts of the Mass itself. The epitome of the argument for the Communion of the people was the use of the first-person plural consistently, for example, *Orate, fratres,* ("Let *us* pray, brothers. . ."). Argument from these liturgical texts likewise characterized the liturgical movement and encouraged its own campaign for the verbalization of the texts by the laity and, eventually, vernacularization. Methodologically and strategically, therefore, the liturgical movement and the Eucharistic movement reinforced each other.

Chronologically, the international Eucharistic congresses also prepared the way for the popular acceptance of the liturgical movement, simply by virtue of their publicity. Publicity was the whole point of the congresses, for they had been initiated by pious French laity to exalt extraliturgical and paraliturgical devotions to the Real Presence on a massive scale and for the express purpose of counteracting the secularization of France. Intrinsic to success at popularization was the specificity of the Eucharistic movement, for it subordinated all else to the significance of the Blessed Sacrament. Once the devotional lives of most practicing Catholics had turned toward the Eucharist, the avenue opened for the popular acceptance of the ambitious program of the liturgical movement. Despite this evidence, some scholars utterly deny connection between the Eucharistic movement and the liturgy. One such scholar, Linda Lee Gaupin, concluded that, "[u]nfortunately, the growth of Eucharistic piety had no connection with liturgical life."[11] It must be admitted, however, that the historiographical emphasis upon the liturgical movement does not always encourage a clear and bold case for a connection between the Eucharistic movement and the liturgical movement. Father Reinhold painted the connections in these words:

> More Communions as so many added figures can hardly have been the idea of so great a reform. One might say that the greater numbers naturally spread greater fervor, greater purity, more penance, closer intimacy with God, greater love. I think that is true. If it were not, we would have no explanation of our own liturgical movement born of the jealous love of Christ's mysteries.[12]

I contend, however, that the Eucharistic movement helped to make the Mass immensely important to Catholics, if at first only because it was the source of the Holy Communion to be received. Only then, once the Holy Sacrifice became preeminent among the array of devotional practices of the faithful, did the liturgical movement take as its priority to reform the Mass.

By their own natures, the Eucharistic movement and its campaign for frequent Holy Communion were properly theological, embodying and articulating beliefs and, more importantly, shaping attitudes not only about the nature of the Eucharist, but also about the Church, human nature, and the love of God.

Have church historians examined the Eucharistic movement? Minimally. What have theologians produced about the campaigns for frequent Communion? Once again, very little. First, biographers of Pius X, "the pope of the Eucharist," are obliged to refer to the campaigns for frequent Communion but do not delve into his Eucharistic policy, its origins and its consequences, as this monograph does. For example, Fernessole's *essai historique* contextualized Pius within a broad Eucharistic movement, but his study merely alluded to the vitriolic dispute between François-Xavier Godts, CSsR (d. 1928), and Jules Lintelo, SJ (d. 1917), that precipitated *STS*.[13] Fernessole also did not pursue the theological implications of the Belgian conflict.

Church historian Roger Aubert's biographical sketch, "Pius X: A Conservative Reform Pope," did name principal colleagues of Godts and Lintelo, and summarized Godts's conservative position as one that held "the absolute necessity of doing away with premeditated venial sin before one could expect to be admitted to frequent Communion."[14] But virtually each word in this quotation requires explication for the sake of understanding veiled theological attitudes;

such explication was beyond the biographer's task. Aubert used his subject's writings as a starting point and thus gave the impression, mildly buffered, that Pius X *initiated* the campaign for frequent Communion.[15] My research dispels that notion.

On the other hand, scholars addressing the institutional topics prove more satisfying to liturgiologists. For example, André Haquin's *Dom Lambert Beauduin et le renouveau liturgique* devoted an entire chapter to "le mouvement eucharistique et les décrets de s. Pie X." Haquin conveyed well the ethos of the Eucharistic congresses and emphasized the Communion decree of Pius's immediate predecessor, Leo XIII (d. 1903). Further, Haquin perceived in the Eucharistic congresses significant, but theologically naive, remote preparation for the liturgical movement that consisted mostly in the ever-increasing importance of the Eucharistic cult as a result of the congresses. Finally, Haquin opined that the way in which frequent Communion was promoted lacked a liturgical context but that the relationship between the two movements was neither purely derivative nor completely independent.[16]

The French encyclopedists of religion of the twentieth century documented generously the topic of frequent Communion. Joseph Duhr, for example, in the *Dictionnaire de spiritualité* faithfully contributed a valuable overview of the sacramental practice of Communion through the centuries. Similarly, the *Dictionnaire de théologie catholique* gave a thorough and panoramic review of frequent Communion, its sources, and its issues. Its author, Dublanchy, was more interested than was Duhr in textual sources for *STS*. Still, he took at face value the decree's own assertion that the pope's actions were largely anti-Jansenistic.[17]

These encyclopedists are not above expressing opinions. Duhr perceived that the success of the campaign for frequent Communion was particularly abetted by its precursor and parallel, the seismic liturgical shift accomplished by Prosper Guéranger. This, Duhr maintained, led to a reconceptualization of the Eucharist as a sacrifice more than a Real Presence.[18] Note that this reverses the flow of influence as perceived by Haquin, who emphasized the impact of the Eucharistic movement upon the liturgical movement. Surprisingly, Dublanchy in the *Dictionnaire de théologie catholique* insisted that the Jesuits did not properly belong to the camp promoting frequent Communion. He did helpfully emphasize the preparatory role of Saint Alphonsus Liguori in the Belgian Communion disputes at the turn of the twentieth century.[19]

The introduction to Herbert Bohl's magisterial *Kommunionempfang der Gläubigen* begins with the bold statement, "Pius X brought to an end the centuries' long epoch of the Eucharistic atrophy of the faithful."[20] My book goes beyond and behind, as well as into, Pius's role. Bohl analyzes the Second Vatican Council and subsequent documents, and he finds them unsatisfactory in reintegrating Communion into the sacrifice of the Mass. He then reviews the meager patristic evidence provided by Clement of Alexandria, Tertullian, Cyprian, Pope Siricius, and various councils and synods. A lengthy section demonstrates how the Council of Trent and its ramifications, in responding to Protestant attacks upon Eucharistic praxis, constructed a distinction between the sacrifice and the receiving of Holy Communion. A pastoral dimension of Bohl's work seems to parry concerns that frequent Holy Communion, insofar as it has been implemented, is somehow unworthy.

The English-language scholarship on frequent Holy Communion and its theological upshots is woefully inadequate. For example, John A. Hardon's promisingly titled essay, "Historical Antecedents of St. Pius X's Decree on Frequent Communion," omitted the precipitating controversy between Godts and Lintelo altogether. It also refused to discuss the consequences of the decrees.[21] The bulk of periodical literature on frequent Communion propagandized for it relentlessly or promoted the canonization of Pius X.

More helpful works in English, though more primary materials than analysis, include Juan Ferreres's *The Decree on Daily Communion: A Historical Sketch and Commentary* and Thomas M. Schwertner's *The Eucharistic Renaissance, or the International Eucharistic Congresses.*[22] The former, a translation from the Spanish, is boosterism for frequent Communion rather than scholarship, but it amply reviews the issues and the documentation. The latter simply chronicles the congresses without concern for their theological grounding. The English translation of Jules Lintelo's *The Eucharistic Triduum: An Aid to Priests in Preaching Frequent and Daily Communion According to the Decrees of H.H. Pius X* serves to lay out at length the thought of the victor, Father Jules Lintelo, in the dispute about the frequency of Communion.[23] Donald H. Marshall's dissertation, "Frequent and Daily Communion in the Catholic Church of Spain in the Sixteenth and Seventeenth Centuries," sheds light upon the societal tumult that followed from the presumptuous "fad" for frequent Holy Communion.[24]

Joseph P. Chinnici's article, the single most satisfactory essay about the Eucharistic movement in the United States, pictured the movement as a worthy successor to the "devotional revival" of nineteenth-century American Catholicism.[25] Chinnici not only characterized the movement as "the most vital spiritual movement of the first fifty years of twentieth-century American Catholicism" but also showed that the movement aptly symbolized the Church in the United States at the time.[26] The major issue was identity, and Chinnici saw the Eucharistic movement as a privileged arena wherein the Church might clarify its "self-perception" and define itself in relation to "American society."[27] In addition, the Eucharistic movement explored the tensions between clericalism and the empowerment of the laity, as well as between highly privatized devotional life and what came to be called Catholic Action. While quite theological, stressing ecclesiology and the nature of the ordained ministry, the essay does not interest itself in the major *liturgical* upshot of the Eucharistic movement, the implementation of frequent Communion.

Quite helpful in establishing a sociopolitical impetus for the campaign is the essay by Peter A. J. Nissen. He argues that pastors, in the face of secularization in Europe in the latter part of the early twentieth century, embraced all efforts to increase the rate of reception even though there was opposition among moral theologians at the time. Thus the church would "keep its hold on the masses." He also cites some localized data, Dutch and Belgian, on trends in rates of reception through the time of Vatican II, and perceives that *QS*, in which Pius X lowered the age of first Communion, was actually an additional tactic in the campaign for more frequent Holy Communion.[28]

Frank C. Senn's comprehensive *The People's Work: A Social History of the Liturgy* deftly summarizes Antoine Arnauld's *De la fréquente communion* (1643) and Fenélon's rebuttal, and maintains that increases in the frequency of reception reflect a general trend toward all Christian churches meeting individual needs for sanctity to the detriment of a communal sense.[29]

Margaret M. McGuinness's major contribution, "Let Us Go to the Altar: American Catholics and the Eucharist, 1926–1976," among other aspects does detail compellingly the means by which the official campaign for frequent Holy Communion enlisted multiple allies—the Holy Name Society, Sodalities, and so on—starting in the 1920s. The efforts of these allies, when coupled with the ongoing efforts of the Fathers of the Blessed Sacrament and with modifications of the rules for fasting, granted ultimate but limited victory to the campaign. For the sake of its focus, this book does not pursue the special initiation ritual to the Lord's Table, the first Holy Communion, nor does it examine the proper etiquette of receiving.[30]

As this quick survey reveals, nowhere does the literature, either historical or theological, cover the campaign for frequent Holy Communion. Given that more, and more frequent, Communions was a momentous change in ritual practice, the Catholic Church's development into a frequently communicating church deserves extensive research and theological reflection. A change in worship—sacramental reception of Communion by the layperson, when once this was reserved to the priest—would signal, and perhaps even cause, adjustments in a range of attitudes. The classical statement of this relationship is *Lex orandi, lex credendi.*[31] But in this case the ritual change does not indicate any fundamental change in Catholic sacramental dogma. To discern causes and effects accurately when a single component of a complex system changes is immensely difficult. The more complex the system, and the more the one system interacts with neighboring systems, the greater the difficulty in rigorously proving causes and effects. At issue here is the single change of greater frequency of Communion, which rippled ever outward to reinforce other liturgical and devotional practices, and ultimately several allied theological themes.

Here are two hypothetical connections between the successful campaign for frequent Communion and changes in liturgical and sacramental practice. They can be here viewed as instances of the law of unintended consequences.

(1) The precipitous decline in the American Roman Catholic use of the sacrament of penance, while it occurred immediately after the Second Vatican Council, finds its most paradoxical and significant cause—namely, a sacramental and ritual one—in this campaign for frequent Communion.[32] It is a historical fact that this campaign deliberately and concertedly worked at breaking the connection between confessing and communicating.[33] Yet how often the popular Catholic press laments the decline in the use of confession and begs for an explanation![34] This is not to deny that numerous other causes helped penance to fade, given that the paradigm has shifted on the nature of sin, morality itself, and so forth.[35] Indeed, some commentators hopefully observe that the receiving of Holy Communion itself as the eminent sacrament of reconciliation recaptures the earlier practice of the Church.[36]

(2) When Holy Communion was unabashedly infrequent, a distinction between the clergy and the laity was ritually embodied by the priest receiving at every Mass while the laity received annually, fulfilling an obligation imposed by numerous councils and synods, most famously by the Fourth Lateran Council in 1215. Of course, many other practices have separated the clergy from the laity, not least of which were literacy (until the 1800s), knowledge of Latin (until the vernacularization of worship after Vatican II), and priestly celibacy (still). To communicate "with" the priest within the action of the Mass itself was a persistent and divisive issue between some leaders of the Eucharistic and liturgical movements, and this is addressed, theologically, in the final chapter. Greater reception of Communion at the liturgically correct moment in the Mass coheres with an erosion of the divide between the priestly and the lay castes. Thus the priesthood of all the baptized, a concept completely submerged well into the twentieth century, was given *ritual* occasion to bloom in the decrees of the Second Vatican Council.[37]

*Lumen Gentium*'s chapter "The People of God" follows its citation of Apocalypse 1:6 with the following:

> The baptized, by regenerating and the anointing of the Holy Spirit, are consecrated into a spiritual house and a holy priesthood. Thus through all those works befitting Christian men they can offer spiritual sacrifices and proclaim the power of Him who has called them out of darkness into His marvelous light. . . .

Though they differ from one another in essence and not only in degree, the common priesthood of the faithful and the ministerial or hierarchical priesthood are nonetheless interrelated. Each of them in its own special way is a participation in the one priesthood of Christ. . . .

It is through the sacraments and the exercise of the virtues that the sacred nature and organic structure of the priestly community is brought into operation.[38]

As prelude to this apostolic constitution, a burgeoning stream of Eucharistic piety and reflection in the early twentieth century identified the participation of the laity with the priest's action as both co-offered through and with Jesus. The most significant ritual enactment of this union was, of course, to receive Communion, especially at the liturgically "correct" time, on the heels of the priest's receiving. Indeed, many changes in the Roman Catholic Church in the wake of Vatican II resonate with many more people going to Communion. But the complexity of these events and attitudes softens any claim that the Eucharistic decrees of Pius X *caused* the reforms.

As the most powerful sacrament, Holy Communion is bound to reflect tensions among Catholics. Although this study is largely historical, its understandings of fairly recent ritualistic modifications may resonate with some common issues of the early third millennium. Have active and fairly devout American Catholics lost reverence for the Eucharist? Do they even believe in the Real Presence? Does the popularity of recently rekindled Eucharistic devotions such as perpetual adoration point to a decline in the rate at which Catholics receive Holy Communion? Will such devotions recover the allegedly lost reverence? Should we conclude that the near evaporation of confession simply means that Americans are in denial about their sinfulness? Should American bishops deny Holy Communion to Catholic politicians because of their votes on abortion? This book cannot attempt to answer the current and specific juridical, administrative, and pastoral concerns, but it can demonstrate that ritual change, even if unaccompanied by textual redaction, is but one current in a broad historical river.

# NOTES

1. Robert A. Taft, "The Frequency of the Eucharist Throughout History," in *Beyond East and West: Problems in Liturgical Understanding* (Washington, D.C.: Pastoral Press, 1984), 71.

2. John F. Baldovin's review of Robert Taft's *The Precommunion Rites*, vol. 5 of *A History of the Liturgy of St. John Chrysostom*, in *Worship* (2002): 288.

3. Margaret M. McGuinness, "Let Us Go to the Altar: American Catholics and the Eucharist, 1926–1976." In *Habits of Devotion: Catholic Religious Practice in*

*Twentieth-Century America*, edited by James M. O'Toole (Ithaca, New York: Cornell University Press, 2004), 181. For a yet more detailed report of patterns of Communion reception in the Netherlands consult Peter J. A. Nissen, "Mobilizing the Catholic Masses through the Eucharist: The Practice of Communion from the Mid-19th Century to the Second Vatican Counsel," translated by D. Mader, in *Bread of Heaven: Customs and Practices Surrounding Holy Communion*, edited by Charles Caspers, Gerard Lukken, and Gerard Rouwhorst, Essays in the History of Liturgy and Culture / Liturgia condenda 3 (Kampen, The Netherlands: Kok Pharos, 1995), 117–18.

4. Catholic Church, Sacred Congregation of the Council, *DECRETUM de Dispositionibus Requisitis ad Frequentem et Quotidianam Communionem Eucharisticam Sumendam. DE QUOTIDIANA SS. EUCHARISTIAE SUMPTIONE. Sacra Tridentina Synodus*, in *Acta Sanctae Sedis* 38 (1905): 400–6; English translation, "On the Daily Reception of Communion," in *The New Liturgy: A Documentation, 1903–1965*, edited by R. Kevin Seasoltz (New York: Herder & Herder, 1966); henceforth *STS*, with pages referring to this translation.

5. Hans Ansgar Reinhold, *The Dynamics of Liturgy* (New York: Macmillan, 1961), 29.

6. Charles Ledré, "Pius X, Pope, Saint," *New Catholic Encyclopedia*.

7. Hans Ansgar Reinhold, "Frequent Communion, Accessible and Integrated," in *St. Pius X and Social Worship, 1903–1953* (Elsberry, Missouri: Liturgical Conference, 1953), 67.

8. Paul Marx, *Virgil Michel and the Liturgical Movement* (Collegeville, Minnesota: Liturgical Press, 1957), 95.

9. United States Conference of Catholic Bishops, "Happy Are Those Who Are Called to His Supper: On Preparing to Receive Christ Worthily in the Eucharist," 14 November 2006 (Washington, D.C.: USCCB, 2006).

10. *STS*, 12.

11. Linda Lee Gaupin, "First Eucharist and the Shape of Catechesis Since 'Quam Singulari'" (PhD diss., Catholic University of America, Washington, D.C., 1985), 149.

12. Reinhold, "Accessible and Integrated," 69.

13. Pierre Fernessole, *Pie X: Essai historique*, 2 volumes (Paris: P. Lethielleux, 1953).

14. Roger Aubert, "Pius X, a Conservative Reform Pope," in *The Church in the Industrial Age, History of the Church*, 9, edited by Hubert Jedin and John Dolan, translated by Margit Resch (New York: Crossroad, 1981), 403.

15. Aubert, "Conservative Reform Pope," 404–5.

16. André Haquin, "Le mouvement eucharistique et les décrets de S. Pie X." In *Dom Lambert Beauduin et le renouveau liturgique*, 30–60, Recherches et synthèses, section d'histoire 1 (Gembloux: J. Duculot, 1970), 47, 57, and 59.

17. E. Dublanchy, "Communion eucharistique (fréquente)." *Dictionnaire de Théologie Catholique* 3, no. 1 (1923): 515–52; henceforth, CEF.

18. Joseph Duhr, "Communion Fréquente," *Dictionnaire de Spiritualité*, 1283, 1291; henceforth, Duhr.

19. This is the usual English version of the saint's name.

20. Herbert Bohl, *Kommunionempfang der Gläubigen: Probleme seiner Integra-tion in die Eucharistiefeier, eine liturgiewissenschaftliche Untersuchung*, Disputatio-nes Theologicae 9 (Frankfurt: Peter D. Lang, 1980), 1.

21. John A. Hardon, "Historical Antecedents of St. Pius X's Decree on Frequent Communion," *Theological Studies* 16 (December 1955): 493–532.

22. Juan Bautista Ferreres, *The Decree on Daily Communion: A Historical Sketch and Commentary*, translated by H. Jimenez (London: Sands, 1909); Thomas M. Schwertner, *The Eucharistic Renaissance, or the International Eucharistic Con-gresses* (New York: Macmillan, 1926).

23. Jules Lintelo, *The Eucharistic Triduum: An Aid to Priests in Preaching Fre-quent and Daily Communion According to the Decrees of H.H. Pius X*, translated by Francis M. de Zulueta (London: R. & T. Washbourne, 1909); henceforth, *ET*.

24. Donald H. Marshall, "Frequent and Daily Communion in the Catholic Church of Spain in the Sixteenth and Seventeenth Centuries" (PhD diss., Harvard University, Cambridge, 1952).

25. Joseph P. Chinnici, "The Eucharist, Symbol of the Church," in *Living Stones: The History and Structure of Catholic Spiritual Life in the United States, The Bicen-tennial History of the Catholic Church in the United States* (New York: Macmillan, 1989), 146.

26. Chinnici, "Eucharist," 146.

27. Chinnici, "Eucharist," 148.

28. Nissen, "Mobilizing the Catholic Masses," 145–64.

29. Frank C. Senn, *The People's Work: A Social History of the Liturgy* (Minneapo-lis: Fortress, 2006), 260–61; Senn has also surveyed Protestant use of the sacrament in "The Frequency of Celebration and Reception of Communion in Protestantism," *Proceedings of the North American Academy of Liturgy* (1990): 98–118.

30. Carrie T. Schultz, "Do This in Memory of Me: American Catholicism and First Communion Customs in the Era of 'Quam Singulari,'" *American Catholic Studies* 115, no. 2 (2004): 45–66; Margaret M. McGuinness, "Is It Wrong to Chew the Hosts?: Changing Catholic Etiquette and the Eucharist, 1920–1970," *American Catholic Studies* 110 (1999): 29–48.

31. In fact, the original phrasing of Prosper of Aquitaine was "Legem credendi lex statuat supplicandi." Paul Bradshaw, "Difficulties in Doing Liturgical Theology," *Pa-cifica* 11 (1998): 186. Pope Celestine I (d. 432) is the putative source for the more ex-pansive saying, "Lex orandi est lex credendi et agendi," or "The rule of prayer is the rule of belief and of action." *Dictionary of Latin and Greek Theological Terms*, 1985.

32. Thomas F. O'Meara, interview by the author, July 1995.

33. Jesuit Karl Rahner's defense of devotional confession does not perceive any connection between use of penance and Holy Communion, although the historical increase of the two in tandem is well documented. Karl Rahner, "The Meaning of Frequent Confession of Devotion," in *Theological Investigations*, vol. 3, *The The-ology of the Spiritual Life*, translated by Karl-H. and Boniface Kruger (Baltimore: Helicon, 1967).

34. O'Toole attributes the drop in recourse to penance in the United States to a seismic shift in morals and also, liturgically, to the very brevity of the sacramental

encounter in the confessional and the introduction of the Saturday evening vigil masses. James O'Toole, "Empty Confessionals: Where Have All the Sinners Gone?" *Commonweal* 23 (February 2001): 10–12.

35. For a thorough examination of the collapse of confession in the United States, see James M. O'Toole, "In the Court of Conscience: American Catholics and Confession, 1900–1975," in *Habits of Devotion: Catholic Religious Practice in Twentieth-Century America*, edited by James M. O'Toole (Ithaca, New York: Cornell University Press, 2004).

36. Joseph A. Favazza, "Forum: The Fragile Future of Reconciliation," *Worship* 71, no. 3 (1997): 240.

37. On the origins of a separate priestly "caste" and its connection to the Eucharist, see Nathan Mitchell, *Cult and Controversy: The Worship of the Eucharist Outside Mass* (New York: Pueblo, 1982), 72ff.

38. *Lumen Gentium*, 27–28, in Second Vatican Council, *The Documents of Vatican II*, edited by Walter M. Abbott and Joseph Gallagher, introduction by Lawrence Shehan (New York: Guild Press / America Press Association, 1966).

# Chapter One

# History of the Frequency of Holy Communion

This chapter sketches the history of the frequency with which Holy Communion has been received by the laity. Information about sacramental practice through the ages is minimal and suggestive, local, pastoral, and episodic. Some is tendentious, as it comes from propagandists for frequent Holy Communion. For centuries, Communion was so rare that bishops, theologians, and mystics continually pleaded for more.

## BEFORE JANSENISM

The witnesses to the practice of the primitive church already suggest a variety of rates of receiving, but clarity proves elusive. In Jerusalem, there may have been daily communicating. "All who were present at the Divine Liturgy were expected to receive the Holy Communion."[1] On the other hand, Acts 20:6–11 may indicate a weekly Eucharistic gathering. Both Dublanchy and Duhr, the premier chroniclers of Communion practice, argue for the great likelihood that whenever the faithful "broke bread," all present would consume it, but they concede that the frequency with which the community gathered and broke bread remains uncertain.[2]

Perhaps the earliest documented changes in the enactment of the Lord's Supper also established a trajectory that ultimately discouraged communicating. The structure of the Last Supper was threefold: breaking of bread, eating of a meal, and blessing of wine. As early as 40 C.E., the breaking of the bread and the blessing of the wine had become a "liturgical unit" concluding an agape meal.[3] But this profound rearrangement of the structure admitted the elimination of the meal entirely, to be replaced by the liturgy of the word.[4] Edward J. Kilmartin, SJ, implies that the rite came consequently to emphasize

1

the institution narrative and the actions of the presider. Two very early consequences for frequency of Communion follow, then. First and directly, this
loss of the agape meal reframed the Eucharist; it lost both associations with
and the very process itself of eating. Second, as the active role of the presider
grew along with emphasis on the Eucharistic prayer, the congregation grew
more passive, and hence less likely actually to communicate.

After the apostolic age, attendance at Mass continued to entail receiving
Communion. One early second-century witness to the universality of com-
municating is Justin Martyr's *First Apology*. "Communion followed [the
Eucharistic prayer] in which the celebrant, deacons, and people received the
eucharistic bread and wine."[5] That *all* those present communicated may be
inferred from the deacons' conveying Communion to the absent faithful.[6]
But Justin indicated, as did the very similar *Didache*, a Eucharist only on
Sunday.[7] Tertullian (d. 225) reveals an innovation in sacramental practice:
Mass was offered more often than on Sundays alone; Communion was still
presumably taken by all in attendance.[8] And Bohl finds in Tertullian already
a growing dissociation between Mass as a sacrificial offering and as a meal.[9]
Western fourth-century witnesses to daily Communion include the life of
Melanie of Rome and remarks by Augustine, Chromatius of Aquila, Zeno of
Verona, Hilary of Poitiers, and Ambrose, who claimed that daily Communion
was normative throughout the Church.[10] Further, Ambrose accused the Eastern Christians of communicating seldom, and John Chrysostom corroborates
this, saying, "'Every one that partaketh not of the Mysteries is standing here
in shameless effrontery' (Hom. III. in Eph.)."[11] He also complained, "'At
other times [than Easter] ye come not, no, not though often ye are clean. . .
. O! the force of custom and prejudice! In vain is the daily sacrifice, in vain
do we stand before the altar; there is no one to partake' (Eph., Hom. III)."[12]
Chrysostom's word *prejudice* may suggest a longstanding custom of rare
recourse to Communion, even in the fourth century.

Who was eligible to communicate? Only the baptized and orthodox, united
in faith with all the other local churches, could share the Eucharistic table.
The issue of how to advise potential communicants, however, complicated
this clarity. Saints Jerome and Augustine deferred to the communicant's own
judgment.[13] Jerome, however, may have insisted upon abstention from sexual
intercourse as a way to prepare oneself for Communion; this very notion
could easily have contributed to the decline in recourse to the sacrament, yet
the notion prevailed in the Middle Ages.[14] John Chrysostom demanded of the
communicant "'sincerity and purity of soul' (Hom. III in Eph.)."[15] He was
combating pervasive Arianism and so emphasized the divinity and remote-
ness of Christ.[16]

The legalization of Christianity under Constantine may have contributed to the decline in the use of Communion. Kilmartin, drawing a parallel between the changes in the baptismal milieu that were occasioned by the legalization of Christianity, says, "This new body of Christians, many of whom entered the Church for reasons of expediency rather than for purely religious motives, undoubtedly exerted great influence on the traditional attitude of Christians toward the Eucharist."[17] But in simple terms of ritual action, a large and permanent body of catechumens, unwilling to go "all the way" into baptism, created a group of noncommunicating congregants, at least until the moment of their dismissal before the Eucharistic prayer in each Mass. This exclusion may have planted a seed for a practice of attendance at Mass but real neglect of the Lord's Table.

The numerous injunctions to communicate frequently in the late fifth and early sixth centuries indicate that Holy Communion of the laity itself seems to have become extinct. Consider Saint Patrick's second synod, held between 450 and 462 C.E., which decided to discover those who did not communicate even on Easter and wanted to declare these persons no longer members of the Church. Similarly, the Council of Braga in 506 C.E. decreed that if persons did not communicate on the major feasts of the year—Nativity, Easter, and Pentecost—they were no longer Christian.[18] Rome in the eighth century seems to have been an exception to the trends in most of the Latin Church, for Venerable Bede reported in a letter to Egbert (around 733 C.E.) that weekly reception of the Eucharist was common among all the unmarried and among the married who practiced the "usual continence."[19] Reception of Communion in Great Britain Bede deplored as too infrequent; because of inadequate teaching, the people accepted Communion only on the Nativity, Epiphany, and Easter.[20] By the end of the eighth century, it seems that the major feasts of Easter, Pentecost, Ascension, and Christmas were general Communion days.[21] During the ninth century concerns were articulated about the infrequency of Communion and its corollary, the dispositions suitable for communicating.[22] Witnesses include the Council of Chalon-sur-Saône (813 C.E.), and Jonas d'Orléans (d. 844 C.E.).[23] Requests for special, individualized permission to receive frequently attest to how unusual the practice was.[24] Late in the eleventh century appears the earliest known articulation of the efficacious discouragement to frequent Communion, the idea that to receive required absolute freedom from venial sins. So said Abbot Durandus of Troarn in Bayeux (d. 1088 C.E.), although he did urge daily Communion because our faults are committed daily.[25] Raoul Ardent (d. 1101 C.E.) observed that some did receive Communion daily and that, though worthy to receive, some abstained to exhibit their respect. Ardent also considered the world so evil that very few were worthy to communicate at all.[26] By the twelfth century, a Cistercian named Herbert was absolutely astonished that a pious widow of Meaux had received Communion every Sunday for ten years—the astonishment testifies to the persisting infrequency of Communion.[27] In this same century, distinctions were made between clerical and lay sacramental patterns.

Josef Jungmann observes that this distancing of clergy from laity seems to result from a "stress on the temporal character of the Church and its juridical-hierarchical apparatus."[28] This latter he sees also as coherent with a loss of distinction between Christ and God the Father, an identification of the Church with the state, and a steady loss of "the Christian's sense of sancity."[29] He continues, "A negative attitude dominates the scene from the ninth to the eleventh century. Self-accusation, confession of personal unworthiness and sin recurs with endless monotony, even in our best known texts—those of prayers for monks and clergy."[30] This attitude, according to Jungmann, arises because the "supernatural world has receded: this world is to the fore."[31] Consequently,

> frequency of Communion becomes less and less, until people have to be urged to make their yearly Communion. This is not to be explained simply by saying that the laity were luke-warm in those days. Too great a tension has been allowed to develop between the holiness and sublimity of what was received and the sinfulness and nothingness of him who received.[32]

This resounding echo of anti-Arianism affects the frequency of Communion well into the High Middle Ages.

Receiving among the laity has been roughly but readily corroborated by the practices of religious orders, also nonclerical but presumably more inclined to use the sacrament.[33] As with all the tesserae of evidence so far adduced, communion patterns varied greatly by order, by particular monastery, and by era. Although Francis of Assisi himself recommended frequent Communion, it seems to have remained unusual among his followers, for Brother Egidius's (d. 1262 c.e.) receiving Communion every Sunday and on the major feasts was considered remarkable.[34] The Dominicans, especially Tauler, Savonarola, Saint Catherine of Siena, and Saint Vincent Ferrer, urged frequent reception of Communion of the laity.[35] This order had been founded specifically to extirpate the Albigensians, Manichaean dualists who denied that matter possessed any worth or goodness. Thus it seems logical for the Dominicans to have promoted the sacraments, which confirm ritually that matter itself can be a vehicle of the transcendent. Conciliar canons for legally minimal reception of the Holy Eucharist and continuing injunctions for frequent Communion both imply that sacramental reception remained rare.

Another important indicator that sacramental Communion remained exceptional was a burgeoning devotionalism that strongly emphasized the viewing of the Eucharistic host. Simply put, gradual and growing investment in the sight of the host may be proportional to, and in part caused by, the decrease in frequency of Communion. Jean de Marienwerder, the biographer of the mystic Dorothy of Danzig (d. 1394), admits as much.[36] If the origins of the valorization of viewing the host are, in fact, to be located in the decline of Holy Communion, then the ramifications through the centuries—the elevation during the Mass, the various species of Benediction, and the vast and elaborate processions to honor the Blessed Sacrament—may indicate a proportionate and even accelerating decline in the frequency with which Communion was received by the laity.[37] "Ocular Communion," available cheaply because it came without the demands for fasting, continence, confession, and penitential actions, which were once justified as highly beneficial, drove out the more expensive sacramental Communion.

On the threshold of the Reformation in England, participation by the laity centered unequivocally on visual contact with the Host. Holes were cut into the woodwork of the church buildings so that the Host could be adored; these holes merit a technical name, "elevation squints."[38] Dark curtains were drawn across elaborate reredos at the moment of the "sacring" (i.e., consecration) so that the raised Host would be suitably foiled.[39] Also, candles were lit specifically at the time of the elevation to enhance the sighting.[40] Bell peals just before the elevation seem to have met the demands of the laity that they be warned about the time of the elevation so they would not miss this powerful action.[41] And even the times of Masses were staggered so that the faithful could gaze upon many Hosts in quick succession.[42] "Behind all was the sense that those cut off from the opportunity of hearing Mass devoutly and seeing the Host were being deprived of precious benefits for body and soul. Mothers in labour could secure safe delivery, travelers safe arrival, eaters and drinkers good digestion, by gazing on the Host at Mass."[43] This piety of the gaze that saves is important because it reflects the near disappearance of Communion by the laity except for their Easter duty, which was almost universally fulfilled.[44]

Such an enduring treatise as *The Imitation of Christ* by Thomas à Kempis (d. 1471) shows continuity with an insistence upon greater use of Communion throughout the later Middle Ages. The persisting infrequency of Communion in the fifteenth century in England is evidenced by two liturgical excrescences that substitute for Communion, the paxbred and the blessed loaf of bread distributed at the end of Mass, whose equivalent in France was the *pain bénit* and in the Eastern Churches is still the antidoron. These two accretions to the liturgy instance the creativity with which the Church compensated for the absence of properly liturgical and sacramental and sensory contact with the transcendent through Holy Communion.

The Council of Trent confidently urged that all the laity who attended Mass should receive Communion. Trent often rejected Protestant practices simply to maintain the identity of the Catholics, and early Protestants often advocated frequent Holy Communion. Still, Trent could support more frequent Holy Communion because the ideal of it had been echoed for over a thousand years. Trent decreed that all those assisting at the Mass should receive Communion, and in this the council seems to have relied upon Aquinas.[45]

> The holy council wishes indeed that at each Mass the faithful who are present should communicate, not only in spiritual desire but also by the sacramental partaking of the Eucharist, that thereby they may derive from this most holy sacrifice a more abundant fruit; if however, that is not always done, it does not on that account condemn as private and illicit those masses in which the priest alone communicates sacramentally, but rather approves and commends them, since these Masses also ought to be considered as truly common, partly because at them the people communicate spiritually and partly also because they are celebrated by a public minister of the Church, not for himself only but for all the faithful who belong to the body of Christ.[46]

This passage became the banner of the movement for frequent Communion during the campaigns at the turn into the twentieth century. Trent was then regarded as virtually infallible, and its decrees were not read contextually, but as proof texts.[47] The Catechism of the Council specified the ideal and implied that the injunction of the Fourth Lateran Council (1215 C.E.) for an annual partaking of the Lord's Supper was, in fact, minimal: "Let not the faithful deem it enough to receive the body of the Lord once a year only; but let them judge that Communion ought to be more frequent; but whether it be more expedient that it should be monthly, weekly, or daily, can be decided by no fixed universal rule . . . (Part 2, chapter 4, note 58)."[48] The implementation of the pronouncements of Trent and its interpretive catechism remained largely in abeyance until the definitive "interpretation" of Trent by *STS*, the decree of Pius X that more than three centuries later ratified the very idea of frequent reception of Holy Communion. Note that the very title of the decree alludes to the Council of Trent.

The success of the first campaign for frequent Communion, which was part of the Catholic Reformation but definitely not attributable to Trent's decrees in themselves, belongs to Saint Ignatius Loyola and the Society of Jesus. Surely Ignatius was not the only founder to advocate frequent Communion—others were Saints Antonio Maria Zaccaria and Cajetan (Gaetano da Chieti or da Thiene)—but "by sheer force of their numbers and international character, they [the Society of Jesus] became its most effective spokesmen."[49] The success of the campaign was circumscribed, too, to Spain and Italy.

Once he had embarked upon the establishment of the Society of Jesus, Ignatius promoted frequent Communion variously. He advised the practice in spiritual direction,[50] encouraged it in the formation of seminarians, arranged for polemics in its favor,[51] and organized a confraternity in his hometown for the purpose of moving members to communicate once per month.[52] Communion seems to have become already a distinct devotional unit, for "they regularly administered the sacrament before or after mass, or at some other time in the morning, as was the widespread custom."[53]

Whether the pristine Church communicated frequently, as Ignatius believed, the people of his day experienced the very idea and its implementation at best as newfangled.

> So novel was it at that time to communicate more than once a year, except in danger of death, that, if one wished to communicate oftener, he betook himself, in order to forestall gossip, to the hermits in their cells, because such a practice [receiving Communion often and in public] would cause no less excitement, as one of St. Ignatius' hearers told Father M. Pérez, than to see a bullock fly.[54]

In Paris, because of the use of frequent Communion, Loyola himself was nearly horsewhipped.[55]

Loyola's own practice and advocacy of relatively frequent Communion was of a piece with the Catholic Reformation in Spain. Of the two campaigns that history records, this one is the earlier by three hundred years, and, although one of its literary relics became a spark for the latter campaign, this Spanish effort did not succeed.

The push for both more and more frequent Holy Communion aroused heated opposition. Marshall contextualizes the campaign as "a [Spanish] episode in a widespread tendency to religious enthusiasm" that accompanied the Catholic Reformation all over Europe.[56] In so representing the campaign, he discounts theological differences between those supporting and those opposing the campaign. He documents how the proponents—as part of a groundswell of enthusiasm, in the negative sense—very often linked frequent Communion with "devotional emotions, ecstatic trances, visions and revelations." He also helpfully connects this enthusiasm with a Spanish phenomenon of the "illuminated" (*alumbrados*).[57]

The opposition to frequent Communion in those days may seem inexplicable from a historical distance and from a theological perspective. In part, the opposition flowed from humanity's resistance to any change, especially of immemorial custom. Theologically, success provoked concern for the propriety of such frequent use of the sacrament. Overuse, even if not sacrilegious, could have resulted in a casual attitude that, in a world quite sensitive to decorum, would have insulted the Real Presence. Because at the same time the

Real Presence was under attack by some Protestants, this doctrine needed vigorous protection. The balance between respect for Jesus in the Host and the will of Jesus in instituting the Eucharist specifically to be available to human beings seemed to have been found in methods for apportioning the spiritual dispositions of the recipients with degrees of frequency. Such a balancing had been adumbrated by a few medieval commentators such as Bonaventure.[58] Through the Catholic Reformation, the baroque era, the Enlightenment, and the disestablishment of the Church in the nineteenth century, even until *STS* at the dawn of the twentieth, rates of receiving Communion were tied to dispositions for it.

In addition to this theological rationale, promoted by a few small but influential groups in Spain, for opposing the sudden surge of Communion, other forces become apparent. The authority structure of the Church was challenged by the qualities of enthusiasm and special revelation so closely allied with frequent Communion. These gyrations raised suspicions that their nature was no less than "diabolic."[59] In the same manner, the proponents in some cases were perceived as "religious radicals" because they disdained the sacrament of penance completely and thus undermined the configuration of pieties that was centered in Holy Communion and that was intended as a linchpin for the Catholic reform of Spain. For example, the circle of Agustin Cazalla both rejected penance openly and received Communion several times a day.[60] Another extreme occurs in the writings of Antonio Velásquez Pinto, who, garlanded with approbations from universities and religious orders, asserted in 1662 that *daily* reception of Communion was *necessitated* by divine precept.[61] Such developments were revolutionary (and thus upsetting), pastorally unsound, and theologically indefensible.

Fueling the opposition to frequent Holy Communion was the perceived superiority of the frequent communicators, and this induced resentment. "The complacent, holier-than-thou attitude of some of the purveyors of the new piety contributed a good deal to provoke the annoyed response which these small groups encountered."[62]

These Spanish controversies shed light on the comprehensive goal of the proponents of encouraging frequent recourse to the sacrament. Marshall summarizes the literary remains:

> These documents suffice to show that frequent communion had its place in the scheme of reform because, tied as it was to confession, it would keep alive the sense of sin and Christian obligation, and because of its own solemn nature, would sustain popular devotion. But these results could be expected only if the use of the sacraments were [sic] accompanied by the careful preparation which the theory of their operation demanded. Otherwise they would become mere ceremony or easy devotions.[63]

The configuration of sacramental piety did not isolate the receiving of Holy Communion from its extensive ritualized context—confession, fasting, set prayers—or from the theology that insisted, with more vigor than ever, on the Real Presence. Insofar as the emphasis upon communicating isolated it from the complex system of attention to matters moral and spiritual, the sacrament, despite its frequency, could not remain the pivot upon which the spiritual reform rested.

But these early campaigns were not so successful as to influence church architecture. At least the piety of adoration of the reserved Host was still determining the shape and fabric of the building, as Freiberg's study of the north transept of the Lateran basilica in 1600 indicates:

> In the absence of documentation spelling out the iconographical program, the author becomes a detective who considers every clue, whether fresco, sculpture, or architectural element, which can reveal the mind of the pope and the artists he chose. He [Freiberg] makes an absolutely convincing case for a unified plan centering on devotion to the Corpus Domini, the eucharistic bread in the ciborium on the altar.[64]

Given the absence of data on the actual reception of Communion, reading such architectural evidence helps to mitigate reports of increasing use of Communion. Marshall confirms this by stating that in Spain, despite the literary volume and the prominence of the campaign in Spanish church history, the practice of frequent Holy Communion was very limited.

While the most famous proponents of frequent Holy Communion in this era include Saints Philip Neri and Charles Borromeo, both Italians, some Spanish authors, because of their place in the lineage of the dispute into the late nineteenth century, require mention. The Franciscan Joseph de Santa Maria (published 1616) and two Benedictines, Alfonso de Chinchilla (d. 1631) and Peter de Marcilla / Marzilla (published 1611 and 1613), sustained the Jesuits' influence. Marzilla is especially important for the early twentieth-century disputes because he emphasized that the state of grace was the only necessary disposition for receiving Communion and that once the state of grace was entered, it could prevail for a "chain" of Communions. He asserted furthermore that the confessor had no right to deprive of Communion any disposed toward receiving. In fact, this castigation of confessors was aimed particularly at the Jesuits, and incidentally this shows how, in general, the Society had retreated from its advocacy of frequent Communion for the laity.[65]

Marzilla seems to have agreed substantially with the influential Carthusian Antonio de Molina (d. 1612),[66] but Molina did insist upon the confessor's role in determining recourse to the sacrament and also elaborated upon the notion of proper intentions in receiving; this concept became commonplace and finally definitive in *STS*.[67] Like Marzilla, Molina argued that the proper dispositions for receiving, unless mortal sin intervened, obtained indefinitely.[68] The only and minimum requirements for receiving, according to Christopher de Madrid / Madridius (d. 1573), included this right intention of Molina, and, of course, as long tradition had insisted, freedom from mortal sin.[69] Freedom from venial sin—a state of extraordinary virtue—was, according to de Madrid, a fruit of communicating rather than a prerequisite.[70] Those who used the Lord's Table often and regularly would "be filled with evangelical trust and confidence, rejoice in their Christian liberty, [and] be rendered strong and sharp for action [and] ardent and fervent in prayer."[71]

In the Spanish model for spiritual regeneration, the increase in the reception of Holy Communion would have accompanied a corresponding increase in the use of the sacrament of penance.[72] When Communion had been received only annually, confession normally preceded it closely, for to receive Communion while in the state of mortal sin was the most heinous sacrilege, "worse than cold-blooded murder in a church" or assassination.[73] Because of the stream of thought that coordinated frequent Communion with greater piety, indeed even with striving for perfection, penance tended to a "devotional" application as frequency of Communion developed—that is, confession was for the dispatching of venial sins.[74] In addition, this linkage of frequent Communion and frequent confession accorded the confessor control over access to Holy Communion, so much so that the confessor would give permission to communicate, for he was to judge both the dispositions and the benefits from a regimen of frequent Communion.[75]

Opposition to the campaign reached the highest level in the request from the bishop of Brescia in Lombardy to the Sacred Congregation of the Council to restrict the distribution of Communion to the laity in his diocese to Sundays and feast days, as well as Wednesday and Friday. He wrote:

> Frequency of Communion has become so common during the last few years in the diocese of Brescia that laymen, simple people, and even married men, in a word, persons whose minds are entirely taken up with the things of this world, not satisfied with the weekly reception of this sacrament dare to receive every day. In consequence of this practice reverence towards the Blessed Sacrament on the part of those who communicate is lessened, and on the other hand many are scandalised to see that married men, men of business, and others not particularly conspicuous for their religious piety approach daily the Holy Table.[76]

It seemed to the bishop, if he were above the fractiousness that the campaign generated, that the laity who were receiving Communion daily were ill-prepared for the sacrament and, by virtue of their occupations, too enmeshed in the world to be preparing adequately.[77] His request reveals either the success of the proponents for frequent Communion, at least in this particular diocese, or the magnitude of the dispute. Many seem to be receiving Communion weekly, and this is, in view of the total history of patterns of reception, quite often.

The council denied the request in a letter to the bishop, dated 24 January 1587. Its denial rested upon two grounds: No precedent could be found for such a limitation, and neither the operations of God's grace nor the worthiness of soul of the prospective communicant could be so constricted or so precisely determined.[78] The council's letter to the bishop, referring to the actions of the Council of Trent, observed that Trent had recommended daily use of the Eucharist but had not imposed any limitations or demanded specific requirements for this devout, daily practice.[79] Rather than pursuing arbitrary means of limiting the distribution of the sacrament, the bishop was, according to the congregation, to bestir himself to consider admission to Communion on an individual basis. The crucial determination for each case was that the frequency of reception correlate with a communicant's "measure of devotion and fitting preparation."[80] Confessors in the diocese were to "insist on the careful preparation required for the reception of the most Holy Sacrament."[81]

While it conceded that consciences are difficult to know, the response did advise that businessmen in particular be subject to their confessors in determining the frequency of Communion, for confessors know their hearts intimately and would know, too, how particular patterns of reception may be benefiting them.[82] The letter did not codify the manner of preparation or proper dispositions, except to emphasize a general unworthiness. Rather, it depicted the daily communicant as the exceptional nun, "conspicuous by purity of conscience or fervour of soul."[83] "Conspicuous" mitigated one explicit premise of the letter that the workings of the conscience are, outside the confessional, unknowable. A person holy enough to communicate every day should look and act holy. To the extent that preparation for Communion and devotions can be observable, however, a correlation was posited between these and the frequency of receiving the sacrament. The pastoral problem of less respect for the Eucharist derives from two popular perceptions: first, those who communicate frequently should benefit from the sacrament and become less worldly (i.e., they should become patently holy), and, second, the majesty of the Real Presence demands piety and rectitude.

This letter of the Congregation of the Council to the bishop of Brescia is in essence the same as the decree *Cum Ad Aures* (12 February 1679). In addition to forbidding the arbitrary restriction of Communion to certain days of the week, it condemned Pinto for claiming the *necessity* of daily reception. Also, it advocated very careful preparation for Communion and provided guidelines to confessors on frequency of communicating by state in life.[84] Perhaps

most significant for the subsequent history of disputes about the frequency of
Communion, *Cum Ad Aures* officially makes the priest responsible for admitting people to Holy Communion on an individual basis:

> It rests with the confessor to whom the secrets of their hearts are unfolded to
> give the final decision. He may advise in each individual case to married men
> and to tradesmen what he thinks more suitable for their spiritual welfare ac-
> cording to their purity of conscience, the profit they derive from frequent Com-
> munion and the progress they make in virtue.[85]

Clearly, this prerogative of the confessor was even then quite venerable.

By the end of the seventeenth century, we know that frequent Communion
had waxed and waned in some few instances in Spain and Italy. Disputes
about the practice resulted in formulating the notion that dispositions of soul
would coordinate with frequency of receiving. In the most ambiguous terms,
Communion should be as frequent or infrequent as best suited the individual.
No evidence suggests, however, that Communion was any more frequent than
annual for the preponderance of laypeople outside of Spain and Italy. But
France, too, had its controversy about frequency of Communion, and this is
the most famous and complex case.


## JANSENISM

*De la fréquente Communion* (1643), the incendiary book of the Jansenist Antoine Arnauld, presents the extreme demand of irrefutable sanctity for access
to Holy Communion. The title misleads, for the epitome of Jansenism, according to Sainte-Beuve, who brought Jansenism into our cultural consciousness, was "le dogme de la non fréquente communion."[86] Jansenism is at the
intellectual-historical heart of the matter of frequent Holy Communion.

Even the particular circumstances of its composition reveal the book's centrality. The French controversies were born from the Spanish: The Princess
de Guéméné, who was involved with the Jansenist enclave at Port-Royal,
about twenty miles from Paris, was scandalized by the frequent Communions
of the Marquise de Sablé, whose spiritual director was a Jesuit named Sesmaisons. At the request of the marquise, Sesmaisons justified the practice in
writing, and this memo, basically a summary of Spanish Carthusian Antonio
de Molina's *Instrucción de sacerdotes . . . debidamente*, was passed from
Saint-Cyran (born Jean Duvergier de Hauranne), the Jansenist leader, to Arnauld so that the latter could write a refutation, which became the tome *De la
fréquente Communion*.[87]

Its publication provides evidence for its impact, for the first edition sold out in a couple of days, and it went to four editions within the first six months.[88] Ronald A. Knox quips, "We are sometimes told that it was the most popular book of devotion in its day; if so, it offers dreadful proof that this was an age morbidly interested in theology."[89] Indeed, its size justifies the accusation, for the book was "a stout volume of more than 700 pages in duodecimo."[90] As to its influence, Saint Vincent de Paul, the "outstanding opponent of Arnauld," blamed it for a precipitous decline in numbers of Communions at Saint Sulpice in Paris; some of the faithful even refused viaticum and ignored their Easter duties.[91]

In his classic *Enthusiasm: A Chapter in the History of Religion, with Special Reference to the XVII and XVIII Centuries*, Knox explains the "manifesto" of Jansenism's attitude toward the Blessed Sacrament and penance in this way.

> All these interminable quotations from antiquity have been worked up into a manifesto, the argument of which can be quite simply put. In the early days of Christendom, sinners were frequently denied restoration to the unity of the Church for a year, or for a period of years. Therefore, in the first place, it is not merely the confessor's right, but the confessor's duty, to delay absolution until he feels assured, from the patience shown by the penitent, that his regret for his sins is genuine. And in the second place it is a pious practice, not to be stigmatized as eccentric, when devout souls, in attestation of penitence for their old sins, withdraw themselves for a time from Communion, as a kind of supernatural fast. . . .
>
> Holy Communion, being what it is, how dare we run the risk of its being profaned, even once, by an unworthy reception? . . . Priests were to be encouraged to think with the mind of the early Church, and defer the absolution of every penitent until he should attest, by repeated applications for pardon, the genuineness of his sorrow. . . . Your rigorist does not understand the maxim *sacramenta propter homines*; he will let the generality of men perish in a dry wilderness, while an *élite* of souls, "pure as angels, proud as Lucifer," forms the bodyguard of the Holy Eucharist.[92]

Arnauld transforms the very highest ideals for receiving the Blessed Sacrament into the minimum requirements; this stems from his conceiving of the Eucharist as truly heavenly food, so that only those with the purity of heaven should approach the sacrament.[93]

The most influential opponent of Arnauld, among many polemicists, was Jesuit Denis Petau (d. 1652), who wrote under the name Petavius.[94] His answer, the book *De la pénitence publique et de la préparation à la communion* (1644), was "typical of the critical analysis to which Arnauld's treatise was subjected."[95] Petavius launches a resourceful attack, but lest his accusation of the "novelty" of the Jansenist idea of dispositions for Communion via penance give the impression that Communion was in fact frequent for the laity, consider the actual practice of Communion in the days when Arnauld was freshly published.

> While clerical diaries [from France] from the period [the second half of the seventeenth century] show that although the paschal communion was widely observed, only between one-third and one-quarter of Catholics received the sacrament on the major feast days and a very small proportion on a monthly or weekly basis.[96]

Proponents of frequent Communion continually, explicitly, and persistently blame Jansenism for the cessation of daily Communion and the virtual elimination of frequent Communion well into the twentieth century.[97] Despite Vincent de Paul's remarks, is this attribution just? The prior question is, What exactly is Jansenism?

"A Jansenist is a Calvinist saying Mass."[98] Some claim that Jansenism was a phantom heresy, conjured by the Jesuits to consolidate their opponents in order to combat them more effectively,[99] and Giovanni Cardinal Bona (d. 1674) defined Jansenists as "some fervent Catholics who do not love the Jesuits."[100] Others imply that Jansenism was at root a feud between the Arnauld family and the Jesuits, for Antoine Arnauld's grandfather had written a "famous speech demanding the expulsion of the Jesuits" that has been tagged the "original sin of the Arnaulds."[101] Knox disagreed with this lineage but did observe that the "persecution of Port-Royal . . . is one of persons rather than ideas, of the heretic rather than of his heresy."[102] John McManners saw the Jansenist controversy not so much as religious as the product of "political cynicism," and in this McManners follows Sainte-Beuve, who "lifted his subject [Jansenism, in its center at Port-Royal les Champs] almost single-handedly out of obscurity, 'inventing' it, so to speak."[103] When the political dimensions are segregated from the theological, however, the conscious motivations of the actors are obscured. "The story of Jansenism after the death of Louis XIV is indeed a story of the war of the parlements against the crown; . . . of the rising discontent of the lower clergy, demanding economic justice and a share in the government of the church; of the convulutionist movement, a strange spiritual underworld of masochism and miracles."[104] Perhaps it is, finally, incorrect to sort the political from the spiritual elements of the phenomenon. "Jansenism is a concept the elements of which are so complex that it is impossible to enclose them by a definition. Popular speech confuses it with rigorism, with which it is connected only in an accidental way."[105]

*Rigorism* is, in this use, an attitude that manifests itself coherently in a dour worldview, in its turn exemplified in the practice of penance.

The type of piety that developed out of Jansenism was inflexibly rigorist and was characterized by the tension experienced by souls weighed down by the thought of damnation. For them, human nature was corrupt, conditioned on the one hand by concupiscence and on the other by the mysterious attraction of efficacious grace. Sacramental absolution, they thought, did not remit sins but simply declared that they had been forgiven, and was valid only if the one who confessed already loved God perfectly. For the proper reception of Holy Communion a certain perfection on the part of the dispositions of the recipient was a necessary prerequisite.[106]

The exact relations between Jansenism strictly speaking and a prevailing rigoristic ethos are murky.[107]

Still, Jansenist rigorism indicates a profound theological error with regard to the nature of the Godhead. Jansenism "takes away from God all the long-suffering and compassion with which his grace pleads with a sinner to the very last; it converts our most loving Creator into an arbitrary tyrant, imposing upon man laws too severe for his weak nature, without giving him supernatural power to fulfill them."[108] No wonder then that the popes condemned Jansenism, both in Jansenius's *Augustinus* (1640) and in its political machinations, at least four times in such documents as *Ad Sanctam Beati Petri Sedem* (1656), *Regiminis Apostolici* (1665), *Vineam Domini* (1705), and *Unigenitus Dei Filius* (1713). The later Jansenists "made common cause with the Gallicans of the parlements," that is, those who believed themselves "guardians of the holy decrees of the Gallican Church and of the Pragmatic Sanction of Bourges," and Gallicanism was condemned by Leo X (1516), Alexander VIII (1690), Pius VI (1794), and even the *Syllabus of Errors* (1864). Still, authorities differ on whether Arnauld's treatise was, itself and specifically, condemned.[109]

Long lists of undisputed, official, and perhaps politically motivated condemnations clearly show the endurance of Jansenism. Indeed, the swan song of institutional Jansenism may well have been the Synod of Pistoia (1786). Observers have claimed that Jansenism—still plagued by denotative layers— reached into very recent times. As Cognet says, "The 19th-century Jansenist circle, a very closed one, lived on memories."[110] Even early in the twentieth century, the bishop of Frejust and Toulon wrote, "How many practical remnants of that hateful heresy [Jansenism] still afflict us, in spite of the strict orthodoxy of our faith! Habits are more tenacious than doctrines."[111] By this time, when the campaign for frequent Holy Communion was on the verge of its ratification by *STS*, Jansenism may have been a synonym simply for a repugnant avoidance of Holy Communion. Thus Pope Pius X blamed Jansenism for the desuetude of Holy Communion: "Piety, however, grew cold, and especially afterward because of the widespread plague of Jansenism, disputes began to arise concerning the dispositions with which one ought to receive frequent and daily communion; and writers vied with one another in demanding more and more stringent conditions, as necessary to be fulfilled."[112] He then characterized infrequency of Communion as "rigorism." The pedigree of Jansenism as an object of papal condemnations was impeccable and it was, presumably because of this famous pedigree and Arnauld's fame, preeminently culpable for the abandonment of Holy Communion, the other causes for not communicating notwithstanding.[113]

Jansenists were often linked to Gallicans by virtue of their opposing the authority of both pope and king; this perception was popularized by Sainte-Beuve's influential *Port-Royal* (1840–1848).[114] Specifically, the essence of the tense drama of Port-Royal seemed, to Saint-Beuve, to be "the preservation of freedom of conscience."[115] The prevailing ideology of ultramontanism and antimodernism at the turn of the nineteenth century would have invited Pius X to scorn Jansenism for its political antiauthoritarianism and for its repellent intellectualism.

A yet more compelling reason for Pius X to play the Jansenist card in his campaign for more frequent Communion is that the entirety of the Eucharistic movement was, from its inception, aimed at reversing the vast de-Christianization of France, primarily, and eventually of all of Europe, too. Jansenism—or perhaps more precisely Jansenistic rigorism—was generally considered, even well into the early part of this century, the primary cause of this declination. For example in the 1920s, l'abbé Charrier wrote, "Jansenistic doctrines and the theological disputes to which they gave birth are the principal causes of the vitiation of the faith by which we are so saddened. Jansenism is indubitably and in very large part responsible for the virtual disappearance of the faith in the region of Auxerre, hithertofore so Christian."[116] The reasoning is straightforward but ignores the complexities of historical change, such as industrialization. Jansenistic extremities alienated the faithful from religion entirely because the demands were too daunting. As Joseph F. Smith describes it, "Jansenism, intertwined with Pelagianism, taught a false perfectionistic state attainable by human effort alone that allowed for no mistakes; it also stressed a rigorous spirit of penance for sins and inevitable mistakes as well as a constant fear of divine wrath."[117]

Specialists are now stating with some diffidence that "Jansenism . . . remains a permanent component of French religiosity," but they ask, in the same breath, such questions as "What place has Jansenism generally in the culture of France, and in particular in its political culture? What is the connection between the upheavals of Jansenism and secularization?"[118] Frequent Communion sought to reverse trends toward secularization, and secularization and avoidance of Communion were commonly blamed on Jansenism.

Although no one really knew what Jansenism was, all knew it was to be reviled.

Because Communion remained infrequent, and because the many devotions that centered in the Eucharist seem to have sprung up from this paucity, a false simplicity would classify such devotions as discouraging a return to Communion. In part, this may be the dynamic, but the issue needs to be pursued. The single, very popular devotion that compels our attention is the visit to the Blessed Sacrament, effectively popularized by Saint Alphonsus de Liguori about a century before the official start of the Eucharistic movement.

Liguori stands in history as a most influential great-uncle, if not grandfather, of the Eucharistic movement and hence of frequent Communion. Liguori and the Redemptorists, which he founded, structured and popularized the visit to church to pray in the presence of the Blessed Sacrament. As an astonishingly productive pastoral and moral theologian, Saint Alphonsus revitalized the notion of the love of God manifest in Jesus; this attitude also reconfigured the practice of penance in the late eighteenth century. Liguori reformed confessional practices to the extent that a Redemptorist son of Saint Alphonsus, François-Xavier Godts, one of the Belgian combatants whose dispute provoked *STS*, opined, "But even more than refuting the heretical Jansenists in print, Liquori wanted to demolish them in his way of living. The best *Treatise against Jansenism* is actually the life of Saint Alphonsus."[119]

Liguori's book, *Visits to the Holy Sacrament and the Blessed Virgin for Every Day* (1745), "republished 109 times between 1815 and 1908," helps gauge the immense popularity of this devotion, this technique of prayer.[120] Indeed, a recent biography of Liguori describes the results of the little book in these words: "Perhaps no other work, with the possible exception of *The Imitation of Christ,* has ever had such an effect on devotional practice throughout the whole Catholic world."[121] Papal indulgences issued by Pius IX in the 1850s specifically for visits using Liguori's prayers augmented Liguori's influence.[122] Ralph Gibson characterizes this book as a "refinement" of devotion to the Real Presence, but he also places devotion to the Blessed Sacrament in opposition to reception of Communion. Actually, several elements of visits explicitly *encourage* frequent Communion.

Clearly Liguori's manual makes the Real Presence the doctrinal focus, but he, with an eye to the pastoral, emphasizes that the point of Real Presence is to manifest the love of God in Christ. The content of the visit draws deeply from the tradition of reparation, popularized by Saint Margaret-Mary Alacoque and thus entwined with devotion to the Sacred Heart. These devotions hinged upon the ability of the devotee to "repair" and compensate in some way for abuse of the Real Presence, whether in scornful inattention or outright sacrilege. Liguori's contribution to the development of personal piety was to place in greater prominence attention to the reserved sacrament. By contrast, Sacred Heart devotions took as their devotional center, though not exclusively, the image of the heart of Jesus.

The prayer of the visit does not stop at the Real Presence but psychologically prepares the devotee to communicate by its thrice-repeated component, the "Spiritual Communion." Within *Visits*, Liguori cited Aquinas's definition of spiritual Communion: It is an "ardent desire to receive Jesus in the Most Holy Sacrament and in lovingly embracing him as if we had actually received him."[123] Liguori's method for the spiritual Communion, within the visit, contains the essential ingredients common to all valid spiritual Communions:

1. An act of faith in the real presence of Jesus Christ in the Blessed Sacrament.
2. An act of desire, accompanied by an act of the love of God with sorrow for one's sins, of worthily receiving sacramental communion if it were at the time possible and thus uniting oneself with Jesus Christ as in sacramental communion.
3. An act of thanksgiving as if Christ had been received sacramentally.[124]

The visit seems to have approached sacramental Communion in both sentiments aroused and spiritual benefits. It could only do such because real, sacramental Holy Communion was so exceptional.

The regnant sacramental theology of Liguori's day did privilege the sacraments with power. He explained that, while in its own sphere the visit was an optimal method of prayer because it focused upon the mystery of the Real Presence, this whole pious exercise remained a quantum below the merit of the sacraments. In other words, howsoever beneficial the visit was, according to Liguori, sacramental reception was far superior. "Certainly amongst all devotions, after that of receiving the sacraments, that of adoring Jesus in the Blessed Sacrament holds the first place, is the most pleasing to God, and the most useful to ourselves."[125] That the campaigns for frequent Communion in the twentieth century did not strive to extirpate the spiritual Communion may indicate that the campaigners thought that the explicit intentionality of the spiritual Communion to move the devout to receive sacramentally, when energized by the campaigns themselves, would serve to increase sacramental Communions.[126]

Second, Liguori the pastoral theologian partook with immense effect in the transformation of the Catholic religion from a nexus of fear to one of love, with consequences on the administration of the sacrament of penance. A contemporary of Liguori summarized the difference between Liguori's attitudes toward confession and that of another moral theologian of the early eighteenth century:

> The *Pratica* of Father Liguori is replete with unction, full of charity, sweetness and moderation. The *Istruzione* of Concina [a Dominican] breathes fury, passion, sternness, and fanaticism. . . . The first proceeds methodically, opens the way and marks the road to repentance with equilibrium and balance. The second is nothing more than a medley, confused and with unbalanced opinions which make confession an odious burden.[127]

His influence penetrated France with immense rapidity.[128] Liguori there became, according to the historian Ralph Gibson, the "champion of probabilism."[129] More precisely, Liguori was the defender of equiprobabilism.[130] His long life and his writings show signal adjustment on approaches to penance. In fact,

> it took Alphonsus over twenty-five years to work out the speculative side of the problem [of equiprobabilism] to his own satisfaction and to devise a system which could not be assailed either on theoretical or pastoral grounds. He published eleven separate dissertations during his lifetime on the whole question of conscience formation in moral theology.[131]

Probabilism "was basically the doctrine that where a moral law was not absolutely clear, i.e., where it had been contested by reputable theologians and where the contrary proposition was 'probable' in the Latin sense that a reasonable case could be made out for it, a confessor must not impose it—even if he were personally convinced of its validity."[132] Greater refining yields equiprobabilism, "the moral system according to which in a doubt of conscience concerning the morality of a certain course of conduct, a middle way between law and liberty is to be taken."[133] In pastoral application of this theory, Liguori's attitude toward penance was completely different from that of the French rigorists. Saint Alphonsus "taught that the confessor was a father to his penitents, and no matter how sinful they were he should never let them despair."[134] Liguori's approach to penance entered France through Bishop Alexandre-Raymond Devie of Belley (d. 1852), the Jesuits, and the Oblates of Mary Immaculate.[135] These two orders, incidentally, crusaded as well for Holy Communion.[136]

But Liguori's writings specifically on the frequency of Communion do not, admittedly, abet the cause. Saint Alphonsus agreed that frequent Communion would be good, but he articulated a proportionality between frequency of Communion and devotion. Thus, in terms of Communion, Liguori was a "mitigated rigorist."[137] Liquori not only "represents the prevalent theological opinion before . . . Saint Pius X," but greatly influenced that opinion by dint of his own authoritative teaching.[138] As Hardon explains, "Writing for confessors [in *Homo Apostolicus*], he [Liguori] cites the directive of Benedict XIV: 'It is undoubtedly wrong to allow frequent Communion to such as fall often into mortal sin, or to such as approach Holy Communion with affection to deliberate venial sin with no desire of amendment.'"[139]

On the one hand, penitents who seem particularly in danger of mortal sin may be permitted to receive often so as to prevent the sin. On the other hand, those who sin often and grievously and those who sin venially, but deliberately and without "desire of amendment," should not be allowed by their confessors to communicate frequently—that is, more than weekly.

> It is indeed proper at times to grant Communion to some who are in danger of falling into mortal sin that they may gain strength to resist; but in regard to those who are not in such danger, and who are in the habit of committing deliberate venial sin, and show no sign of improvement or desire of amendment, it is best not to allow them Communion oftener than once a week. It will, moreover, be good to deprive them of Communion sometimes for a whole week, so that they may gain a greater horror for their faults and greater reverence towards this Sacrament.[140]

For the sake of conveying forcibly to the penitent his obduracy in venial sin, the confessor may deprive him even of this weekly Communion. However, under certain conditions frequent, even daily, Communion may be permitted:

> To certain souls who desire it for their greater growth in the love of God, I judge the director can hardly without scruple deny Communion frequently and even daily, with the exception of one day in the week in accordance with the practice of some directors of experience, and with the exception also of the periods for which they may decide to deprive their penitents of Communion, as a proof of their obedience and humility, or for any other good reason. Such souls, however, should live free from affection to any venial sin, and should moreover be much given to mental prayer and strive towards perfection, no longer falling into sin, even fully deliberate venial sin.[141]

Even the most pious souls, daily communicants, should forego Communion once in the week to exercise the virtue of humility.

> The rule is not of universal application, but needs to be further qualified if certain contingencies arise: If, however, it be afterwards noticed that, notwithstanding frequent Communion, a person makes no progress in the path of perfection, and does not free himself from deliberate faults, even though venial, but for example still clings to the pleasures of sense in sight, hearing and taste, and is fastidious in dress, in this case it would be well to restrict the use of Communion deliberately, to the end that such a person may take serious thought of amendment, and look to his progress in spirit.[142]

Liguori pastorally responds to the realistic case of a frequent communicant not making spiritual progress. If the Eucharist is so unquestionably powerful, but progress is not discernible in either the communicant's exterior or interior forum, the rate of communicating should decrease. Given the doctrine of the Real Presence, something is amiss if there is no progress, and so Liguori, suspecting a deficiency in the communicant's preparation, advises a cessation of reception so that this problem can be addressed by the communicant's greater efforts.

Insofar as receiving Communion was a public act, frequent Communion became a sign of the communicant's aspiration to spiritual perfection. Likewise, admission to the table at a grandiose first Communion ceremony, a marking of adulthood and the completion of religious instruction, gave Communion the semblance of a reward. A third ingredient contributed to this idea of Communion as a reward for apparent spiritual progress: Even the daily communicant was advised to forego Communion once in the week for the virtue of humility. How is this? In the worst interpretation, not to communicate could indicate that one was not minimally fit for the sacrament, that one had fallen from grace, had sinned mortally. While Liguori wanted the faith of the communicant in the power of the Real Presence, met in the sacrament, to be confirmed and evidenced by spiritual growth, this complexity was easily misconstrued in a Jansenistic world where Communion was a reward for moral perfection.

Liguori described the other extreme, and in so doing confirmed that the nature of the Eucharist is not to reward progress but to prevent sin. Liguori allowed that, in case of danger of mortal sin, Communion acts as a preventative and diminishing the use of the sacrament in this grave situation is impossible, other circumstances notwithstanding. So long as the sacrament effectively prevents sin, and so long as the temptation remains nearly irresistible, receiving may continue.

These Communions in time of peril are not, of course, exempt from either the minimal requirements or from the techniques of preparation and thanksgiving. Even in the case of nearly irresistible temptation, the communicant must have the correct intentions and be in a state of grace, and, given that jeopardy prowls, this communicant is well advised to heroic prayerfulness. Communion, despite its mystical fruit of union with Jesus, cannot function as a pill; receiving Holy Communion requires immense application—fasting and the often formally structured preparation and thanksgiving—naturally encouraged by the doctrine of the Real Presence. Sin, despite the power of the Precious Body, may nonetheless occur, as human freedom and the power of evil readily testify. Only penance, reconciliation with Jesus through the Church in her ministers, will admit the penitent again to Communion.

In the sphere of Communion practice, Dublanchy lists no fewer than fourteen moral theologians who follow Liguori's lead.[143] Liguori's "rules" on the proportionality between the spiritual status of the penitent and frequency of Communion were codified by Clément Cardinal Villecourt and publicized by Godts in the early twentieth century; these rules were invalidated by *STS*.[144]

This analysis of Liguori's theology of penance manifests the revolution in pastoral practice and moral theology he and his order effected throughout the Church. "Among the major events in the history of the Church in the nineteenth century was the progressive rallying of moralists and of the clergy to the moral thinking of Saint Alphonsus. In eliminating rigorism, in facilitating access to the Sacraments, he infused a new youth into Christianity."[145] Liguori's advice to confessors is especially important for two reasons. First, Saint Alphonsus presumed that the reception of the Eucharist usually followed closely upon sacramental confession, and confession was tantamount to spiritual direction. The priest-confessor knew the individual well and judged progress in virtue either from observation or the reports of the penitent. Second, Liguori wanted the client to discern the benefits of the penitential regime. This regime included frequent Communion.

Like Saint Alphonsus, Saint Thérèse of Lisieux (d. 1897) is a doctor of the church, despite her lack of formal theological education and her death at the age of twenty-four. One of her letters provides evidence of a naive but confident anti-Jansenism. Thérèse's nineteen-year-old cousin had written to her about her fears of receiving Holy Communion because of her scrupulosity. The sixteen-year-old novice wrote back from the convent:

> You did well to write me, and I understand everything, everything, everything, everything! . . . You haven't committed the shadow of any evil; I know what these kinds of temptations are so well that I can assure you of this without any fear, and, besides, Jesus tells me this in the depths of my heart. . . . Go without any fear to receive Jesus in peace and love. . . . What offends Him and what wounds His Heart is the lack of confidence.[146]

This was written in the north of France at the same time the Eucharistic movement was very active there.

Because all sacraments are the work of Christ, the tenets of *ex opere operato* guarantee that the recipient makes some spiritual progress so long as the sacramental actions are licit. Holy Communion, if received with even the minimal and legal requisites—that is, freedom from mortal sin and proper intention, including the faith of the Communicant that the sacrament is a most profound encounter with Jesus—must benefit the receiver. Human intervention, on the other hand, for example, in the preparations for and thanksgiving after receiving Communion, can affect the sacrament.

After *STS*, the relative contributions of God's grace and the recipient's actions were clearly defined, consonant with the dogmas of God's omnipotence and an individual's free will. So long as the sacrament is received legitimately, a mystical union with Christ benefits the communicant. This union completes the work of God in baptism and creates a loving union that assures of salvation in appropriating to the individual the historical sacrifice of the Cross. This union occurs *ex opere operato*, whether felt, perceived, or experienced by the communicant or not.[147] The efforts of the communicant to live with utmost rectitude and to pray with ever-increasing devotion and fidelity, efforts guided by the confessor, may yield tangible results in the life of the penitent and may even witness powerfully and evangelically to the social milieu of the penitent; still, her efforts pale in comparison to the impact of the Real Presence, the salvific action of Jesus and the Passion.

## DATA ON COMMUNION RECEPTION

What was actual Communion reception in Europe in the second half of the nineteenth century and into the twentieth? No statistics exist to answer the question broadly. However, some information does exist for certain dioceses and parishes, largely in the Netherlands. The data suggest that, fortuitously, impressionistic accounts of trends in Communion practice, such as H. A. Reinhold's in the introduction to this book, are valid. "Local studies certainly do let us see that, as the end of the nineteenth century approached, a gradual increase in communion frequency began to be visible."[148] A longitudinal study, based upon the number of hosts used, sheds some light on trends in one parish in the village of Bladel in North Brabant, "in the Catholic south of the Netherlands."[149]

In the middle of the nineteenth century the average believer there went to Communion five times a year. During the last two decades of the nineteenth century, there was a distinct increase that resulted in a practice of monthly communion; in 1900 twelve hosts were distributed per communicant per year. After the decree of Pius X, an increase appeared once again. In no way, however, did this result in the practice of daily Communion that the pope had hoped for, nor even in the practice of Communion several times a week. Around 1920 the prevailing average Communion frequency was around forty times a year. This meant something less than the practice of weekly Communion.[150]

A study of the diocese of Ghent, home diocese of Jules Lintelo, SJ, reveals that "communion frequency between the middle of the nineteenth century and the middle of the twentieth more than doubled, but nonetheless still stalled with the practice of monthly communion."[151] Unhappily, no such data exist for the United States; our case study of the United States follows in chapters 4 through 6.

Why did calls for more frequent reception of Holy Communion, calls that echoed largely ineffectually for hundreds of years in Europe, bear fruit finally in the twentieth century in the United States? To answer this question, the historical antecedents to the campaign for frequent Communion need rehearsal. First to appear are the official considerations of the issues by the hierarchy of the United States. Then some anecdotal windows will be opened through which to glimpse Communion reception in the nineteenth century. Then, we review "sacramental evangelicalism," the dominant sacramental and liturgical activity in American Catholicism during the second half of the nineteenth century.[152] This seems to have prepared the soil very well for the Eucharistic movement. We examine Irish American Catholic Jansenism, a likely impediment to the success of the campaign for frequent Communion. Finally, this section extrapolates from the works of Jay Dolan, Ann Taves, and Robert Orsi to explain why the American campaign for frequent Communion seems to have succeeded in the United States in the early part of the twentieth century.

## THE INSTITUTIONAL CHURCH IN THE UNITED STATES

The hierarchy in the United States first officially addressed the subject of receiving Communion in its pastoral letter of October 1833. On the subject of the sacraments generally, the letter noted that sacramental graces require reception and then cited the classic Eucharistic passage of John 6 for support; the letter also couched its advice in terms of unquestioning compliance with authority. Next, the letter urged confession before receiving lest an unworthy reception "be our ruin."[153] The laws of the Church on Easter Communion, originally formulated at the Fourth Lateran Council, followed—including the penalty of excommunication. On the subject of Holy Communion, the letter seems contradictory:

> Thanks be to our heavenly Father: our hearts have been greatly consoled by the increasing multitude that since our last Council has on every side exhibited itself to us, pressing forward to this life-giving food [Communion]. We have indeed been made joyful by the vast increase; still we have to lament the absence of numbers. Oh that they would reduce their principles to practice! That they would feel the importance of providing for eternity! That they would follow the plain and explicit declarations of the incarnate Son of God, rather than hazard every thing upon the miserable sophistry of deceitful world! Brethren, we openly announce to you that there is no other name under heaven in which you can be saved but by our Lord Jesus. And there is no salvation in His name but by means of His institutions, and these are principally the sacraments which

He has established. We beseech, we conjure you not to continue the criminality of this neglect.[154]

The explicit claim that Communions have been increasing since the earlier council, only three years previous, need not command credibility because the bishops remained displeased and exhortatory.

The decrees of the Second Plenary Council of Baltimore (1866) touched upon many Eucharistic topics, such as the extension of the period in which to satisfy one's Easter duty and priestly responsibilities to prepare first communicants, but the subject of Holy Communion was not central. Because a large chasm may separate the ideals and desires that the bishops were articulating from actual communion practice, anecdotal evidence follows.

John Hughes (d. 1864), the archbishop of New York, writing in 1858, opens a tantalizing but blurry window onto the practice of receiving Communion: "In a letter to Rome recounting his twenty years['] experience in New York, Hughes said that a 'great body' of people received communion 'once or twice a year; and very many, once a month, and even once a week.'"[155] Ten years later James Parton, writing in *Atlantic Monthly*, reported that, at Sunday Mass at six on a winter's morning at Saint Stephen's Church in New York City, five men out of approximately one hundred in attendance communicated, and that twenty women out of a thousand did likewise. Later that day, at the children's Mass, ten to fifteen of the two thousand children present received Communion.[156]

This contrasts remarkably with a glowing account of the sacramental practice of American Catholics in the mid-1880s—just twenty years later—written by the English convert Richard Frederick Clarke, SJ. He sets the scene as a Mass on a wintry Sunday at five in the morning, attended by thousands; the church is cramped. The congregational singing of the refrain "Adeste, fideles" indicates that Clarke is describing a Mass in Advent or Christmastide.

> At length the bell rings the *Domine, non sum dignus*. The stream, the throng of communicants includes nearly all of that enormous congregation. Not women chiefly, scarcely a majority of the female sex—but old men, men in the prime of life, men in their early manhood, youths and boys, and innocent children. Three priests come in to assist the celebrant in giving Communion, and he, as the Mass has already been a long one, administers to a few railfulls and then returns to the altar. But the assistants go on with that work of love which seems as if it would never end. On and still on follows the unceasing stream of those who come to receive their God. On and still on, though the Mass is over, and the long procession has wound its way out from the sanctuary—on and still on, though another Mass has now begun—on and still on, until once more the *Domine non sum dignus* is said, and a fresh stream of communicants mingles with those who have been patiently waiting their turn ever since the High Mass began.[157]

That Clarke begins his account with the admission that such a scene could occur in either Chicago or Detroit indicates that his description is at best typical and representative rather than journalistic. At worst for our purposes, the description could be a propagandistic charade to encourage English Catholics to greater Communion. Because we shall later examine very closely the disputes about precisely when Communion was to be distributed, please note that Holy Communion is essentially continuous in this account.

Saint Elizabeth Seton's remarks upon receiving Communion provide compelling witness to the emotional dynamics of abstaining from Communion. This practice "for humility" was considered virtuous, as Liguori's rules indicated. In this, she represents the prevailing attitude and so may be regarded as typical. "Unusual sweetness and consolation at Communion the more sensibly felt, because ungrateful self indulgence kept me absent the two former appointed days—renewed the *entire* sacrifice fervently yielded *All* and offered every nerve fiber and power of Soul and Body to sickness, Death, or any and every appointment of his blessed Will."[158] The "appointed days" were presumably when Communion was allowed her by her confessor. Further, during the campaigns for *daily* Communion in the twentieth century, the emotional exultation that accompanied the rare Communion urgently needed redirection.

Now look at Saint Elizabeth's milieu, at the status of Catholics in the United States in the first half of the nineteenth century. Few Catholics practiced their religion; they lacked enthusiasm for the faith and did not receive the sacraments.[159] The reasons for this were primarily geographic and demographic: Catholics, a tiny minority of the population of the United States, were widely dispersed; the shortage of priests was acute.[160] While the hierarchy responded with much conciliar activity, European-born priests responded by running Catholic equivalents of Protestant revival meetings. Called "parish missions," they resembled uncannily the Protestant meetings but were derived from European practices.[161] They proved astonishingly effective. Catholic parish missions targeted preeminently lapsed or nominal Catholics and culminated in reception of the sacraments of penance and Communion, and so the parish missions created a phenomenon of "sacramental evangelicalism."

Often, this sacramental reincorporation of the *lapsi* by confession and Communion was celebrated in a most public way by a ritual renewal of baptismal vows.

> It was an impressive ceremony; . . . journalists seldom failed to comment on [it]. Invariably the church was packed with people. . . . In the sanctuary of the church stood the baptismal font, richly decorated with flowers and candles together with all the paraphernalia necessary for the sacrament of baptism. No baptism was to take place, however.[162]

The conversions had been individualistic; the concluding ceremony, this renewal of baptism, was public and intended to "encourage perseverance in the people."[163] According to Jay Dolan, "Like Janus, the Roman god, evangelical Catholicism had two faces. It was both individual and communal."[164] The legacy of sacramental evangelicalism for Catholic piety in the twentieth century was an "experiential" piety, and for the Catholic Church as an institution the legacy was an augmentation of its power.[165]

Dolan contrasts experiential religion and ritualistic religion, and holds as axiomatic that these two emphases occur in cycles. While Ignatius Loyola advocated greater frequency of Communion and Alphonsus Liguori maintained a proportionality between one's dispositions and morality and frequency of Communion, both find homes in Dolan's camp of preachers of conversion, that is, in experiential religion.[166] The most prominent orders in American Catholic revivalism were the sons of Ignatius and Alphonsus; their sons prepared well the way in the United States for greater Communion.[167] A Redemptorist handbook on giving missions in the United States stresses the preservation of the faith, a prolongation, as it were, of the experience of the highly emotional parish mission.

> The entire fruit of the Mission is lost, if the people do not frequent the sacraments; and experience proves how slothful people generally are especially in this respect. . . . The people must be told in plain words that one Communion a year is not enough to keep the soul in the state of grace; then, how often they should receive. In places where the faith in the Real Presence has become weak with the greater part of the people, the first part of the sermon should be on the Real Presence.[168]

Holy Communion was the means par excellence of fidelity after the mission was over, for it continued contact with Jesus. The broader impact of Liguori may be seen in his serving as a source for so many of the derivative homilies of the American clergy.[169]

From the liturgical point of view, of course, experience is not an opposite of ritual, as Dolan perceives. But Dolan, describing a vast panorama, refers to highly emotional and ultimately personally appropriated conversion events—peaks in a spiritual journey—as *experience*, and he rightly observes that such events, either in an individual or in a social organism, cannot be sustained. Dolan sees the sum total of devotions, quite individualistic in the praying but managed by the parish priests, as that which sustained the conversion experiences of the parish missions.

"The 'flying visit' of the revivalist toned up the body religious, but it did not end there. Conversion was but the first step; sacramental nurture and the practice of devotional piety were also deemed necessary to sustain and perfect conversion."[170] In other words, after the mission-band priests departed, the local parish priests would attempt to sustain the effects of the missions by encouraging routine devotions, including the sacraments. Dolan's work points, then, to increasing sacramental practice generally, and this would include greater frequency of Communion. Documentation of this aftermath of the parish missions does not exist, but Joseph Chinnici has noted that even as this sacramental evangelicalism was thriving, harbingers of the American Eucharistic movement were, providentially, beginning to appear.

Beginning in 1865, various species of tabernacle societies established themselves, nocturnal adoration groups began in Boston in 1882 and the institution spread to many large cities, and a Confraternity of Perpetual Adoration was endowed with a rescript from Rome in 1893. All such groups promoted adoration of the Blessed Sacrament, especially in the individually conducted visit and in the communally celebrated Benediction and Forty Hours' devotion. One part of this adoration was the making of reparation for the insults and neglect to which the sacrament was subjected, a leitmotif of Sacred Heart devotions. Concurrent with the piety of adoration, these various clubs and institutions promoted the more frequent reception of Communion.[171] Remember that no distinction existed, at least in the common parlance of that day, between devotions and sacramental reception of Communion.

The sacramental system of Catholicism accords with this psychological reality of the uniqueness of conversion by restricting baptism to once in a lifetime; the system also accommodates the need to sustain this unique conversion by encouraging Communion. Baptism represents the "peak" event as the Rite of Christian Initiation of Adults now makes evident; baptism betokens irrevocable membership in the Body of Christ. The baptismal commitment can be revivified by the Eucharist, which is encountered for the first time, significantly, as one important element within the rites of initiation.

Dolan perceives alternations between conversion phenomena and sustenance phenomena in the religious experiences of a denomination through several generations. If we apply his paradigm to the Eucharistic movement, (literal) sustenance of the faith and routinization of the conversion experience, through frequent participation in the ritual of receiving Holy Communion, naturally follows the period of Catholic revivalism. This is confirmed by Chinnici, who wrote, "Emerging from the devotional revival in the second half of the nineteenth century, the Eucharistic movement was the most vital spiritual movement of the first fifty years of twentieth-century American Catholicism."[172]

What aspects of American Catholic culture, in addition to sacramental evangelicalism, contributed to this success? As an institution, the official Church, largely through the use of indulgences, appropriated popular devotions in order to enhance its own institutional clout. This is manifest in an investigation of Roman Catholic devotional manuals in the middle of the nineteenth century. This continues trends in Europe, too, after Trent: "Church officials promoted devotions in order to bind the laity more closely to the institutional church, both to ensure the church's survival in this world and to ensure the orthodoxy of the laity and thus their survival in the world to come."[173] The Church's "system of parochial conformity" aimed to central-ize and standardize both liturgical and devotional practices.[174] Indulgences did this in two ways: First, their legal promulgation depended upon the pope, around whose office an astonishing cult developed.[175] Second, the most munificent indulgences insisted upon recourse to confession and Holy Com-munion, as well as prayers for the intentions of the pope, for the bestowal of their merits; in this way the popular devotion was placed under the control of the institutional Church.[176]

A case study of the same pattern of the co-opting by the institutional Church of popular devotions treats the *feste* in Italian Harlem, and this social history occurs simultaneously with the campaign for frequent Communion. The *feste* was originally a popular and communal devotion of the Neapoli-tans; it was religious without being otherworldly.[177] Its practice in the United States alarmed the largely Irish Catholic prelates of New York City. They perceived that the *feste* actually impeded the Americanization of the Nea-politan immigrants. Still, the festival could not be banned entirely because it would alienate the entire immigrant community from the Church. So the chancery officials over the years reshaped the *feste* so that finally it was encouraging the participants to go to church and receive Communion—very "otherworldly" rituals.[178] The success of the prelates' actions was aided by such larger historical trends as the dispersion of the community of Italian Harlem to the suburbs after the Second World War. So, by 1953,

> the pastor urged all those who were planning to attend the celebration to make sure they went to confession and communion during the feste. . . . The meaning of the feste had become interior, controlled, a matter of the heart and not of the street. The people have come not to march and eat and cry in the hot streets, but to go to church.[179]

The Eucharistic movement itself fits the pattern noted by Taves and appli-cable to both devotional books and the *feste*. "Virtually all general devotions began as local devotions, often receiving papal sanction as general devotions only after vigorous lobbying efforts on their behalf."[180] But of particular inter-est are the institutional dynamics of power and resources and control.

Holy Communion offered to the laity, according to standard sacramental theology and in the context of a vast menu of devotions, the most rewarding spiritual benefit; to the institutional Church, it thus offered control over a most precious and desirable commodity, and this control, in turn, contributed to institutional robustness. On the local level, the customary link between confession and Communion allowed confessors supervision of the morals of their flocks. On a national level in the United States, Communion provided a ritual action more powerful than any particular devotions from the homelands of the immigrants, and so it could replace or subordinate those old-country devotions. Simultaneously, the Blessed Sacrament as a devotional focus united the Church in the face of an exclusively and sometimes militantly Protestant ethos, wherein the Bible was the "central devotional symbol."[181] More particularly, frequent Holy Communion added yet another distinction, in addition to the Latin language and celibate clergy, with respect to Protestants.[182]

The Catholic Church, united in America as a securely Roman Catholic Church, could then assert both its Americanness as well as its patriotism in response to accusations of its political allegiance to Rome. The decorations for the International Eucharistic Congress in Chicago witness this marriage of genuine Americanness and Catholicity. As the immigrants assimilated, the Church was forced to become American lest it suffer massive abandonment: As Communion replaced ethnic devotions, it facilitated assimilation of the faithful at least into the united and American Roman Catholic Church, if not yet into the mainstream of American society.

An additional aspect of American culture prepared the way for the relatively rapid implementation of *STS* here. Law universally denotes prescriptions for behavior, but in the United States, law is derived by the community through the experience of history and codified by the representatives of the people. The English Jesuit Clarke contrasts the American view of *civil* law to the Catholic view of *ecclesiastical* law, which, by extension, the American Catholic wants to ignore because it seems to him that it is imposed, rather than his own. Clarke is explaining why there has been such a large decline in the practice of Catholicism by those whom he thinks should be practicing:

> But while there is no lawlessness, this is because the laws are the people's laws. It is the uncrowned King respecting his own sceptre. . . . The American view of obedience to civil law is that the law is the people's law framed by the people's representatives for the people's good, and therefore, I as a sensible, self-respecting man, must obey it whether I like it or not.[183]

Thus, laws are to be implemented and obeyed because Americans "own" the laws. Because they must really be implemented, they are actually important to the culture and must remain systematized and lucid.

A very Catholic view of American civil law is manifest in the writings of Isaac Hecker (d. 1888). He considered American civil law a manifestation of

Natural Law, which thus exacts obedience: To obey is to be in harmony with the will of God.

> The individual is not the source of Law; the immediate source of Law is the people as interpreters of the natural Law of God. . . . Hence in the American system the idea of Law is sacred. It is not regarded as a hard master or a tyrant, but as a great strength erected by the people themselves for their protection, and obedience to Law is not only divested of anything like servility, but becomes a duty imposed by the dignity of citizenship itself.[184]

But note that still the law in America is mediated by the people. To the degree that this general attitude toward law lost sight of the authoritarian origins of papal enactments, then, the provisions of *STS* as laws would have been accorded great respect in the United States. In addition, although Jansenism properly speaking may not have pertained in the United States, Irish American scrupulosity goes hand in glove with reactive legalism.

> Without unified national Catholic cultures, as they had known in their European homelands, the American bishops in the nineteenth century convened many councils.
> One area in which the variety of national traditions had created a state of chaos was liturgical practice. . . . To remedy this, the councils sought to impose one common style of liturgical practices as prescribed in the Roman Ritual. . . . To create unity amid diversity the church fathers looked to Europe, especially Rome, for guidance.[185]

This habit of relying upon Rome for solutions to frictions between various ethnic groups likely disposed American clerics to attend to—and attempt to comply with—such decrees as *STS* more energetically than their European counterparts.

By way of contrast, Italian law, far less important to social functions than magnificent spectacles and patronal relationships, resembles a "tropical tangle of statutes, rules, norms, regulations, customs," and its provisions are thus so "numerous, contradictory, and ambiguous" that "nobody knows for certain what some of them really mean." Here is an instance of a liturgical upshot of the Italian legal "system." Godfrey Diekmann described daily Mass during the Second Vatican Council in his journal and notes that the "rump" of the Sistine Choir sang hymns during the liturgy, in direct violation of a recent Vatican directive. He adds, parenthetically, "In Rome they only *make* the laws—but they are to be *observed* outside of Rome."[186]

Reciprocally, Rome was asserting itself in the United States more and more in the years around 1900, and it was generally attempting to control the Church's "spiritual" affairs more efficiently as a consequence of the loss of the Papal States.[187] For example, in contrast to the earlier councils of Baltimore, the Third Plenary was convened by Rome and was presided over by a Roman appointee, not by the honorary primate of the country, the Archbishop of Baltimore.[188] The last factor predisposing Americans to accept the provisions of *STS* was the cult of the pope, which would have depicted the decree on frequent Communion as a clear-cut order from God, and this would have stirred the ardor of those campaigning for the implementation of *STS* as well as the obedient zeal of rank-and-file Catholics.[189]

Frequent Communion was an astonishingly swift change in liturgical practice. Several factors in the United States seemed to encourage this change: The American bishops urged greater use of Communion, not only for the explicit reason of obedience to the injunctions of Trent, but also to help unify a Church of immigrants from diverse devotional traditions. In terms of Church history, greater frequency of Communion may be considered one aspect of the general Counter-Reformation tendency toward centralization and conformity. In terms of the permeation of the Church by broader cultural trends in America, during the late nineteenth and early twentieth centuries, all institutions, including commercial ones, organized on a massive scale. Uniformity of "product" gave the Church an institutional identity pointing toward Rome and superseding ethnic allegiances; this allowed immigrants to become American, but not Protestant. A greater emphasis upon the sacraments made the Church more Roman and more acceptable to the Vatican. The intense energies of evangelical Catholicism naturally flowed into a calmer stream of routinized piety and sacramental practice.

## NOTES

1. Thomas B. Scannell, "The History of Daily Communion," in *Report of the Nineteenth Eucharistic Congress, Held at Westminster from 9th to 13th September 1908* (London: Sands, 1909), 215.
2. CEF, 516; Duhr, 1236.
3. Edward Kilmartin, *The Eucharist in the Primitive Church* (Englewood Cliffs, New Jersey: Prentice-Hall, 1965), 147.
4. Kilmartin, *The Eucharist in the Primitive Church*, 149.
5. Kilmartin, *The Eucharist in the Primitive Church*, 149.
6. Duhr, 1237.
7. CEF, 517.
8. Duhr, 1237.
9. Bohl, *Kommunionempfang*, 162; the earliness of this phenomenon leads Bohl to discount Jungmann's hypothesis about Arianism causing infrequent Communion.
10. Duhr, 1241.
11. Duhr, 1241.

12. Scannell, "History," 218.

13. Scannell, "History," 217.

14. CEF, 520.

15. Scannell, "History," 218.

16. Josef A. Jungmann, "The Overall Historical Picture: The Defeat of Teutonic Arianism and the Revolution in Religious Culture in the Early Middle Ages," in *Pastoral Liturgy* (New York: Herder and Herder, 1962), 11–15.

17. Kilmartin, *The Eucharist in the Primitive Church*, 151–52.

18. Duhr, 1247.

19. Duhr, 1247.

20. CEF, 521.

21. Peter Browe, *Die häufige Kommunion in Mittelalter* (Munster: Regensbergsche, 1938), 10.

22. Browe, *Kommunion in Mittelalter*, 18–19.

23. CEF, 522, and Duhr, 1248.

24. Browe, *Kommunion in Mittelalter*, 18.

25. CEF, 527.

26. Duhr, 1248 and 1249.

27. Browe, *Kommunion in Mittelalter*, 21.

28. Jungmann, "Defeat of Teutonic Arianism," 59.

29. Jungmann, "Defeat of Teutonic Arianism," 62.

30. Jungmann, "Defeat of Teutonic Arianism," 62.

31. Jungmann, "Defeat of Teutonic Arianism," 62.

32. Jungmann, "Defeat of Teutonic Arianism," 62.

33. In fact, the decree *Quemadmodum* (1890), though it touches upon the receiving of Communion in religious houses, figures prominently in the drive to more frequent Communion for the *laity* at the turn of the twentieth century.

34. Duhr, 1262.

35. Scannell, "History," 223.

36. Édouard Dumoutet, *Le désir de voir l'hostie et les origines de la dévotion au Saint-Sacrement* (Paris: Gabriel Beauchesne, 1926), 17.

37. Dumoutet, *Le désir*, 101.

38. Eamon Duffy, *The Stripping of the Altars: Traditional Religion in England, c. 1400–c. 1580* (New Haven: Yale University Press, 1992), 97.

39. Duffy, *Stripping of the Altars*, 96.

40. Duffy, *Stripping of the Altars*, 96.

41. Duffy, *Stripping of the Altars*, 97.

42. Duffy, *Stripping of the Altars*, 97–98.

43. Duffy, *Stripping of the Altars*, 100.

44. Duffy, *Stripping of the Altars*, 95. "But the reception of communion was not the primary mode of lay encounter with the Host. Everyone received at Easter, and one's final communion, the viaticum or 'journey money' given on the deathbed, was crucially important to medieval people." While Duffy has read extensively in vernacular prayer books, wills, and the like, he does not from these provide hard evidence on the rate of compliance with the obligation imposed upon all Christians

to communicate at Easter. He seems to rely on connections between fear of death and fear of a ritually deficient burial for those who have been excommunicated by failure to fulfill this obligation.

45. CEF, 534.

46. Council of Trent, *Canons and Decrees of the Council of Trent: Original Text with English Translation*, trans. H. J. Schroeder (Saint Louis: B. Herder, 1941), 147, 420.

47. J. A. McN [*sic*], "A Plea for Daily Communion," *EPUL* 15 (1909): 92–93, and Albert Tesnière, "Commentary on the Decree of the Sacred Congregation of the Council, December 20, 1905, On Daily Communion," *Ssac* 9 (1906): 263. The preeminent purposes of the council must be recalled. "It was not their [the council fathers'] aim to provide a full and exhaustive exposition of the whole of the Church's sacramental doctrine." Hubert Jedin, *A History of the Council of Trent*, trans. Ernest Graf (London: Thomas Nelson, 1957), 386.

48. Scannell, "History," 224.

49. John W. O'Malley, *The First Jesuits* (Cambridge: Harvard University Press, 1993), 152–53.

50. Scannell, "History," 224.

51. Ignatius asked Salméron, one of the theologians of Trent, to prepare a rebuttal to the opponents of frequent Communion, and his notes were the source for Cristóbal de Madrid's *De frequenti usu sanctissimi Eucharistiae sacramenti libellus*, according to O'Malley "the first book ever published for the professed and exclusive purpose of defending and promoting more frequent reception of the Eucharist." When it appeared in Naples in 1556, it caused considerable civil unrest. O'Malley, *First Jesuits*, 154; Ferreres, *Decree*, 57; Hardon, "Historical Antecedents," 499ff.

52. Hardon, "Historical Antecedents," 499.

53. O'Malley, *First Jesuits*, 156.

54. Justo Beguiriztáin, *The Eucharistic Apostolate of St. Ignatius of Loyola*, translated by John H. Collins (1955), 27.

55. Beguiriztáin, *Apostolate of Ignatius Loyola*, 29.

56. Marshall, "Spain in the Sixteenth and Seventeenth Centuries," 488.

57. Marshall, "Spain in the Sixteenth and Seventeenth Centuries," 178.

58. CEF lists nine authors in this contentious time who favored limiting the use of the Eucharist, and nine who explicitly favored daily Communion. CEF, 535–38.

59. Marshall, "Spain in the Sixteenth and Seventeenth Centuries," 267.

60. Stephen Haliczer, *Sexuality in the Confessional: A Sacrament Profaned*, Studies in the History of Sexuality (New York: Oxford, 1996), 23.

61. Hardon, "Historical Antecedents," 515.

62. Marshall, "Spain in the Sixteenth and Seventeenth Centuries," 51.

63. Marshall, "Spain in the Sixteenth and Seventeenth Centuries," 40–41.

64. Elisabeth G. Gleason, review of *The Lateran in 1600: Christian Concord in Counter-Reformation Rome* by Jack Freiberg, *Church History* 66, no. 1 (March 1997): 199.

65. CEF, 537.

66. Antonio de Molina must not be confused with Miguel de Molinos (d. 1696), the more famous proponent of Quietism or with the Jesuit Luis de Molina (d. 1600),

the more famous moralist and economist whose notion of "pure nature" was attacked by Jansen in *Augustinus*. Luis's *Concordia ligeri arbitrii cum gratiae donis* tried to solve "the problem of free will and God's foreknowledge, providence, predestination, reprobation, [and] efficacious grace." Antonio de Molina's writings were "severely attacked by the Jansenist Antoine Arnauld" in his *De la fréquente communion*, while Miguel de Molinos's slight pamphlet and first published work "might have been written as a deliberate counterblast" to Arnauld. Further complicating the confusion of the two is that Juan Falconi de Bustamante (d. 1638) greatly influenced Miguel de Molinos, and Falconi's work, translated into French only in the late nineteenth century, ignited the bitter controversy that in turn provoked *STS*. Ronald Arbuthnot Knox, *Enthusiasm: A Chapter in the History of Religion, with Special Reference to the XVII and XVIII Centuries* (New York: Galaxy / Oxford, 1961), 299, 302; from the *New Catholic Encyclopedia* (New York: McGraw-Hill, 1967): F. C. Lehner, "Molina, Anthony de"; L. J. Cognet, "Jansenism"; and F. L. Sheerin, "Molina, Luis de."

67. Duhr, 1282.

68. Ferreres, *Decree*, 62. This notion of the "persistence" of qualification to communicate seems to resonate with Juan Falconi's (de Bustamante's) notion of the "single act." Knox, *Enthusiasm*, 267.

69. O'Malley, *First Jesuits*, 153–54.

70. O'Malley, *First Jesuits*, 154.

71. O'Malley, *First Jesuits*, 154.

72. Haliczer, *Sexuality in the Confessional*, 23–24.

73. Haliczer, *Sexuality in the Confessional*, 24.

74. Haliczer, *Sexuality in the Confessional*, 24.

75. Karl Rahner implies that, while it is difficult to prove that Holy Communion is "necessary in itself" for the preservation of the supernatural life, frequent and devotional confession is yet more difficult to prove. Karl Rahner, "The Meaning of Frequent Confession of Devotion," in *Theological Investigations*, vol. 3, *The Theology of the Spiritual Life*, translated by Karl-H. and Boniface Kruger (Baltimore: Helicon, 1967), 179n2.

76. This is a translation of a portion of the bishop's letter itself. Ferreres, *Decree*, 92.

77. CEF, 534.

78. Ferreres, *Decree*, 150.

79. CEF, 534.

80. Ferreres, *Decree*, 151.

81. Ferreres, *Decree*, 152.

82. CEF, 534.

83. Ferreres, *Decree*, 151.

84. Hardon, "Historical Antecedents," 517–19. *Cum Ad Aures* in fact quotes large passages from this letter verbatim. Joseph Nicholas Stadler, *Frequent Holy Communion: A Historical Synopsis and Commentary*, Catholic University of American Canon Law Studies, no. 263 (Washington, D.C.: Catholic University, 1947), 17–18, 29.

85. Hardon, "Historical Antecedents," 517.

86. Duhr, 1279.

87. Duhr, 1278, and Lehner, "Molina, Anthony de," *NCE*; and A. Barnes, "Duvergier de Hauranne, Jean," *NCE*.

88. Hardon, "Historical Antecedents," 505–6, and Duhr, 1278.

89. Knox, *Enthusiasm*, 215.

90. Hardon, "Historical Antecedents," 505.

91. Hardon, "Historical Antecedents," 510 and 508.

92. Knox, *Enthusiasm*, 215–16.

93. Hardon, "Historical Antecedents," 505–6.

94. Hardon, "Historical Antecedents," 509.

95. Hardon, "Historical Antecedents," 509.

96. Edmund H. Hogan, "Jansenism and Frequent Communion—A Consideration of the Bremond Thesis," *Irish Theological Quarterly* 53 (1987): 145. Hogan does not name his sources, and Ralph Gibson asserts, also without naming sources, that in the eighteenth century, "quite a number" did not receive Communion at Easter. Ralph Gibson, *A Social History of French Catholicism, 1789–1914* (New York: Routledge, 1989), 257.

97. Scannell, "History," 225.

98. Knox, *Enthusiasm*, 216.

99. John McManners, "Jansenism and Politics in the Eighteenth Century," in *Church, Society, and Politics: Papers Read at the Thirteenth Summer Meeting and the Fourteenth Winter Meeting of the Ecclesiastical History Society*, edited by Derek Baker, Studies in Church History 12 (Oxford: Basil Blackwell, 1975), 254.

100. Knox, *Enthusiasm*, 186-87.

101. Knox, *Enthusiasm*, 186.

102. Knox, *Enthusiasm*, 183.

103. McManners, "Jansenism and Politics," 257. Richard M. Chadbourne. *Charles-Augustin Sainte-Beuve* (Boston: Twayne, 1977), 122.

104. McManners, "Jansenism and Politics," 253.

105. Cognet, "Jansenism."

106. B. Matteucci, "Jansenistic Piety," *NCE*.

107. "The whole eighteenth-century Church, however, and not just the Jansenists, had adopted a rigorist attitude to the sacrament [of the Eucharist], regarding it as a reward for supreme efforts of virtue, rather than as an ever-present help in time of trouble and a means whereby the soul might enter into communion with a loving God." Gibson, *French Catholicism*, 257.

108. John Dalgairns, *The Devotion to the Heart of Jesus with an Introduction on the History of Jansenism* (Philadelphia: H. L. Kilner, 1854), 21.

109. "A miasma of relations among Arnauld, the Jesuits, the Queen and her prime minister, and bishops who approved of the work of Arnauld make the royal action against Arnauld imperceptible, if not futile." Hardon, "Historical Antecedents," 512–13. "The work, which was a great success and caused lively controversy, was delated to Rome, but the Holy See refused to condemn it." Cognet, "Jansenism." "Rigorism was condemned in 1690 by Alexander VIII." F. J. Connell, "Rigorism," *NCE*. "But in the condemnation of the thirty-one Jansenist propositions by Alexander VIII in 1690, five seem indubitably the essential theses defended by Arnauld." Duhr, 1279.

110. Cognet, "Jansenism."

111. *ET*, 76n1.

112. *STS*, 12.

113. Father Stephen Coubé's influence as an advocate of weekly Communion and his ranking of Jansenism as more pernicious even than the Reformation may be a textual antecedent to *STS*. His speech at the International Eucharistic Congress at Lourdes attracted praise from Pope Leo XIII. See Stephen Coubé, *The Great Supper of God, or Discourses on Weekly Communion*, translated by Ida Griffiss, edited by F. X. Brady (New York: Benziger, 1901), 43, 122–23, 243.

114. Chadbourne, *Sainte-Beuve*, 108.

115. Chadbourne, *Sainte-Beuve*, 119.

116. Dominique Dinet, "Le jansénisme et les origines de la déchritianisation au XVIIIᵉ siècle. L'exemple des pays de l'Yonne," in *Du jansénisme à la laïcité: Le jansénisme et les origines de la déchristianisation*, edited by Léo Hamon. Les entretiens d'Auxerre (Paris: Éditions de la maison des sciences de l'homme, 1983), 1.

117. Joseph F. Schmidt, *Everything Is Grace: The Life and Way of Thérèse of Lisieux* (Ijamsville, Maryland: Word Among Us, 2007), 60.

118. Léo Hamon, "Avant-propos," in *Du jansénisme à la laïcité: Le jansénisme et les origines de la déchristianisation*, edited by Léo Hamon. Les entretiens d'Auxerre (Paris: Éditions de la maison des sciences de l'homme, 1983), 7.

119. François-Xavier Godts, *L'apôtre moderne du T. S. Sacrement: S. Alphonse, docteur de l'église* (Bruxelles: Larose, 1905), 8, henceforth *AM*.

120. Gibson, *French Catholicism*, 256; because Gibson's work is a social history of *French* Catholicism, presumably he is totaling French editions here, but the text does not specify.

121. Frederick M. Jones, *Alphonsus de Liguori: The Saint of Bourbon Naples, 1696–1787* (Westminster, Maryland: Christian Classics, 1992), 191.

122. Ann Taves, *The Household of Faith: Roman Catholic Devotions in Mid-Nineteenth-Century America* (Notre Dame, Indiana: Notre Dame University Press, 1986), 31.

123. Spiritual Communion needs scholarly treatment. The practice was multiform; Liguori outlines one method. It includes declarations of faith in the Real Presence and of love for Jesus on the altar. The prayers themselves concede that the only reason for a spiritual Communion is the inability to communicate sacramentally, and they also admit that union with Jesus to some degree subsists already, while simultaneously imploring Jesus to be present within the devotee. Alphonsus de Liguori, *Visits to the Blessed Sacrament and to the Blessed Virgin*, in vol. 4, *The Holy Eucharist*, of *The Complete Works of Saint Alphonsus de Liguori, Doctor of the Church . . . Holy Redeemer*, ed. Eugene Grimm (n.d.; third revised reprint, Brooklyn: Redemptorist Fathers, 1934), 121, 124ff.

124. H. V. Gill, "Spiritual Communion," *Irish Monthly* 71 (1943): 517–18.

125. Liguori, *Visits*, 116.

126. Gill, writing thirty-seven years after the promulgation of *STS*, concedes that spiritual Communion has spurred frequent and even daily Communion by "numbers in every section of the faithful." His advocacy of recourse to spiritual Communion

for those unable physically or circumstantially to communicate sacramentally may be the best evidence for the obsolescence of the piety. Gill, "Spiritual Communion," 515.

127. Jones, *Alphonsus de Liguori*, 284.

128. L. Vereecke, "Saint Alphonsus Liguori," *NCE*.

129. Gibson, *French Catholicism*, 261.

130. Lawrence Cunningham of Notre Dame University, Indiana, corrected Ralph Gibson on this issue during the defense of my dissertation. See also F. J. Connell, "Equiprobabilism," *NCE*.

131. Jones, *Alphonsus de Liguori*, 281.

132. Jones, *Alphonsus de Liguori*, 281.

133. Connell, "Equiprobablism."

134. Connell, "Equiprobablism."

135. Gibson, *French Catholicism*, 261.

136. Gibson, *French Catholicism*, 257.

137. Duhr provides several examples of the term but does not apply it explicitly to Alphonsus Liguori. Duhr, 1275.

138. Hardon, "Historical Antecedents," 525.

139. Hardon, "Historical Antecedents," 525.

140. Hardon, "Historical Antecedents," 525.

141. Hardon, "Historical Antecedents," 525–26.

142. Hardon, "Historical Antecedents," 525–26. Hardon seems to rely upon only one work of Liguori, *Homo Apostolicus*, specifically composed for confessors and spiritual directors, and shortly after admitting this reliance, he asserts that many *moral* theologians owe a great debt to Liguori. This is just, for this pastoral manual derives quite directly from Liguori's *Theologia Moralis*. Jones, *Alphonsus de Liguori*, 278–84. Godts, in contrast, sees the founder of the Redemptorists as a champion of the middle way between laxism and rigorism on the subject of admission to Holy Communion. In this, Godts echoes Liguori's intention in his *Theologia Moralis* as well as both Pius VI and Pius IX. *AM*, 2–3, 26.

143. CEF, 544.

144. For the text of these rules, see chapter 2; a scholarly edition of Liguori's *Theologia Moralis* introduces its attempt to reconcile Liguori and *STS* in a footnote. Alphonsus (de) Liguori, *Theologia Moralis: Editio Nova*, edited by Leonard Gaudé (Graz, Austria: Akademische Druck-U. Verlagsanstalt, 1954), 3: 221n254.

145. L. Vereecke, "Saint Alphonsus Liguori," *NCE*.

146. Schmidt, *Everything Is Grace*, 187–88.

147. In order to combat the notion that the frequency of Communion would dull ardor, the campaign for frequent Communion depended ultimately upon the concept of *ex opere operato*. In a sentimental and Victorian religious ethos, the campaign discounted emotions and sensibilities associated with reception. How one felt upon receiving Communion did not matter; the action of Jesus mattered, almost exclusively. *Devotion* was defined not as a matter of feelings but as actions of the will, and persisting in Communion when emotions were unmoved seems, to Lintelo, highly meritorious. Communion, as food for the soul, nourishes; nourishment does not need to feel good in order to be effective. *ET*, 96–103.

148. Nissen, "Mobilizing the Catholic Masses," 151.

149. Nissen, "Mobilizing the Catholic Masses," 152.

150. Nissen, "Mobilizing the Catholic Masses,"· 152.

151. Nissen, "Mobilizing the Catholic Masses," 152.

152. Jay P. Dolan, *Catholic Revivalism: The American Experience, 1830–1900* (Notre Dame, Indiana: University of Notre Dame Press, 1978), xvii.

153. Roman Catholic Church, Bishops of the United States, "Pastoral Letter, Issued by the Second Provincial Council of Baltimore, October 27, 1833," in *The Pastoral Letters of the United States Catholic Bishops,* edited by Hugh J. Nolan (Washington: National Conference of Catholic Bishops / United States Catholic Conference, 1983), 74.

154. Bishops of the United States, "Pastoral Letter Baltimore, 1833," 75.

155. Jay P. Dolan, *The Immigrant Church: New York's Irish and German Catholics, 1815–1865* (Baltimore: Johns Hopkins University Press, 1977; reprint, Notre Dame, Indiana: University of Notre Dame Press, 1983), 55.

156. James Parton, "Our Roman Catholic Brethren," *Atlantic Monthly* 21, no. 126 (1868): 433, 434, 436. The report is unsigned, and the author's name comes from Dolan, *Catholic Revivalism,* 238n 1.

157. Richard Frederick Clarke, "Roman Catholics in America," in *Through Other Eyes: Some Impressions of American Catholicism by Foreign Visitors from 1777 to the Present,* edited by Dan Herr and Joel Wells (Westminster, Maryland: Newman, 1965), 77–78.

158. Elizabeth Bayley Seton, *Elizabeth Seton: Selected Writings,* edited by Ellin Kelly and Annabelle Melville (New York: Paulist, 1987), 220.

159. Dolan, *Catholic Revivalism,* 8–9.

160. Dolan, *Catholic Revivalism,* 8–9.

161. Dolan, *Catholic Revivalism,* 11–12.

162. Dolan, *Catholic Revivalism,* 168–69.

163. Dolan draws the contrast between the experience of conversion being "individual" and the baptism renewal as public. While the sacrament of penance was presumably quite private, receiving Communion, insofar as it occurs during the Mass or immediately before or after, was presumably public. In the 1920s, John F. O'Hara of Notre Dame allowed receiving Communion to be quite private, as individual students, according to their own inclinations, confessed and received. In contrast, in France in the nineteenth century, to receive Communion was a political-religious statement. Dolan, *Catholic Revivalism,* 169.

164. Dolan, *Catholic Revivalism,* xviii.

165. Dolan, *Catholic Revivalism,* xviii.

166. Dolan, *Catholic Revivalism,* 186.

167. Dolan, *Catholic Revivalism,* 38.

168. Joseph Wissel, *The Redemptorist on the American Missions, The American Catholic Tradition,* edited by Jay P. Dolan, Paul Messbarger, and Michael Novak, third revised edition (1920; reprint, New York: Arno, 1978), 261.

169. Dolan, *Immigrant Church,* 141–47.

170. Dolan, *Catholic Revivalism,* 179.

171. Chinnici, *Eucharist*, 146–47.

172. Chinnici, *Eucharist*, 146.

173. Taves, *Household*, 89.

174. Taves, *Household*, 95.

175. Taves, *Household*, 51 and 104–5.

176. Taves, *Household*, 28–29 and 95–96.

177. Robert Orsi, *The Madonna of 115th Street: Faith and Community in Italian Harlem, 1880–1950* (New Haven: Yale University Press, 1985), xviii.

178. Orsi, *Madonna of 115th Street*, 54–55.

179. Orsi, *Madonna of 115th Street*, 72–73.

180. Taves, *Household*, 94.

181. Taves, *Household*, 126.

182. Edward Foley explains the decline in the celebration of the Lord's Supper in general in Protestantism: "The various Protestant groups held divergent views on the role and frequency of the Eucharist. . . . Emphasis on the word in virtually every segment of Protestantism, coupled with the influences of pietism and rationalism during the eighteenth century, contributed to a decline in the frequency of Eucharist, even in the most sacramental traditions." Edward Foley, *From Age to Age: How Christians Have Celebrated Eucharist* (Chicago: Liturgy Training Publications, 1991), 135.

183. Clarke, "Roman Catholics in America," 86.

184. Denis J. O'Connell, *A New Idea in the Life of Father Hecker* (Freiburg im Breisgau: Herder, 1897), reprint in Gerald P. Fogarty, *The Vatican and the Americanist Crisis: Denis J. O'Connell, American Agent in Rome, 1885–1903*, Miscellanea Historiae Pontificiae 36 (Roma: Università Gregoriana, 1974), 321.

185. Dolan, *Catholic Revivalism*, 31.

186. Luigi Barzini, *The Italians* (New York: Atheneum, 1964), 103–4; [Helen] Kathleen Hughes, *The Monk's Tale: A Biography of Godfrey Diekmann, O.S.B.* (Collegeville, Minnesota: Liturgical Press, 1991), 223.

187. The condemnation of Americanism by Leo XIII resulted in the "Romanizing" of the American hierarchy and the end of American Catholic intellectual life. Gerald P. Fogarty, *The Vatican and the American Hierarchy from 1870 to 1965* (Wilmington: Michael Glazier, 1985), 177–206.

188. Fogarty, *Vatican and the American Hierarchy*, 28–31.

189. Taves, *Household*, 104–5.

# Chapter Two

# Prelude to Pope Pius X

This chapter sets the scene for the document *STS*, which energized the campaign for frequent Communion. The decree itself addresses one particular but diplomatically veiled dispute: "In our own day the controversy [over frequency of and dispositions for Holy Communion] has been continued with increased heat and not without bitterness, so that the minds of confessors and the consciences of the faithful have been disturbed, to the no small detriment of Christian piety."[1] This chapter examines the two most important adversaries and their main sources in order to see how their dispute provoked and shaped Pius X's decree.

The bulk of the dispute between Father François-Xavier Godts, CSsR, and Father Jules Lintelo, SJ, served up notions and sentiments about the frequency of Holy Communion throughout Church history. In the first round, each party amassed theologians and spiritual writers in support; then, in subsequent rounds, these authorities were demolished, demoted, and dismissed.

A just and expeditious strategy, therefore, to understand Godts and Lintelo is first to investigate the most relevant papal document on frequent Communion, Leo XIII's *Mirae Caritatis* (*MC*), and then to turn to their handling of it; to examine the way each one claims to be derivative of earlier authorities; and finally to examine their own attitudes toward dispositions for Communion as manifested through the set pieties of preparation for and thanksgiving after Communion.

Although the banners under which the disputes were fought did proclaim "frequent Communion," this term, while historically valid because of Arnauld's famous book, does mislead. The question was not really about the frequency of Communion per se; it was a question of the proper dispositions for Communion. As the rhetoric and passions of the dispute quickly absolutized the frequency of reception of Communion, the dispute polarized. Areas of obvious agreement were ignored, the inherent ambiguities of dealing with the realities of the care of souls vanished, and points where clear-cut distinctions could be made hardened. Genuine opposition between the parties resulted.

This fairly typical dynamic was fueled by extraneous issues, such as linguistic culture, personality, and rivalry between religious orders. The dispute, rife with unrestrained appropriation of theological authorities, erased nuances from the theories to which Lintelo and Godts referred.

This analysis is indebted to a "social construction" of the "reality" of heresy. In his treatment of the modernist heresy, Lester R. Kurtz observes that the creation of enemies within—that is, heretics—serves very well to consolidate and to energize a given stance. For the vitriolic disputes that led to the campaign for frequent Communion, Kurtz's model applies even when the larger political situation is taken into account. Godts saw political liberals and anticlericals as enemies to the Church, and he could oppose them in a normal way. But to Godts members of the frequent Communion crowd were more threatening because they were devout but benighted insiders, enemies that should be allies. This type of fraternal opposition provokes a most impassioned confrontation.[2]

The delicate theological balance between the doctrine of the Eucharist as Real Presence and the human need for this sacrament, subjected to a blunt, bitter dispute, resulted in a papal policy whose implementation could be quantified (by the numbers of communions) but whose theological underpinnings were suspect. In its simplest expression, from the "both-and" was to be drawn an "either-or," and Saint Pius X was the personality in the proper historical circumstances to select a winner.

The immediate context of the Lintelo-Godts controversy was the vastly complex Eucharistic movement that originated with the first Eucharistic Congress at Lille in 1881.[3] Within this movement subsisted a groundswell to increase the taking of Holy Communion by the laity. Sociologists and anthropologists remind us that change begins at the margins in large social institutions, and this movement began with a French laywoman. In the case of a devotion—as it was so categorized at the time—such as frequent Communion that had not been the practice of the Church for countless generations, polemic arose rather than mere lobbying to find papal support.

## LEO XIII AND *MIRAE CARITATIS* (*MC*)

One of the final pronouncements of Pope Leo XIII, *MC* could earn for him the title "Pope of the Eucharist." History emphasizes his social teachings, and his devotional and even liturgical impact has consequently been insufficiently examined. His copious devotional writings include nine encyclicals on Mary and the rosary, and his *Annum Sacrum* (1899) "consecrated the whole human race to the Sacred Heart."[4] His last encyclical fused Leo's persistent concern for social issues with his liturgical interest. As such, it manifests the many deep and complex currents of European Catholicism, including the liturgical movement, that connect social justice with worship.

*MC* called greater recourse to Holy Communion one of the "practical measures" to combat rationalism, the spirit of the age inherently inimical to religious faith. The life of Christ, both historically in the Incarnation and sacramentally in the Eucharist, necessitated social consequences. "Everyone is aware that no sooner had 'the goodness and kindness of God our Saviour appeared' (Tit. iii, 4), than there at once burst forth a certain creative force which issued in a new order of things and pu[l]sed through all the veins of society, civil and domestic."[5] Leo posited the unity of charity toward God and neighbor, and noted that the lack of this charity resulted in individualism and social strife.[6] Developing the image of 1 Corinthians 10:17, Leo drew an alluring picture of the social harmony that abided in the celebration of the Eucharist. "Very beautiful and joyful too is the spectacle of Christian brotherhood and social equality which is afforded when men of all conditions, gentle and simple, rich and poor, learned and unlearned, gather round the holy altar, all sharing alike in this heavenly banquet."[7] This Eucharistic encyclical, however, ranked several practices having to do with the most significant symbol of Catholicism.

> This Sacrament, whether as the theme of devout meditation, or as the object of public adoration, or best of all as a food to be received in the utmost purity of conscience, is to be regarded as the centre toward which the spiritual life of a Christian in all its ambit gravitates; for all other forms of devotion, whatsoever they may be, lead up to it, and in it find their point of rest.[8]

While *Sacrosanctam Conciliam*, the Constitution on the Sacred Liturgy of the Second Vatican Council, was to call the liturgy the source and summit of Christian life, *MC* invested in the Eucharist the entirety of the Catholic religion—for the Blessed Sacrament was "the very soul of the Church."[9] Moreover, it was not an object of reverence and ritual distance but was essentially food. This is of crucial importance for the campaign for frequent Communion, and here is Leo's reasoning.

Since the new life, given by Christ in the Eucharist, resembled "natural" life, this new divine life required food as did biological life. A review of biblical anticipations of the institution of the Lord's Supper supported Leo's contention that this food for the divine life is the Eucharist and allowed Leo emphatically to expand access to the Holy Table by castigating those who would restrict it to professed religious.[10] Holy Communion was for all, irrespective of state in life or social standing, who were striving for "the life of blessedness with God."[11]

Leo was careful, however, to retain but not to specify customary pieties of preparation for sacramentally receiving the Eucharist. Indeed, Leo's entire review of the Johannine anticipations of the sacrament served to endow preparing for Communion with dominical authority. "And here it will be opportune to recall to mind on what occasion and in what manner Christ moved and prepared the hearts of men for the worthy and due reception of the living bread which He was about to give them."[12] Preparing for Communion was, at the time, a set piece of piety, and it became a focus of the disputes about Communion frequency.

Pope Leo's citation of the Council of Trent (session 22, chapter 6) included the ideas of the Eucharist as guarantor of social harmony and as real food, but it located the place of the banquet more in heaven than on earth and mitigated the food image with wishes and prayers both for a proper respect toward it and for requisite virtues that would admit to it.

Quite significantly, *MC* defined the Belgian battleground that led to Pius X's interventions in the disputes about Communion frequency in three ways. First, the encyclical recalled the natural symbolism of the Eucharist as food. Second, Pope Leo interpreted the passage from Trent urging sacramental reception of Communion at every Mass at which the faithful assist as a corrective to the injunction of the Fourth Lateran Council that required, with regret, annual reception of the Eucharist to avoid excommunication.[13] This interpretation conceptually distances annual Communion from frequent Communion. Leo did not deduce that Trent wanted *daily* Communion. Third, Leo asserted a historical argument for greater use of the Eucharist by correlating the "virtues of the Christian life" with "frequent reception of the Eucharist."[14] That is, if more Christians were receiving communion more frequently, their lives would be more meritorious, probably obviously so.

While Leo reaffirmed, although somewhat obliquely, the preparation necessary for receiving Communion, he concluded with an unmistakable injunction to partake of the sacrament of the altar more. "But the chief aim of our efforts must be that the frequent reception of the Eucharist may be everywhere revived among Catholic peoples."[15] In other words, preparation for receiving Communion was not to be curtailed in order to increase the quantity of Communions. A phrase such as "food to be received in the utmost purity of conscience" embodies the idea of frequent, even daily, reception while still requiring sterling dispositions. Even as Leo placed, as an ideal, the Eucharist in the center of the Catholic devotional universe, so, too, he made the sacramental reception of Communion an urgent priority.

The encyclical prepared for a general reordering of Catholic devotional life by building first upon the devotion to the Sacred Heart of Jesus. Leo alluded to his own reliance upon the Sacred Heart in his struggle against the hostility and error of the age. Leo wrote, "We directed, as a thing most desirable, that the entire human race should be consecrated by a special act to the Sacred Heart of Jesus Christ our Redeemer."[16] According to Leo, the consecration to the Sacred Heart would be effectively completed by devotion to the Eucharist, and this was the second element of the campaign against the evils of the age. Leo continued, "[We] commend to all Christians, more earnestly than heretofore, the all-holy Eucharist, foreasmuch as it is a divine gift, proceeding from the very Heart of the Redeemer."[17] This official recommendation may have been tinder to the flames of the bitter controversy that quickly elicited from Leo's immediate successor, Pope Pius X, a commitment of the Church's clerical and institutional resources to encourage daily Communion for all the faithful.

## LINTELO AND GODTS ON *MIRAE CARITATIS*

Both Lintelo and Godts necessarily needed to address *MC*, for its plain topic was the increasing of Communion reception by the laity. Their writings, however, largely consisted in pitting authorities against each other; therefore, to focus upon their use of authorities allows us to see the nature of the conflict as a dynamic polarization of very subtle differences.

*MC* interpreted the classic but contested locution of the Council of Trent on the receiving of Communion by the faithful every time they assist at Mass. To Pope Leo, this text meant greater frequency of Communion. Both Lintelo and Godts needed to take into account the canons and decrees of the Council of Trent, which in those days was regarded as virtually infallible. How did Lintelo ratify this interpretation, and how did Godts, though claiming support for an ideal of frequent Communion, deny it?

The fundamental strategy of Godts's *Exagérations historiques et théologiques* (*EH*) was to ignore *MC* punctiliously but to undermine its contents as it appeared elsewhere. For example, the thematic section of *EH* did address some key assertions of *MC*. Godts's inattention to a recent papal pronouncement upon his subject made him extremely vulnerable. Lintelo trumpeted this inattention by contrasting Godts's opinion to Pope Leo's. Lintelo wanted to capitalize upon ultramontanism to discredit Godts and to cast Godts as a naysayer of the pope.

Godts worked with immense speed in composing his tracts and could have conceivably overlooked *MC*, especially if it had not been directly cited by his antagonists.[18] In addition, Godts could have restricted himself for tactical reasons to assaults upon ideas from the Eucharistic movement as a whole. In the encyclical itself Leo had described and applauded the Eucharistic movement, and increasing the use of Communion was evolving into the movement's major thrust. Pope Leo's ideas were not original; the fertile and amorphous Eucharistic movement spawned the encyclical. For Godts to introduce this encyclical into the polemic would have necessitated, given Godts's temperament as a controversialist, a Procrustean interpretation. Such an interpretation would have undermined its own clincher, "But the chief aim of our efforts must be that the frequent reception of the Eucharist may be everywhere revived among Catholic peoples."[19] Yes, Godts could have agreed with frequent Communion as a pious platitude or as a quixotic ideal, but Godts deplored isolating "frequent Communion" as a category. He would rather focus upon the proper dispositions for Communion. Judging from Godts's strategy, *MC*, despite its careful and politic ambiguity, seems to have already been co-opted by the proponents of absolute frequent Communion.

Given this presumed appropriation, Godts's tactic needed to avoid a direct confrontation with Pope Leo. So, when the authority of the Petrine office needed invoking, Godts skipped over this most recent papal pronouncement and mobilized Pope Innocent XI's *Cum Ad Aures* (1679), written more than two centuries earlier.

In the thematic section of *EH*, Godts rebutted the two mainstays of the encyclical without a frontal attack. Pope Leo's main arguments are historical, to which are subordinated the biblical and then the symbolic arguments. Here is a schematic of Leo's reasoning: Holy Communion was received very frequently in the most pious ages of the Church, in the days closest to the historical Jesus; the phrase "daily bread" in the Lord's Prayer meant Holy Communion. Because the matter of the sacrament was patently food, and because food must be taken with frequency to maintain health, the Eucharist should be received frequently.

Godts rebuts the assertion that historically the frequency of reception of Communion has correlated with fervor. Relying exclusively upon the work of Abbé Lejeune, Godts began by denying that the extant but meager documentation supported such a claim.[20] He did deploy some counterevidence: Paul's churches seemed to have met only on Sunday; the churches of the West obviously did not celebrate the Mass daily. Such a schedule would have precluded daily Communion. He also asserted that, even in the primitive Church, freedom from mortal sin did not admit to Communion, despite this tenet of the progressives. Godts answered historical precedent sensibly and convincingly with the observation that as cultural and historical circumstances change, so too would ritual. "The discipline of one century is never able to serve as the discipline of another, unless they are very similar. . . . The example of the primitive Church proves nothing says Petavius. Many are the obsolete customs which it would be absurd to re-introduce."[21] The kiss of peace illustrates Godts's point.

Godts next dismembers Pope Leo's precritical biblical argument that the locution "daily bread" in the Our Father indicated Communion. Of course, *MC* did not declare this equivalence. In fact, this encyclical avoided specifying daily Communion as its end, while it did propose both greater access by the laity to the Lord's Table and increasing the rate of receiving. *MC* referred to the typological relationship between manna and the Eucharist; progressives often supported their agenda by reference to this typology and to the fact that the manna fed the Israelites daily.[22] Leo also quoted the Council of Trent, urging excellent preparation for the "supersubstantial bread" of Communion so that it could be received with greater frequency.[23]

*Supersubstantial* is, as Godts reminded the reader, the alternate and mystifying translation of the famous *hapax legomenon* of the Matthean version of the Lord's Prayer; *daily* from the Lucan version eclipses the indecipherable word, both in Jerome's rendering into Latin and in the prayer formula.[24] While the proponents of daily Communion tried to capitalize upon an alleged equivalence with the daily bread of the Lord's Prayer, supporting this reading with numerous authorities, Godts observed that many scholars—Ceulemenas, Knabenbauer, and Maldonatus—have not equated the two. Their exegesis of the phrase restricted its meaning to the material needs of the body. He added that the Gospel accounts of the institution of the Eucharist are quite remote in time from the instruction of the disciples about how to pray.[25]

Then Godts misreads Louis-Claude Fillion (d. 1927), his source, or Fillion misinterprets the "Greek fathers," for Godts emphasized that the point of the "daily bread" of the Lord's Prayer was to transform itself into our (fleshly) substance.[26] This recalled but significantly subverted an important element of the thinking of *MC*, which dilated upon the life-sustaining nature of the Eucharist as a food. "For there is this difference between the food of the body and that of the soul, that whereas the former is changed into our substance, the latter changes us into its own; so that Saint Augustine makes Christ Himself say: 'You shall not change Me into yourself as you do the food of your body, but you shall be changed into Me' (*Confessions* 1. vii, c.x.)."[27] Godts finally addressed the natural symbolism of food. Not overtly quoting any particular enemy, but rather drawing on a general theme of the progressives, Godts began the section with the false premise of natural symbolism: "The nature of the Eucharistic species clearly indicates that the faithful must feed upon the Eucharist every day."[28] In response, Godts claimed that this was theologically vacuous. His reason was that if the analogy were taken to its logical conclusion, communicating several times a day would follow from eating meals several times a day. Such a Eucharistic practice Godts found absurd. He did not elaborate.

As Pope Leo did in *MC*, Father Godts established a distinction between the life of the world and the spiritual life, and this distinction was the result of two distinct modes of "becoming." Yes, both natural food and the Eucharist gave life: the one, mundane life, the other supernatural, as was promised by Jesus. Natural food sustained the human person; Holy Communion helped the person become like Christ. Bishop Victor-Joseph Doutreloux of Liège (d. 1901), Godts's source, had made the distinction quite differently, shying away from the basic natural analogy: The Eucharist was not the *only* sustenance for the soul, as God had ordained.[29]

Godts thus questioned the pope's rationales for the return to frequent Communion—the asserted connection between virtue and sacramental frequency in the primitive Church, the biblical interpretation that equated daily bread with Holy Communion, and the natural analogy comparing Holy Communion to food. Further, to protect himself against allegations of disloyalty to the Petrine office, Godts limited himself in *EH* to naming opponents who had specified *daily* Communion, which Leo did not explicitly espouse.

Lintelo, in the first of his *Lettres à un prêtre à propos d'une polemique sur la Communion fréquente* (*LP*), acknowledged to his fictitious priest-friend that Godts was attacking only *daily* Communion; thus Lintelo implied that frequent Communion was unimpeachable as a concept.[30] The Jesuit confused *daily* with merely *frequent*, however, by a falsely irenic rhetorical ploy. He wondered about Godts's position on *MC*. "It would be easy for us to begin by finding a common ground between Godts and the magisterial exposition of the doctrine of the Holy Eucharist written by His Holiness, Pope Leo XIII, in his encyclical of 1902."[31]

Recall that, in fact, Godts had scrupulously and prudently stood mum about *MC*. According to Lintelo, Godts had not only attacked a group of priests of impeccable credentials, but Leo XIII, the pope himself.[32] Lintelo claimed that he would be iterating the same arguments that appeared in *MC* and complained that Godts was obnoxious in undermining exactly these papal arguments. In order to enhance the prestige of his own positions, Lintelo hoped to forge a significant alliance with the pope.

Lintelo sought to appropriate Leo to the progressive party through his citing of Trent (session 22, chapter 6) and his use of the classic dismissal of the causes of opposition to frequent Communion as "prejudices" and "vain fears." In a footnote, Lintelo insinuated that Godts had vitiated the interpretation of Trent found in *MC*; in fact, Coppin's booklet had interpreted Trent exactly as did Leo, but politic Godts denigrated only Coppin. Like filings around the poles of magnets, subtle and complex thoughts were being configured into distant and hostile clusters in the social dynamics of the Lintelo-Godts controversy.

It was impossible, after Lintelo's maneuver, for Godts to dodge *MC* any longer, and so he offered his own interpretation in *Réponse aux lettres à un prêtre à propos d'une polémique sur la Communion fréquente par le Père Jules Lintelo de la compagnie de Jésus (RL)*. Godts quoted verbatim Lintelo's hopeful, but apparently disingenuous, search for a commonality between the pope and Godts. Godts boldly answered,

> No, dear reverend father, any common ground is impossible on this subject, because the pope treats the subject vaguely and speaks only in generalities. The pope does not analyze the issues and does not articulate any rules; furthermore, he does not define the qualities of soul for one who wishes to receive Communion every day. The only possible area of agreement to date is found in the decree of Innocent XI [i.e., *Cum Ad Aures*], which has been duly glossed by Saint Alphonsus, among others.[33]

To Godts, *MC* was rife with generalities. In fact, Pope Leo's strategy was to remain complex, nuanced, and even ambiguous because that was the totality of the tradition of discourse on frequency of and disposition for Communion. Furthermore, this ambiguity left open to pastoral discretion what really would be benefiting penitents as individuals, and it is more coherent with the nature of sacraments as places of mystery. It is as if Leo had said, "Yes, Communion should be more frequent; and yes, Communion should be anticipated with pious solicitude; and yes, greater frequency of Communion benefits souls if they are able to prepare better and also to behave better as a result of the Communions."

The injunction of *MC*, "above all else, to labor to insure a revival of the frequent reception of the Eucharist," Godts claims had been his own mission for the previous forty years—in retreats, missions, ministry of confession, and preaching.[34] According to Godts, the presumably standardized plan of the parish mission as given by the Redemptorists had always aimed at drawing the laity to the Eucharist twice during its duration, and their plan for a "renewal" urged four Communions. "We strongly recommend frequent Communion, and even daily Communion to those who are disposed according to the writings of Saint Alphonsus."[35]

The controversy continued to polarize positions and to generate not just recommendations but rules where the discretion of the confessor had been held supreme. So long as the topic was *frequent* Communion, the discussion could abide in comfortable and idealizing generalities. When Godts sought to establish a category, "absolute frequent Communion," this polemical strategy distanced the advocates of frequent Communion from authorities whom they cited because, fundamentally to the mind of Godts, such an alliance was untenable—*frequent* eluded definition. The polarization was accelerated by such sleight of hand as Lintelo's, where calls for *frequent* Communion were transformed into calls for *daily* Communion. In the unfolding of the Lintelo-Godts dispute, this transformation occured covertly in the progressives' interpretations of *MC*. In the mind of Lintelo, what separates receiving Communion frequently from receiving it daily? Certainly, to gain a victory in the polemic with Godts by impressing Leo XIII into his own party, Lintelo muddies the issue, for Leo wrote only of frequent Communion, not daily, and yet daily was the explicit abuse that Godts debunks.

The bound edition of Lintelo's *Lettres* includes a section of point-by-point answers to the accusations of Chatel and Godts, and within his *réplique* to the former occurs a fine instance of Lintelo's misrepresenting of *MC*. Lintelo justifies the expediency (*opportunité*) of engaging in the discussion on the frequency of Communion at all by citing Leo XIII on the necessity of working with great energy to revive the frequent reception of the Eucharist, and to do so by abolishing prejudices and vain fears and false reasons for abstaining from Communion.[36] Lintelo surveys the literature to determine the meaning of these obstacles to the restoration of frequent Communion and then classifies them: "Communion does not suit me; I'm not fervent enough for such frequency of reception; I wouldn't profit enough from it."[37] The effectual responses to such prejudices, presumably again drawn from Lintelo's own survey of the literature, are as follows:

1. Daily and frequent Communion is recommended for everybody.
2. You are pure enough if, being in the state of grace, you have a firm intention of becoming better; you will become ever better by communicating often.
3. You will reap from your Communions a large profit if you only avoid mortal sin. But strive to prepare yourself as well as you can, because thus you will grow greatly in virtue.[38]

Under Lintelo's transforming pen, a general and unremarkably formulaic call of Leo XIII to greater frequency of Communion—which could have meant weekly in many local environments of the Roman Catholic Church at that time—becomes an unequivocal call to daily Communion. Lintelo's loading Leo XIII with unwarranted "meanings" was spurred by the polemics that were destroying a logical alliance.

## THE ANTIQUE SPANISH ANTECEDENTS

The immediate context of the Lintelo-Godts controversy connects to the age-old discussion of the merits of frequency of Communion by skipping both in time and in place to seventeenth-century Spain. One fruit of the Counter-Reformation was, especially in areas of Jesuit influence, a noteworthy increase in the use of Communion. This era—and its own peculiar conflict over the frequency of Communion—was made present to *fin de siècle Francophonie* through an article, reprinted abundantly as a pamphlet, by Father Joseph Coppin, CSsR (d. 1915), which in turn was an avowed distillation of the translation of *Notre pain quotidien, c'est-à-dire le T.S. Sacrement,* a book by a Spanish priest of the Order of Mercy (Mercedarians), Juan Falconi, OdeM (d. 1638). This book was originally published posthumously in 1656, and its approving translation by Eugène Couët of the Fathers of the Blessed Sacrament appeared in 1893.[39]

## PRINCIPAL DOCUMENTS

The most intense and most determinative discussion of the frequency of Communion was bounded, naturally in an ultramontane age, by papal actions, namely Pope Leo XIII's encyclical *MC* (28 May 1902) and by Pope Pius X's *STS* (20 December 1905). Within these thirty-two months flared such an exchange between the two Belgian priests that Pius X himself intervened to quell the flames. Such was the very and avowed purpose of the decree *STS.* Because this decree was occasioned by the dispute between Jesuit Jules Lintelo and Redemptorist François-Xavier Godts, and because the decree admitted as much in its own text, their writings require some attention.

This Belgian conflagration consisted of a fusillade of articles, pamphlets, and books. Godts, temperamentally a controversialist, ignited the dispute with *EH* (2 August 1904).[40] This work attacked the very recent pamphlet by fellow Redemptorist Joseph Coppin, a popularization of a book by Juan Falconi. Lintelo entered the combat with an article, in the form of a letter to an unspecified priest, in the magazine *O Salutaris Hostia* in December 1904. Lintelo continued with some other such interventions in short order. Godts fueled the blaze with a booklet of fifty-seven pages, dated 25 March 1905, *Réponse aux lettres à un prêtre à propos d'une polémique sur la communion fréquente par le père Jules Lintelo de la compagnie de Jésus* (*RL*). Lintelo responded to the response in a book-length work, *Lettres à un prêtre à propos d'une polemique sur la Communion fréquente* (*LP*), consisting of several "letters," both reprinted from periodicals and freshly composed for the dispute. This compilation went into a second and corrected edition within about two months after its first edition and provoked Godts's *Deuxième réponse au r.p. Lintelo* (14 May 1905). Although the final blow aimed at Lintelo in particular was Godts's *Pro Veritate et Justitia* (27 May 1905), Godts speedily produced a number of other works to challenge the progressives.

Godts returned to theological and devotional sources, and in the book *Le quiétiste Falconi et son opuscule "Notre pain quotidien, c'est-à-dire le T.S. Sacrement"* (5 July 1905) Godts dispatched Falconi, already wounded severely. The longest, most theological, and most positive contribution of François-Xavier Godts to this hubbub was his *L'apôtre moderne du T.S. Sacrement: S. Alphonse, docteur de l'église* (*AM*, 8 December 1905). Despite its title, hinting at biography, it is polemical at heart.

Godts was not without his allies. Simultaneous with *EH* appeared the work of Father Fernand Chatel (d. 1924), *Défense de la doctrine catholique sur la Communion fréquente*, also an attack upon Coppin and Falconi. Unlike Godts, however, Chatel seems to have engaged in only this one foray.

Joseph Coppin, beset by both Godts and Chatel, quickly parried their assaults with his *Notes contre notes pour ma défense au congrès de Hasselt*, but this was Coppin's second and last publication on frequency of Communion. Presumably because of the devotional tenor of Coppin's original pamphlet and because of his early withdrawal from the field, the publication of Lintelo's works marks the significant beginning of the controversy with Godts. Lintelo himself, uninvited, allied himself with the Coppin-Couet-Falconi contingent.

Besides generating approximately 450 pages in French, Godts also wrote but never published (out of deference to the wishes of his provincial superior, who considered the work too long) a Latin treatise. This tome, *Frequentiae communionis historia et norma*, comprised over six hundred octavo pages.[41] *STS* explicitly forbade continuation of this vitriolic dispute; Godts, a model of submission, turned his fecund pen to the subject of the Blessed Virgin Mary.[42]

## THE VERNACULAR

This polemical bulk raises this question first: Why the vernacular, French, rather than Latin, as Godts himself proposed? I offer four hypotheses and allow Godts himself to explain.

First, the most comprehensive context for the dispute was the Eucharistic movement, including the congresses, and the movement was largely francophone.

Second, the religious who specialized in Eucharistia, the Fathers of the Blessed Sacrament, were founded in France.

Third, the immediate causes of the controversy appeared in French—both Couet's translation of Falconi and Coppin's popularization and simplification of Falconi. Incidentally, Gennari's influential commentary, though published originally in Italian (*Sulla communione frequente e sul decreto "Quemadmo-dum"*), spread quickly among the controversialists in French.[43]

Father Godts excused the vernacular by virtue of expediency. He felt pressed to prepare his essay for the Eucharistic Congress at Hasselt in August 1904, which was to convene only months after Coppin's brochure had come to his attention. While brief Latin passages pepper another of Godts's vernacular salvoes, *AM*, one five-page segment appeared here in Latin because its "high theology" would be harmful to "timorous laypeople."[44]

Lastly, by temperament Godts was a controversialist; presumably he enjoyed a larger audience than the Latin-literate clergy, and French afforded this expansion. Pius X's *STS* was provoked, by its own admission, by this Belgian uproar in its pastoral dimensions; had the dispute remained in the realm of the clergy and thus rather academic, as had the discussion of frequent Communion since the seventeenth century, no papal intervention would have been required.


## GODTS AND SAINT ALPHONSUS LIGUORI

Lintelo's and Godts's respective champions are treated in their own historical order. Godts's patron saint was Alphonsus Liguori. Besides being the founder of Godts's own religious congregation, the Redemptorists, several other characteristics recommend him to Godts as a redoubtable champion. Saint Alphonsus had been a controversialist himself on the question of Communion practice, he was famously a foe of Jansenism, and finally he was the most significant moral theologian in the early nineteenth century.

Lintelo's princely protector was Casimiro Cardinal Gennari (d. 1914). Gennari first published specifically on the question of frequent Communion in 1893, and this work, because it so influenced Lintelo and more importantly because it demonstrates a concerted expansion of the applications of Leo XIII's *Quemadmodem* (*QMM*), requires attention. Additionally, Gennari was instrumental in the production of *STS* and composed a commentary upon the other and later Communion decree of Pius X, *Quam Singulari* (*QS*).

Throughout the dispute, Godts depended confidently upon the teachings of the founder of the Redemptorists, Saint Alphonsus Liguori, and it is Godts's reading of Liguori, rather than Liguori considered more academically and disinterestedly, that is of importance in showing the way in which the dispute generated interpretations of the literature.

Because Liguori's moral theology seemed to the Church and to Pope Pius IX the eminently centrist position between laxism and Jansenism, the Vatican had largely adopted both Alphonsian—as the French would say—principles of moral reasoning and Alphonsian Eucharistic pieties. In the words of a moral theologian of the early part of the twentieth century, "St. Alphonsus Liguori is recognized as the Doctor of moral theology as St. Thomas [Aquinas] is of dogmatic. By his writings he drove out of the church the last remnants of rigorism. . . . Moral theology is still what St. Alphonsus left it. There is general agreement in the schools, a common doctrine which all accept."[45] The heart of Godts's *AM* justifies three rules distilled from Saint Alphonsus Liguori's writings that apportion the various rates of receiving Communion with dispositions for the sacrament.[46] Such rules indicate a system of *proportionality*, and these rules brand Godts and his conservatives. Godts and his side will be the conservatives, for "anti-frequent-Communionites" proves too cumbersome and ultimately misleading, at least in the initial stages of the dispute; Lintelo and his side will be the progressives. The conservative program, had it prevailed, may actually have resulted in greater frequency of Communion than was the benchmark at the time, but not nearly so much as ensued from the dispute and then Lintelo's victory. Lintelo is progressive both in that his emphasis upon more frequent Communion was widely perceived as innovative and in that he did, indeed, catalyze a change in sacramental practice in Catholicism.

Because both Godts and Lintelo were arguing from authorities, Godts took pains to establish the credentials of his order's founder. Testimonials to the value of Saint Alphonsus, both to the particular issue of frequency of Communion and in his capacity as a moral theologian, flowed from pens both prominent and representative—an unnamed secular priest of the diocese of Malines, an anonymous member of a religious order, and Abbé Lejeune. Other choristers praising Liguori were Bishops Victor-Joseph Doutreloux (d. 1901) and Louis Gaston de Ségur (d. 1881), both lionized for disseminating Eucharistic devotions.[47] Two Vatican bureaus—the Holy Inquisition and the Penitentiary—explicitly claimed the writings of Liguori in their judgments upon questions about Communion practice.[48] Importantly for Godts, the sources upon which Saint Alphonsus drew—the Eucharistic decrees of Pope Innocent XI, most especially *Cum Ad Aures*, and his own vast pastoral experience—demonstrated his immense erudition in moral theology.[49] The liturgy itself, Godts proudly observed, called Saint Alphonsus "the faithful herald of the divine mystery."[50] Godts recalled Liguori's dispute about the frequency of Communion with a certain Cyprien Aristase and placed himself, at least implicitly, in Liguori's shoes.[51]

In staking a claim to Liguori, Godts undermined the progressives' similar maneuver. Typical in this pamphlet war, it repays consideration. For instance, Godts demolished Canon Stefano Antoni's appropriation of Liguori by pointing out the canon's audacious wishful thinking—that is, misinterpretation.[52]

Godts's ire shows through. "It is an outrageous misrepresentation of Liguori's mind, character, and faithfulness to his mission, ordained by Providence, to maintain that he concealed the truth out of a spirit of prudence. If this saint was prudent, he was even more so strong; strong in struggle, struggle against lax errors and doctrines."[53]Antoni, according to Godts, also wished to distance Liguori from Bishop de Ségur, the most celebrated personage in the Eucharistic circles in the mid-nineteenth century and also someone appropriated by the progressives.[54] With assurance, Godts quoted de Ségur and argued convincingly from the context that when de Ségur had written "frequent" he had actually meant "weekly," and so de Ségur's prescription of each category of dispositions for the schedule of weekly Communions concurred exactly with Liguori's.[55]

While both sides in this battle mustered luminaries, Godts, in his final offensive, disseminated the teaching of Alphonsus Liguori on the specific question of dispositions for and proportional frequency of Communion. This ambitious work, *AM*, seemed to answer an accusation that Liguori's thinking was old-fashioned and irrelevant. Perhaps the inauspicious use of the word *moderne* in the title is telling of Godts's disconnection from his times. The Church was on the brink of condemning modernism as the "heresy of heresies" with the famous encyclical *Pascendi Domini Gregis* (1907) of Pius X. Before delineating the rules for confessors, Godts argued that guidelines in such a matter enhance the credibility of the sacraments. He ascribed to the proponents for absolute frequent Communion a dangerous dismissing of the very concept of rules and a glorifying of "equality." In other words, Godts saw in the admission to daily Communion on the conditions only of freedom from mortal sin and correct intention at the exact moment of receiving Communion as an insidious leveling. He depicted from his imagination that casual daily Communion would equalize an exemplary pious virgin and a hungover philanderer, the seminarian and the rough-and-ready factory hand, and so on.[56]

The Alphonsian rules, as served by Godts, in turn relying upon Cardinal Villecourt, number three:

One: Weekly Communion is advised and even recommended very earnestly to those who, although they commit ordinary venial sins, do try to avoid the same and at least make a firm purpose to avoid them.

Two: Frequent Communion, that is, made several times in a week, necessarily requires three conditions: 1) avoidance of all fully deliberate venial sins and the absence of any affection for even one such sin; 2) a striving for perfection, accompanied by a sincere desire to receive Communion with an intention of growing in the love of God; 3) practice of mental prayer and mortification of the senses and of the passions.

Three: Daily Communion is allowed to those who, having surmounted for the most part their evil inclinations, apply themselves fervently to mental prayer and also to mortification, and who have attained to some degree of perfection. Even for these, the confessor should forbid Communion once a week.[57]

These rules differ from the discussion of frequency of Communion to be found in Liguori's *Homo Apostolicus*. Rhetorically they offer legalistic simplicity and thus, presumably, consistent parochial application.

Two main differences need elaboration. The first is in the creation of categories of frequency of Communion. *Homo Apostolicus* offers four categories: (1) weekly, (2) weekly but withdrawn occasionally, (3) daily but withdrawn occasionally, (4) no longer daily. This last category is for those whose program of daily Communion lacks evidence of efficacy in spiritual and moral growth. Significantly, this last category, absent from Godts's rules, indicates a pastoral sensitivity to the realities of struggling for spiritual perfection; the emphasis is on the person.

Godts's rules create, implicitly, three categories, here reorganized so as to form a continuum: (1) weekly but withdrawn occasionally, (2) more than weekly but less than daily, (3) daily but withdrawn occasionally. Godts does not acknowledge an inefficacious program of intense reception of Holy Communion and simply moves the qualifications for daily one notch higher than required for Communion more than weekly and less than daily. For example, *frequent* communicants will do mental prayer; *daily* will do lots of mental prayer. Notice that Godts's categories themselves reflect an overarching concern for making frequency proportional to moral and spiritual status. The emphasis is clearly upon the dispositions and not upon frequency in itself.

The second important difference is that while *Homo Apostolicus* admits to daily Communion those who are striving for perfection, Godts admits only those who have largely "surmounted for the most part their evil inclinations" and who have "attained to some degree of perfection." Although Godts has claimed Liguori as his own because of Saint Alphonsus's reputation for opposing Jansenism, here Godts's position does smack of the elitist and pessimistic heresy. Godts's Alphonsian rules, though they interpret a long lifetime of Saint Alphonsus's grappling with the issues, did not change during the sixteen months of the Lintelo-Godts controversy. Godts and Liguori both did adhere to proportionalism. The progressives either ignored Liguori, or, as we saw in the case of Canon Antoni, they attempted boldly and heavy-handedly to subvert him into one of their allies.

In summary, Godts and the party of the conservatives he represents, driven by social-psychological dynamics, strove to formulate and then safeguard ultimate reliance upon a confessor's judgment for the fruitfulness of Communion for the individual and upon the suitability of the individual's dispositions for Communion. His writings were occasional and responsive to the discursive maneuvers of his opponents. Godts's temperament and polemical bent did not allow significant advance in his thought. Quite to the contrary, the dynamics and passions of the quickly boiling controversy pushed Godts into misrepresenting his own avowed champion, Saint Alphonsus Liguori, and into revealing his own Jansenistic leanings.

## LINTELO AND CASIMIRO CARDINAL GENNARI

Liguori, Godts's preeminent source, died about fifty years before the Redemptorist was born and was both a canonized saint and doctor of the Church. Lintelo's fountain was Casimiro Cardinal Gennari (d. 1914), only twenty-three years Lintelo's senior. In fact, Lintelo's biographer, Severin, refers to Gennari as a friend of Lintelo, but the biography suggests that their friendship was professional rather than personal, for it reports only that Gennari and Lintelo were in close communication while *STS* was under advisement in the Sacred Congregation of the Council, of which Cardinal Gennari was prefect.[58]

Lintelo acknowledges his dependency on Gennari, for his second "letter" refers the reader to the cardinal for a scholarly and balanced examination. Lintelo's introduction to the anthology of his part in the dispute, *LP*, asserts that Gennari's works are "lucid" and "authoritative."[59] Gennari serves, then, not only as a source for Father Lintelo, but also as an indicator of the mind of the cardinal who was so important in the formulation of *STS*.

Gennari's *Sulla communione frequente e sul decreto Quemadmodum* (DD) had first been published in 1893, but it appeared in French in 1904 in two popular venues, just when the Belgians were girding for battle. A later edition of Father Coppin's pamphlet rendered Gennari's ideas in summary fashion, and a full translation appeared as an appendix to Bastien's comprehensive summary of canon law with respect to religious, *Directoire canonique a l'usage des congrégations a voeux simples*. Gennari's little work (*opuscule*) proposed to comment upon the decree of the Sacred Congregation for Bishops and Religious, *QMM* (17 December 1890), during the pontificate of Leo XIII.

In this decree the Pope disapproves of the fact that the superiors of many congregations, institutes, and pious sodalities either of women with simple vows or of unordained men, go so far as to prescribe by their own authority the days on which their subjects have either to abstain from or to receive Holy Communion. In consequence, the Pope lays down the following rules. . . .

All prohibitions or permission in connection with the frequency of Communion may come only from the confessor, either ordinary or extraordinary. The superiors have no powers whatever to interfere in this matter, except in the case in which one of their subjects has been a cause of scandal in the community by committing a notoriously grievous sin after the last confession: in which case the Communion may be forbidden until the delinquent approaches the tribunal of penance.

The Pope advises all to do their utmost to insure a due disposition for Holy Communion, and wishes them to receive it on the days appointed by their rules, and whenever the confessor judges that anyone on account of his greater fervour or progress in virtue is worthy of more frequent Communion he may allow it. But he who obtains this permission is bound to manifest the same to his superior. Superiors may put before the confessor their objections to such permission, but they must always acquiesce in his decision without the slightest hesitation.[60]

In August 1891 the same Sacred Congregation of Bishops and Religious summarily eliminated all provisions of constitutions of religious orders of nonclerics that restricted the Communion days.[61] The obvious goal of this decree was to shift control over the sacramental practice of nonclerical religious from the nonclerics themselves to priests. Indisputably, this centralization of control was part of a vast and multifaceted process in the Church throughout the nineteenth century. The decree definitively limited the power of religious superiors over their charges to matters of observable behavior, and it simultaneously enhanced the role of the confessor and the sacrament of penance in the lives of religious.

Despite its claim to be a commentary on *QMM*, Gennari's vernacular commentary announced at its very beginning an astonishing expansion of its supposed theme: "It is not only the teaching, but also the desire of Holy Church that *all the faithful* approach the Holy Table each day" (emphasis added).[62] No wonder that on the short list of those who earnestly promoted frequent Communion appears the name Gennari along with Giuseppi Frassinetti and Amédée Curé.[63] He claims in his first paragraph that *all* theologians support *daily* Communion for all. His mainstays are the more recent passages from the Council of Trent, its catechism, and excerpts from Pope Innocent XI; he weaves throughout the text, however, a cornucopia of supportive quotations.

Immediately following his opening statement, Gennari cites Trent's session 22, chapter 6: "The holy council wishes indeed that at each mass the faithful who are present should communicate, not only in spiritual desire but also by the sacramental partaking of the Eucharist, that thereby they may derive from this most holy sacrifice a more abundant fruit."[64] Oblivious to the historical development of the liturgy, he reasons that, since Mass is said each day, Communion should be distributed each day to all the faithful at the Mass. This is "without doubt" the case.[65] If Gennari's essay were completely governed by the decree *QMM*, as the context would strongly imply, then for him to write as if daily Mass and Communion were the standard would merit an iota of credibility, for he would be referring exclusively to professed religious. But no, he is urging daily Communion upon all Catholics.

Gennari speaks at great length about the apparent conflict between Trent's allegedly desiring daily Communion by all the faithful and the time-honored insistence by many spiritual writers upon married people abstaining from conjugal relations for three days before participating in the Eucharist. Cardinal Gennari anticipates one objection to his interpretation of Trent that would argue that daily Communion for all the faithful cannot be what Trent intended, for the married faithful could not submit to such a discipline as perpetual abstinence. He meets this objection with the adage, "The exception proves the rule," and, without elaboration, details how certain types of marital relations do not bar from Communion.[66]

His exegesis of Trent on the advisability of all the faithful communicating at Mass studiously begs the question. Session 22, chapter 6 is self-evident, according to Gennari: Daily Communion is the premise of Trent. The curial decision, a refusal to allow the bishop of Brescia to restrict the days for the laity to communicate to only a couple per week, confirms to Gennari's satisfaction the premise and interprets Trent correctly.[67] A closer look at the language of the response of the Sacred Congregation, or its historical context, was superfluous to the prelate. So Trent, as well as its catechism, promoted daily Communion, and with these assertions Gennari claims to have demonstrated coherence between the Counter-Reformation teaching on Communion and *QMM*'s teaching on sacramental use by professed religious.

In fact, this document touched upon Communion practice in any generally applicable sense to all of the laity in only two ways. First, it urged that communicants be "duly disposed" to receive but prudently did not elaborate upon this cliché. Second, it described a proportionality between the frequency of Communion, as one term, and "fervour and virtue," as the other. Two questions must be addressed: What connection is there between the decree of Leo XIII in 1890 about religious life, and, strictly speaking, the controversies about how frequently any Catholic was to communicate? Did Gennari parlay this conservative stance of Leo XIII into a progressive one, in favor of frequent Communion, in this pivotal commentary?

Disputes and discussions about the frequency of Communion for the laity in general funneled quite naturally into questions about the particular ramifications of this trend with respect to religious houses.[68] Some constitutions and rules of religious specified the days of Communion, and these rules were growing archaic as Communion gradually was becoming more frequent as a result of the Eucharistic movement. Thus, religious rules and constitutions, instead of encouraging frequent Communion relative to the practice of the nonreligious as they once had, were impeding the spread of yet greater frequency of Communion, even among religious who presumably were thoroughly disposed for it. The legal nicety was the confessor's power to override a clause of an order's rule in order to allow more frequent Communion.

In summarizing the question of admission to Communion, Gennari judged unhelpful questions of classes of persons. In this respect, Gennari superseded *Cum Ad Aures*, which had specifically addressed the arbitrary restriction of Communion to businessmen. Gennari thus divulged, for the second time and in this case an apparent inadvertence, that his *opuscule* was not limiting itself to religious congregations.

Crucial in the discussion of Eucharistic reception, in Gennari's treatment, are dispositions. Gennari, the canon lawyer, focuses first upon the indisputable laws of the Church on the topic: The faithful must receive Easter Communion and are forbidden to receive more than once per day.[69] Determinations of the frequency of reception fall, Gennari insists, outside the realm of law, but in the realm of advice (*conseil*). Because it was possible to "sin venially" by neglecting Communion entirely or, at the other extreme, by communicating every day but "without piety," the entire vast matter reduced itself to the judgment of the confessor.[70]

Allowing the confessor ultimate authority in admission to Communion and avoiding general rules and regulations about Communion practice, was, in fact, the essence of Innocent XI's decree, *Cum Ad Aures*, as interpreted by Gennari. He listed the results of this seventeenth-century pronouncement:

> From whence it follows: 1) that frequent and daily Communion is a holy thing, certainly recommended; 2) that a fixed rule about the frequency of communicating may not be established; 3) that no class of persons, neither businessmen nor merchants, can be refused Communion; 4) that the confessor, who knows the recesses of their consciences, alone has the competence to judge the matter of frequency of Communion for individuals.[71]

What, then, must the confessor know, besides that the penitent has freed herself from mortal sin and its attendant disqualification from Eucharistic reception?

As *Cum Ad Aures* had advised, the conscience must be pure and benefits must flow from the Holy Communion.[72] The benefits, or fruits of Communion, seemed inadmissible as a disposition *for* Communion, simply by virtue of temporal logic. In other words, to Gennari, the dispositions were *pre*dispositions. The confessor, then, would only be able to judge the benefits of frequent Communion because he remained apprised of the state of soul of the communicant.

Gennari opines that the confessor is absolutely forbidden to refuse Communion to those who are properly predisposed. These predispositions included purity of conscience—namely, freedom from grave sin and no attachment to venial sins. Toward the end of the commentary, he puts these opinions in the form of rules: "Third Rule: Confessors who counsel penitents who are very well disposed for Communion may not, without error, refuse permission to receive Communion every day, unless the confessors believe that denying them Communion one day in the week will benefit them as a test of their virtue." Note that this rule makes denying Communion to the daily recipient more the exception than the standard procedure, as Liguori's rules and general custom prescribed.

Alphonsus's somewhat more difficult definition of appropriate predispositions, demanding a regimen of prayer and desiring to make progress in the love of God, did not provoke an attempt by Gennari to square with the purity of conscience required by Innocent XI and interpreted by Benedict XIV.[73] Recall, too, that Saint Alphonsus operated under a system of proportionality, in which one's virtues and piety cohered with the frequency with which one could communicate. Dramatically and with dispatch, Gennari's rules eliminate this idea of proportionality: "Fourth Rule: If it so happens that some penitents, lacking such excellent dispositions as described above, but nevertheless possessing the state of grace and the correct intentions, it is neither obligatory nor forbidden to permit frequent and even daily Communion."[74] A rule that says that rules are not the best approach! Pope Innocent's *Cum Ad Aures* had emphasized the inherent limit of rules and policies and general directives; it is epistemologically humble.

> The manifold recesses of the human conscience and the distractions of those minds which are mostly occupied with the things of this world are veiled from us, and the supernatural gifts which God bestows upon his children are not revealed to human eyes; consequently nothing can be pronounced by us as to the worthiness and purity of a soul and its fitness to receive daily the bread of life.[75]

This mystery is best understood in the privileged relationship between the confessor and the penitent. Or, at least it is best dealt with where the mystery meets church discipline. Actually, the only rule is to do what is most beneficial to the penitent.

> Fifth Rule: The best rule for the confessor is that he is to search thoroughly into what would most benefit the penitent: and thus, he may determine that frequent and daily Communion is helpful, even if its only benefit is preservation in the state of grace, or increase of this grace through the power of the sacrament, and thus to procure for the penitent the gift of perseverance. In this case, the confessor must not hesitate to allow frequent Communion.

This pragmatism seems quite conformable to the pastoral sensitivities of Alphonsus Liguori. Godts, representing Alphonsus, conceded that frequent

Communion was admissible even in the hypothetical case of a person, grievously tempted, who did not fulfill the prescriptions for a preparation for
Communion. This is not to deny that, generally speaking, preparation and
thanksgiving of considerable effort were apposite to receiving the Second
Person of the Trinity under mere accidents of bread.

To this point, the description of the relations between the confessor and
the penitent largely and basically reiterated *Cum Ad Aures*. But Gennari
does not allow the confessor absolute power in determining the frequency
of communicating: "Sixth Rule: The penitent behaves meritoriously in obey-
ing the confessor in all things which pertain to Communion. However, it is
not obligatory, under penalty of sin, to obey in this regard, at least insofar
as the instructions of the confessor do not have as their end the satisfaction
of natural, divine, or ecclesiastical law." Could Gennari have been obviating
the inertia of priests resistant to allowing daily Communion? Remember that
the avowed purpose of *QMM* was, on the other hand, to assign exclusively to
the confessor of nonclerical religious communities control over admission to
Communion and thus to remove control from the hands of the superior. Was
this a loophole, then, for the superior to influence Communion practices in
the local religious houses?

The earlier rules in the conclusion of Gennari's DD did return to the almost forgotten context of the essay, the decree *QMM*, for they counseled
daily and frequent Communion for *religious* especially. But note that they
continued Gennari's expansion of the theme of this supposed commentary
to *all* the faithful. "First Rule: It is necessary to cultivate in all the faithful,
and in religious persons especially, the practice of frequent and even daily,
Communion." The second rule kept the same antecedents, "tous les fidèles,
et particulièrement aux personnes religieuses."[76] "Second Rule: It is also
necessary to impress upon all the importance of receiving Communion with
exemplary dispositions." These rules, then, conclude the supposed commentary upon *QMM* with blatant signals that the "commentary" may merely be
piggybacking upon *QMM* in order to further the agenda of frequent, even
daily, Holy Communion.

Was Gennari really a proponent of frequent Communion, at least in this
influential essay? In his very simplistic reading and application of Trent, conditioned, perhaps, by the context of dealing with consecrated religious, Gennari sounds a clarion note *pro* frequent, even daily, Communion. Elements
of his essay seem to be sources for *STS*. For example, the cardinal perceives
that much of Alphonsus's thrust was in opposition to Jansenism, during Liguori's lifetime at full tide in Naples, and this might explain the references to
Jansenism in Pius's decree.

The cardinal concludes, however, with a carefully crafted, even politic, hedging of positions, bolstered by approving appropriation of the key papal documents hitherto, *Cum Ad Aures* and *QMM*, as well as the writings of Liguori. Dublanchy's assessment of Gennari is that he, like the others lumped with the pro-frequent-Communion camp, wanted to avoid making absolute rules and quantifications because he believed in the discretion of the confessor.[77]

## DISPOSITIONS FOR HOLY COMMUNION

The controversy between Lintelo and Godts is much more than a battle between those in favor of frequent Holy Communion and those opposed. Do not be blinded by the upshot of the controversy or by its feverish rhetoric. The controversy seems a bludgeoning by pamphlet, but its rancor did not, at first, necessitate theological or pastoral polarization.

The feuding Belgians actually agreed, in principle, that an increase in the frequency of receiving the Eucharist by the laity would benefit both church and society. The liberals and conservatives agreed on the rules of the dispute: Both depended upon the writings of the Fathers and theologians, and upon the authority of both precedent (that is, justifications of practices) and history (reports of practices). Rhetorically, too, they concurred in demonstrating the passion with which they espoused their positions, and so the writings were laced with sarcasm and invective. Perhaps these spices boosted readership. The enmity was a genuine provocation of *STS*, as this *motu proprio* admits, and thus a historical cause of all the subsequent campaigns for frequent Communion. Finally, the antagonists agreed on an ultimate pastoral goal — what is best for the salvation of souls.

The essential disagreement between Lintelo and Godts, perhaps, was about terminology. Godts tried to replace the term "frequent Communion" in the polemic for two reasons: It mislabeled the heart of the problem, which was actually and in his view the *dispositions* for Communion, and it allowed those who wanted to absolutize the receiving of the Lord's Body to appropriate all the theologians and spiritual writers who had praised and encouraged frequent Communion through the centuries. Godts in fact tried to refine the discussion by coining the phrase "absolute frequent Communion" to refer to those who seemed to want access to Communion considerably eased.[78] According to Godts, this new category was the goal of the progressives, and the coinage helped to clarify the discussion because the term *frequent* usually meant a relative increase in the frame of reference of the writer. Godts contrasted absolute communion (*communion absolue*) with usual communions (*communions ordinaires*).

Because virtual unanimity existed that frequent Communion was a good, Godts wanted the entire conflict resolved to three interrelated questions: First, what were the proper dispositions for receiving Communion? Second, what were the fruits of receiving Communion? Third, given the intrinsic nature of the Eucharist both as the person of Jesus and as a literal embodiment of faith itself, would it be pastorally prudent to emphasize *more* Communions as a good to be pursued by rule or by urgent injunction rather than by determination of the actual fruits of receiving for individual cases? In other words, should quantity be pursued more than quality? Quality would largely depend upon dispositions and preparation.

Godts's conservative stance argued for a proportionality between frequency of admission to Communion, on the one side, and piety and moral virtue, on the other. Piety and virtue together form the proper dispositions; the greater these two are, the more frequently a person may, or should, communicate.

Most Catholics, according to Godts, would be preserved from mortal sin by receiving Communion seven or eight times a year so long as they were adequately and properly disposed to this rate of receiving.[79] With respect to prevailing practice at the turn of the century, which was to fulfill the Lateran precept of Easter duty once a year, Godts's proposal meant remarkably "frequent" Communions. Thus, to style Godts as an opponent of frequent Holy Communion because of his opposition to Lintelo is inaccurate. To receive Communion more frequently, and even daily, demanded greater piety and adherence to a moral code, or, in the language of Liguori's rules, avoidance of "deliberate venial sin."

Lintelo saw greater piety and moral exemplariness as *results* of frequency of Communion, rather than as prerequisites to it. Because the Eucharist would be fruitful, as were all sacraments, *ex opere operato*, the layperson would be stimulated to greater piety and more virtuous living by greater frequency of Communion.

## PROPORTIONALITY

Proportionality as outlined by the rules attributed by Godts to Alphonsus Liguori insists that each element of the disposition for *frequent* Communion be enhanced or upgraded or intensified to become a disposition for *daily* Communion. The frequent communicant does not commit any venial sins willfully and has no affection for venial sins; for daily Communion, even the evil inclinations—apparently something like defects of character or instances of temptation—should be mastered. For frequent Communion, one is striving for perfection, as indeed the struggles to extirpate venial sins would seem to indicate. This is somehow linked to the desire, to a serious yearning to receive Communion. For daily Communion, some "degree" of this perfection, logically a degree greater than the degree of perfection indicative for merely frequent Communion, should have been achieved. While frequent Communion follows from an ardent desire to communicate, receiving daily itself manifests and confirms a yet more intense desire. For frequent Communion, a Christian must mortify the senses; for daily, the mortification must be done fervently—presumably, that is, with an emotional component.

These descriptions of interior and emotional states may console Godts; they seem usably qualitative and quantitative. But unless confessors know the spiritual states of their penitents intimately, such descriptions are unhelpful. Admission to Communion was to be governed by the confessor who, knowing well his penitent, could gauge the value of Communion at a recommended rate. Be mindful that the benefits of Communion obtained not only to the individual but also to the parish and that receiving Communion entailed a heavy commitment—fasting and prayers, and public witness to one's faith by the act of communicating. While at root Godts's approach is very traditional and proportional—apportioning "holiness" and the rate of receiving Communion—it is far from mechanical. On the contrary, it is consummately pastoral, for it accommodates to the needs and capacities of the individual, and it preserves respect for the sacrament, which in turn reflects the doctrine of the Real Presence.

> We all believe in the presence of our Lord Jesus Christ in the holy Eucharist. We all believe that He is present as God and as Man, with soul and body, truly, really, and substantially, these words being taken in the meaning and sense which Catholic tradition and the Church's teaching apply to them. . . . We all believe that Christ as God and as Man is deserving of our adoration—as Man on account of the mysterious union of the divine and human natures in Him, which we call hypostatic.[80]

Following from this dogma, the reception of the Eucharist demanded a decorous preparation, above and beyond the minimal canonical requirements for the avoidance of sacrilege. Both Godts and Lintelo could concur with this general principle, so proved by custom. These minimal juridical requirements were freedom from mortal sin, usually enacted by the faithful by having gone to confession on the vigil of Communion day, and observance of the fast.

With respect to the additional preparation, many factors bolstered demands for decorum. In European society, which was still socially stratified, worldly etiquette insisted upon deferential behavior to superiors. How much more deferential a communicant must be in welcoming the Godhead into his own body! Eucharistic taboos (such as strict avoidance of physical contact with a chalice, even empty), the prevailing practice of infrequent Communion among the laity, and extraliturgical, extrasacramental, grandiose devotions (such as Corpus Christi processions), all effected a *lex orandi* that reinforced the doctrine of the Real Presence. Inasmuch as they filtered to the laity, the Latin texts of the Mass itself preach meticulous purification from sin. The *Domine, non sum dignus* serves as embassy for the many penitential prayers for Communion. With the adoption of frequent Communion, the venerable piety of the preparation for Communion seems to have disappeared. In fact, it was transformed: The preparation prayers of the faithful, an individualistic array of devotions performed independently of, but during, the Mass, emerged as a sacramentally, if not quite liturgically, focused program. The preparation had always been coupled with a suitable thanksgiving, and methods for doing the two filled many pages of many popular devotional manuals.

Sacramental theology accommodated these pieties of preparation and thanksgiving, although they were far from liturgical. The essence of the Eucharist was Jesus's Paschal sacrifice, reenacted ritually *ex opere operato*. In Communion, Jesus again acts to a perfect and intended goal; human cooperation, however, with the graces thus made available forms a contrasting *operans operantis*. This effort on the part of the communicant is apparent in the preparation and thanksgiving that bracket the Holy Communion.

If Godts's entire structure of thought follows from the idea of the Real Presence, then Lintelo's follows from a foundational principle, almost identical but more comprehensive in that it applies to sacramental action generally. Lintelo's principle declares that Jesus, not humans, acts in the sacraments and that therefore the sacraments are efficacious, *ex opere operato*, so long as they are received licitly. A succinct articulation of this principle occurs in Zulueta's preface to the translation of Lintelo's most comprehensive work on frequent Communion: A legal and correct Communion must be "necessarily meritorious and profitable, whatever be its lack of ulterior improvements and perfections. By it grace must inevitably be increased *ex opere operato*, a sacramental effect too commonly underrated, while the worth of personal pieties, the *opus operantis*, is unduly magnified and falsely made the qualifying test of a worthy Communion."[81]

With respect to the actions of Jesus in the sacrament, then, notions of preparation and disposition reduce to trifles. The point is, however, that even in their foundational theological principles, the controversialists are distinguishable by emphasis or by articulation rather than by substantive theological divergence.

Another discussion of daily Communion in Lintelo appears at a point of definite and explicit agreement between Lintelo and Godts, and depends upon Thomas Aquinas, as interpreted by Francisco Cardinal Toledo (d. 1596). Toledo follows the distinction in venial sins with respect to Communion that Aquinas had—venial sins may be antecedent to the act of communicating or may be committed in the act itself, as by, for example deliberate, momentary inattention. Such a venial sin does not, however, impair the reception of grace, so long as the communicant receives licitly. This leads Godts to concede that, in the hypothetical case that a Christian could avoid committing a mortal sin only by receiving Communion daily, she should receive despite committing venial sins of irreverence in the very act of communicating.[82] As hypothetical, such a case taxes the imagination. Lintelo rejoices that here the school of Godts agrees with his own progressive school, for Godts practically admits that frequent Communion serves as a prophylaxis to sin, rather than as an end product of conversion.

Lintelo exults in his triumph by citing Godts's apparent inconsistency, for Godts had written, "We said earlier, and here we repeat it, that, as a general rule, it is not permissible for the confessor to allow frequent or more frequent Communion, unless the penitent's conversion is complete."[83] Saint Liguori's three rules apply a principle of proportionality and, of course, fit the vast majority of cases. An important and paradoxical exception allows daily Communion to a person who, though quite far from the near perfection that would admit to daily Communion, is beset by urgent temptations to commit mortal sin.[84] Alphonsus maintained, however, that a weekly Communion was sufficient for the vast majority to avoid damnation.[85]

The conservative Chatel, author of the pamphlet *Défense de la doctrine catholique sur la Communion fréquente* (1904), similarly maintained, according to Lintelo, that frequent and daily Communion might be accorded to those who urgently need the sacrament as a preservative of purity, even if these imperiled persons do not exhibit such pure dispositions as Chatel had described. Chatel says that youth are especially in need of the Eucharist for this particular reason. Lintelo fires these questions at Chatel:

When does the individual not need this prevention from falling into mortal sin? . . . If the individual in fact ceases to need this extraordinary use of Communion, doesn't the risk of sinning return with an end to daily Communions? When the individual has ceased to be in such danger of sinning mortally, hasn't she become much more pure and fervent, and so would it be necessary to forbid Communion so frequent?[86]

It appears, then, that Lintelo has hoisted the conservatives on their own petards.

For much of the history of disputes about the frequency of Communion, the most authoritative decisions of the Church, though the product of specific requests and circumstances, refused to specify any laws about the frequency of admission to the Lord's Table. The response of the Sacred Congregation of the Council (1587) to the request of the bishop of Brescia, who wished to curb the abuse of too many laity communicating too frequently, instances this wisdom well. In essence, the response justified its refusal to let the bishop allow Communion only on Sundays, feast days, Wednesdays, and Fridays. The response says both that such a restriction would be unprecedented and that the Council of Trent (session 22, Chapter 6), while not insisting upon more frequent Communion by all the faithful, did express the wish that Communion would be taken by all the faithful at every Mass at which they assisted.[87] Ultimately, the Church opted to depend upon the prudence and sagacity of the confessor to determine not merely fitness of a soul for Communion, but the likely benefit from Communion.

A truly pastoral confessor estimates the benefit to the individual penitent as well as to the local ecclesial community. Blessings to the individual are the text of Liguori's rules; blessings to the entire community undergird his counsel.

The first rule of Alphonsus Liguori proposes that weekly Communion suffices for most Christians. Liguori, as mediated by Godts, does not coordinate this with the laws of the Church regarding attendance at Mass and how these laws developed. The state of Communion frequency and Mass attendance by active Catholics at the beginning of the twenty-first century seems to support the idea that this periodization of Communion reception coheres with the religious aspirations of most of the laity. Despite Pius X's ratification and promotion of the idea of daily Communion and his own subsequent canonization as the pope of the Eucharist, this goal remains unreached.

The rules of Liguori strive to preserve, on the individual level, a realistic and humane scheduling of demands upon the faithful layperson and a healthful respect for the dangers of routinization that would supposedly vitiate reverence for the Eucharist. Ultimately, weekly Communion would (in the studied opinion of Liguori) and did (from his pastoral experience) suffice for the preservation of the individual in the state of grace. This recommendation of weekly Communion was, both in the time of Liguori and in the time of Godts and Lintelo, an ambitious recommendation in light of general levels of reception of Holy Communion.

What is the pastoral benefit to the Church as a whole, then, especially as reflected in the Liguorian system of proportionality? First, consider that the individual and the communal benefits are not at odds. For individuals to receive weekly and preserve the state of grace blesses Church and society.

These benefits follow from the avoidance of sin, both demanded by the sacrament of penance and encouraged by the awareness of the love of God, which was, in turn, fostered by the intimacy of sacramental Communion. Communal benefits pertain to the faith itself, and hence pastoral theology influences dogmatics, as Prosper of Aquitaine declared, *Lex orandi, lex credendi.*

In the thick of this controversy, no dichotomy arises between pastoral theology and dogmatics. The acrimony of the debate between Godts and Lintelo suggests that each party judged the stakes high. Godts saw that the emphasis was wrongly placed on the numbers of times a person received rather than upon proper preparation and disposition for Communion, and so he attempted to reframe the discussion into a concern for the dispositions. Emphasis upon numbers would result in carelessness with Communion practice, and the *lex orandi* would inexorably mar the faith, *lex credendi.* Rather than merely trafficking in attitudes, here Prosper's maxim would indeed affect a dogma of sacramental theology. Here is the "slippery slope" that Godts anticipated from "absolute" frequent Communion.

Suppose the distortion of absolute frequent Communion, and not *better* and more frequent Communion, wins the day. Priests become fixated upon increasing the numbers of Communions, and seepage from a scientific ethos compels priests to gather data. A fine example of this is the methodology of the prefect of religion at the University of Notre Dame, Father John F. O'Hara, CSC.[88] The leadership of the priests is effective and numbers of Communions do soar. Without a continuing emphasis upon the preparations and thanksgivings for Communion, Communion reception becomes casual and easily degenerates, then, becoming routine and finally even sacrilegious. So much for the individual soul, advised to frequency of Communion without corresponding advancement in the spiritual life—now a mortal sinner, compounding immoralities with sacrilege.

Godts continues to imagine how this process affects observers. Skeptics at first wonder, "How can Catholics 'eat God,' the creator of the universe, without some visible tokens of this momentous contact? If Catholics really believed in the Real Presence, wouldn't that register in some special way?" Yet more significantly than evidences of piety alone, without some discernible correlation between the morality and the piety of the communicant, skeptics question, "Does this going to Communion, which Catholics believe is such intimate union with God, really do or mean anything? Does it affect people's lives?" Without the faith, so profound that it would draw the believer to Holy Communion, impacting the world dramatically, and without the witness value of uprightness and a sense of detachment from the world that should follow from frequent Holy Communion, the very holy sacrament loses its meaning. *Ex opere operato* guarantees an efficacy to the sacraments.

This efficacy should give some fruit in the lives of the frequent recipients of Communion. Frequent Communion without effects undermines the doctrine of the Real Presence.

## PREPARATION FOR AND
## THANKSGIVING AFTER COMMUNION

Dispositions, the linchpin of Godts's policy, were enacted devotionally in all of the ritual activities prior to Holy Communion as well as in the pieties of the preparation for and thanksgiving after Communion. These became central to the Belgian conflict between Godts and Lintelo, and they also suffered a fairly rapid disappearance as the campaign for frequent Communion gathered momentum. Evidence of this is that Pius XII decries the loss of the thanksgiving after Communion in his liturgical encyclical *Mediator Dei* (1947).[89] Simultaneous with the decline in preparation and thanksgiving, praying the Mass and the preeminent aid to this piety, the missal, steadily grew in popularity. In schematic terms, then, the devotional (individualistic preparations for and thanksgivings after Communion) retreated before the liturgical (the vernacular missal that enabled the laity to pray the Mass in union with the priest). Union with the priest in verbal prayer and union through ritual sacramental participation in the actual receiving of Communion reinforced each other.

Remember that common notions of purity, if not canon law, demanded the layperson confess his sins, usually on the vigil of receiving Communion. This alliance between the two sacraments had become almost inviolable. Notions of purity would have entailed a scrupulous avoidance of the most minute of venial sins in the interval between confession and Communion. Confession itself required examination of conscience and revelation of faults and failures to the priest and then, to complete the sacrament, performing prescribed devotional actions and saying certain prayers. The requisite fast for Eucharist was a "natural" fast from the midnight prior to Communion; a natural fast precluded even the taking of water.[90]

Additional pieties for Holy Communion, cultivated during the long centuries of rare use of the Eucharist, attained status as a set performance, which nonetheless admitted considerable latitude and personalization; it acquired the name *preparation*. *Thanksgiving*, likewise a set performance and likewise subject to considerable variation, still invariably followed communicating. Godts saw these as crucial in the discussion of the frequency of reception of Communion.

Godts's evisceration of Father Falconi's *Notre pain quotidien, c'est-à-dire le T.S. Sacrement* consists largely in lively descriptions of one abuse that flowed from his alleged advice—daily Communion without any preparation. Falconi had been condemned as a quietist, and thus quietism and advocacy of daily Communion in many ways overlap. Godts's strategy is to impute guilt by association to demonize those struggling to implement absolute frequent Communion.

The abuse of skipping preparation Godts flags by means of a historical prospectus: Spanish priests of greater zeal than education misapplied the "daily bread" petition of the Lord's Prayer to Communion. Women, especially given to enthusiasm and sentimentality, took such teaching to heart. Godts reports that nuns would, at the sound of the bell that signaled the consecration of the host, "hop from their beds" and "drop their chores" without considering in the least making preparations for Communion.[91] Indeed, they seemed to have skipped Mass altogether. Laywomen, because of their domestic duties, would insist upon having Communion at home—even in bed—as a "divine right" (*droit divin*).[92]

The spiritual readiness of the offensive women is not the issue for Godts; rather, the issue is an evident lack of respect for the Real Presence. Godts simply applies, though does not make explicit, the maxim *Lex orandi, lex credendi*. By receiving Communion so casually, without what a class-conscious culture would consider gestures of respect for a being so infinitely above the human, such women enact for themselves and convey to their communities that the sacrament is not an encounter with the Godhead. Thus, to Godts lack of preparation equals faulty disposition, which in turn equals disrespect, and this equals a very real, if not doctrinal, denial of the Real Presence.

No less an authority than Aquinas does Godts use to outline his case for the importance of "making" a preparation for Communion in order that the Communion will be of benefit. "It is indubitable, says Saint Thomas, that frequent, and even daily, Communion is not very beneficial [*utile*] in itself; nor is it fitting for everybody, undiscriminatingly, not even for those faithful who are in the state of grace. Rather, it is beneficial only to those who are well-disposed and well-prepared."[93] A famous early advocate of *weekly* Communion, and therefore eagerly claimed by both progressives and conservatives, Stephen Coubé, echoed Aquinas in a series of immensely influential lectures at Lourdes: "It would be both baneful and imprudent to recommend it [daily Communion] indiscriminately, at the present day, as the majority of the faithful have neither the time nor the requisite dispositions for receiving it."[94] These texts explode the very idea of absolute frequent Communion.

What is it to "make" a preparation? Godts sketches a sample preparation. He distinguishes between its remote and proximate modes. Citing Augustine who draws the comparison between receiving Communion and receiving a "grand personage," Godts urges for the remote preparation for Communion an abrogation of all "earthly affections."[95] The recipe for proximate preparation reads, "On the evening before Communion, prepare your heart with acts of love and desire. As soon as you arise in the morning, remind yourself that you will be receiving Jesus shortly; with an ardent sigh, invite the divine Spouse to enter your soul unhesitatingly."[96] Then, just before actually receiving, "you must excite in yourself Faith, Humility and Desire."[97] Faith recalls that the Eucharist is the Real Presence, "our Redeemer . . . really and substantially in the consecrated Host."[98] Humility is characterized by the emotion of astonishment at the condescension of our King, coming to our shanties. From this humility—which Godts reminds the readers is expressed in the liturgical and Matthean phrase, "Lord, I am not worthy that you should come under my roof"—will naturally flow acts (i.e., prayers or expressions) of contrition and hope, for our souls will be so enriched by the graces of this sacrament. Desire, insofar as it is aroused, benefits the recipient proportionally, for it reflects love for Our Lord. In short, these acts of faith, humility, and desire make us recognize who is coming to us, to whom He is coming, and why He is coming. Note that the Latin Mass did not serve, in the thinking of the day, as preparation for Communion.

"L'action de grâces," or thanksgiving after Communion, comprises separate and additional procedures, perhaps of even greater importance than the preparation because of the indwelling of the Real Presence. In both popular piety and serious theological literature, the actual digestion of the host constituted the most privileged time for prayer. Godts finds supporters in such authors as "Cajetan, Suarez, Gonet, Valencia, De Lugo and others," and he describes then a second abuse of the Spanish women—clamoring for larger hosts so that their most efficacious prayers would find a larger window of opportunity with longer digestion.[99]

Godts recommends a format for the thanksgiving, but its stuff was as variable as creative spiritual writers could imagine. During this time, "endeavour as much as you are able to speak with Jesus Christ."[100] Godts blames any diminishment of benefits from communicating, howsoever frequently, to too little conversation with Jesus in these valuable moments. Thus Godts recommends, "If you are not obliged to do something else as a matter of obedience or charity [during your thanksgiving], strive to speak with Jesus for at least one half-hour."[101] The matter of this conversation should above all be importuning Jesus for the grace of perseverance in faith, and should also include "fervent acts of welcome, gratitude, love, contrition, self-offering, and whatever concerns you."[102] If conversation is impossible, a devotional book will suffice. The whole rest of the day should be spent in meditation. Greater frequency of receiving Communion does not result in less meditation; rather, one must then take care to "remain united to" Jesus.[103]

The erosion of preparation and thanksgiving stemmed from the campaign for frequent and daily Communion, but these individualistic brackets around sacramental Communion were not assailed deliberately or theologically or liturgically. No, simple pastoral advice and the desire to find absolute and impressive numbers of communicants spurred this erosion.

Having examined Godts's position, I now examine Lintelo, who holds a contrasting position. His source on the nature of preparation for Communion is Father Denis Petau, SJ, also known as Petavius. Petau's steadfast opposition to Jansenism credentials him for Lintelo.[104] The starting point of Lintelo's four-page summary of Petau is both to define "worthy reception" (*reçevoir dignement*) of Communion and to assert the real cause-and-effect relations of the sacrament upon the soul. Worthy reception demands a "certain perfection of virtues and of gifts, particularly of reverence and devotion." Even Francis-Xavier Godts would find no fault here. But when it comes to precedence, or sequence of events, Petau stresses that such virtues and gifts *follow* the frequent reception of Communion.[105]

The actions that constitute disposing oneself to Communion include what was common practice for the centuries of infrequent Communion—a legally sound sacramental confession and observance of the fast. Lintelo expounds upon the former modestly, noting, perhaps superfluously, that the examination of conscience is to be diligent, that one's mortal sins should be the object of detestation, and that all of one's faults should be mentioned during the confession. In contrast, recall that Liguori specified, for frequent Communion, the absence of affection for venial sins. In addition to a valid confession, preparation includes faith, which is manifest in love (*dilection*). Petau outlines the legal aspects thus, "Moreover, in this disposition is understood *all* which the holy Doctors require for worthily partaking of the Blessed Sacrament" (emphasis added).[106]

All other teachings about disposition, according to Lintelo, treat what is above and beyond necessary (*nécessaires*), and so these supererogations can admittedly be beneficial (*utiles*) and lead to more fruitful (*plus fructueuse*) Communions.[107] Logic and definition together dictate that these latter are not necessary. In fact, according to Petau, this is the crucial distinction in treating preparation to communicate. Petau makes no distinction between preparing for one Communion or many, and he indicates that indeed the more perfect dispositions are "the fruit of a Communion more frequent precisely."[108] This boldly contradicts proportionality. As the campaign for frequent Communion accelerates, this notion blossoms into the common image of a "chain of communions" in which each instance of reception prepares for the next.[109]

Within the body of the "First Letter," Lintelo describes the contemporary pastoral situation in which Eucharistic practice is being abandoned by the young in droves. He is exasperated that in and despite this circumstance, the conservatives are harping upon the proper "dispositions" to communicate.[110] Thus, receiving the sacrament becomes more foreboding. Lintelo is also indignant that his opponent, Godts, implies that the de-emphasizing of preparation for Communion is a concerted and purposeful abandonment of the practice.[111]

Godts quotes a brief, supposed case study from the periodical *L'ami du clergé* of 1899. A woman zealous in the works of the Lord is so pressed for time that she neither prepares for nor makes a thanksgiving after Communion; she demands Communion in the sacristy and then rushes to the train.[112] Godts expresses his incredulity that the woman is called a "veritable apostle" by interjecting "(???)" after the word *apôtre*, and he judges this situation scandalous. True saints value prayer and the interior life over business, and such behavior once provoked a censorious Flemish pastor to honor the Real Presence in a similarly busy communicant's stomach with an escort of altar boys bearing candles.[113] Disrespect is, to Godts, a catastrophic consequence of absolute frequent Communion and its abettor, the enfeeblement of preparation and thanksgiving. Discarding preparation and thanksgiving lead to a denial of the Real Presence and, ultimately, to apostasy. In light of the secularization of Europe of his day, Godts was far from extravagant in his alarm.

Formats for preparation and thanksgiving were largely disjunct from the Eucharistic liturgy and were emphatically individualistic. Early in the campaign for frequent Communion, advocates of more frequent Communion such as Eduard Barbé had dared only to reclassify and to rearrange the stuff of the preparation and the thanksgiving; eventually, progressives articulated and encouraged the practical abolition of these pieties, and even of Communion on demand.

As with many complex and controversial issues, "opposite" positions actually share very much and often become controversies because of social-psychological dynamics. In other words, controversies can mushroom from merely imperfect concord.

First dynamic: movements for any sort and any magnitude of institutional change occur within the supervening culture; both of these interrelated systems generate controversies which become so pitched that intemperance and demonization follow. Daily Communion is but one element, and eventually a preponderant element, of the Eucharistic movement, including Eucharistic associations and confraternities, congresses, devotional literature, and so forth. This Eucharistic movement, in turn, operates within blatantly political systems, for the Eucharistic movement was spawned in deliberate reaction to French anticlericalism and liberalism. These form the larger, cultural envelope.

Second dynamic: as the controversy intensifies, it polarizes the "opponents," who actually differ largely in expression of a common truth. Within the institutional Church, itself embattled at that time, adjustments had to occur to correspond with or respond to changes in the larger systems. The configuration of these adjustments becomes the bone of contention, and the struggle is all the more passionately joined because the antagonists are insiders. In the embattled Church, then, at the turn of the nineteenth century, the demonizing of opponents on the issue of frequency of Communion parallels structurally the condemnations of Americanism and modernism. As with those two episodes, the intellectual content of the dispute seems, in balance, less significant than the social dynamics. As in those cases, the controversy about the frequency of Communion pushed Lintelo and Godts apart, institutionally and in the tone of their language. In essence, Godts's fundamental theology was the Real Presence; Lintelo's was the sacramental principle of *ex opere operato*. Surely, a common ground exists here.

Pastoral strategies fuel the polemic between sincere Belgian priests, and these strategies seem rooted in pastoral experience. Even as the temperaments of the antagonists may be the essential factors in their positions, so too do their priestly experiences contribute to their stances. Lintelo taught high school for much of his career, and his perceiving rich benefits from experiments with frequent Communion may derive from Victorian notions of childhood, purity, and sex. To state the speculation starkly: Sexual purity is coextensive with sinlessness, and prepubescent children are therefore pure. In the perceptual grid of the Victorian era, their purity, without elaborate trappings of preparation and thanksgiving, sufficed to "prepare" them decorously for receiving the Real Presence in the Eucharist. With great fidelity to Communion, the children seemed to remain pure.

Godts, in contrast, while he did spend some years in teaching at a house of formation for the Redemptorists, occupied himself greatly in parish retreat work. Jay Dolan's *Catholic Revivalism* details how the retreats and missions given in the United States, contemporaneous to Godts's years of ministry and patterned upon European models, focused upon reclaiming lost souls. We speculate then that much of Godts's experience was with the morally and spiritually lost, which gave rise to his opinion that very few of his contemporaries were free from mortal sin and hence eligible for eternal happiness. Preservation of the Real Presence from indignity in itself was, naturally, his genuine concern, but not a concern centered in the sacramental species. Rather, Godts imagines the dire long-term consequences of inadequately prepared but frequent and casual Communions: no less than the end of faith.

It may well be that culture, taste, and temperament did more to shape these disputes than theology did. The dispute in which Godts and Lintelo engaged subsists in divergent and very basic ways of perceiving the world and human nature—that is, temperament and culture. Consider whether Godts's view on dispositions for Communion coheres with his perspective on human nature, his theological anthropology, as it were: Quintessential to another of Godts's controversies was the number of souls who would be saved, and on this issue his book *De Paucitate Salvandorum quid Docuerunt Sancti* (1899) opposed Father Castelain. Godts held that very few, indeed, would attain salvation. Father Dryvers wrote, concerning this earlier controversy, "The propositions of Father Godts sound a bit harsh upon our ears, but Godts wore himself out in pushing as many as possible through the door which he depicted so narrow."[114] In his writings on the dispositions for Communion, Godts surmised that a minute fraction of Catholics could communicate without sacrilege—that is, most of the congregation was in the state of mortal sin.[115] Temperamentally, then, Godts seemed to see humanity in a dismal light. In two ways Godts resonates, then, with the Jansenists: They both consider that salvation is only for the few, and they both emphasize sublime worthiness for Communion. Both Godts and the eponymous Cornelius Otto Jansen were Flemings.[116]

Cultural differences may explain, too, differences in theological anthropology and practical sacramental theology. The mother tongue of Lintelo and Couët was French; and that of Godts, Flemish. Significantly, Godts introduced cultural conflicts into his polemics; for instance, in his introductory prayer to *EH* he wrote, "May the Lord preserve us Flemish from this craze of the French!"[117] In the movie *Babette's Feast*, the exiled *cusinière* provides a gratuitous and totally unmerited taste of heaven through a festive and most extravagant banquet to her dour, Danish employers. Analogously, Lintelo, the Walloon, wants a taste of heaven—Communion—absolutely frequently and, insofar as preparation is minimized, gratuitously; Godts, the Fleming, insists upon being admitted only by the confessor to the banquet, and works very hard at worthiness to feast.

## NOTES

1. *STS*, 13.
2. Lester R. Kurtz, *The Politics of Heresy: The Modernist Crisis in Roman Catholicism* (Berkeley: University of California Press, 1986).
3. This date is, of course, subject to correction. For example, research into the life of Saint Pierre-Julien Eymard suggests that he himself was a "latecomer" to Eucharistic projects and that the real center, in France, of rekindling interest in the Eucharist was Mother Dubouché, foundress of a religious congregation of women whose particular apostolate was "adoration of reparation." "Cave, III-V: Eucharistic

Projects for Men (1851–1856)," typewritten document, Provincial Archives of the Blessed Sacrament Fathers, Cleveland (Highland Heights), Ohio; Schwertner, *The Eucharistic Renaissance*, provides a history of the Eucharistic movement.

4. J. M. Mayeur, "Leo XIII," *NCE*.

5. Pope Leo XIII, *Epistola Encyclica Sanctissimi Domini nostri Leonis Papae XIII de Sanctissima Eucharistia. Mirae Caritatis*, in *Acta Sanctae Sedis* 34 (1902): 650; English translation from *The Papal Encyclicals: 1878–1903*, edited by Claudia Carlen (Raleigh, North Carolina: Consortium / McGrath, 1981), 505; henceforth, *MC*.

6. *MC*, 503.

7. *MC*, 504.

8. *MC*, 505.

9. *MC*, 505.

10. John 6:14ff; John 6:27ff; John 6:48ff; *MC*, 501.

11. *MC*, 501.

12. *MC*, 501.

13. *MC*, 505.

14. *MC*, 505.

15. *MC*, 506–7.

16. *MC*, 499.

17. *MC*, 499.

18. Godts's biographer observes that Godts's writing was quite careless, especially upon being so praised for his earlier publications, and that the fecundity of Godts's pen was "frightening." Maurice de Meeulenmeester, *Le révérend père François-Xavier Godts, rédemptoriste* (Louvain: S. Alphonse, 1929), 50–52.

19. *MC*, 506–7.

20. "La Pratiq. de la S. Com." is the title; no other information is provided by the author. François-Xavier Godts, *Exagérations historiques et théologiques concernant la Communion quotidienne* (Roulers: Jules de Meester, 1904), 17n1; henceforth, *EH*.

21. *EH*, 39.

22. *MC*, 501.

23. *MC*, 505.

24. *EH*, 37.

25. *EH*, 35–36.

26. Godts cites the explanation of Fillion simply as "FILLION, in *Matth*, VI, 18, page. 132." *EH*, 37n2.

27. *MC*, 501.

28. *EH*, 37.

29. Godts refers to the bishop's "Lettre du 15 Juil. 1900," presumably published. *EH*, 39.

30. Lintelo, *Lettres à un prêtre à propos d'une polemique sur la Communion fréquente*, second and revised edition (Tournai: H. & L. Casterman, 1905), 17–18, henceforth *LP*.

31. *LP*, 18.

32. *LP*, 18.

33. François-Xavier Godts, *Réponse aux lettres à un prêtre à propos d'une polémique sur la Communion fréquente par le Père Jules Lintelo de la compagnie de Jésus* ([Bruxelles: Albert De Wit], 1905), 9; henceforth *RL*.

34. *RL*, 9.

35. *RL*, 10.

36. The passage from *MC* is cited in the French translation. *LP*, 73.

37. *LP*, 73–74.

38. *LP*, 74.

39. *EH*, 16.

40. *ET*, 84.

41. François-Xavier Godts, *Deuxième rèponse au R. P. Lintelo* (Bruxelles: Albert De Wit, 1905), 12.

42. Meulemeester, *Godts, rédemptoriste*, 57.

43. Casimir Gennari, "De la Communion fréquente et du décret 'Quemadmodum,'" in Pierre Bastien, *Directoire canonique a l'usage des congrégations a voeux simples*, 392–421, translated by Pierre Bastien (Maredsous, Belgium: Maredsous Abbey, 1904).

44. *AM*, 125.

45. Thomas Slater, *A Short History of Moral Theology* (New York: Benziger, 1909), 48–50.

46. *AM*, 170–73.

47. *EH*, 65–66.

48. *EH*, 68–69.

49. *EH*, 67.

50. *EH*, 68.

51. "Cyprien Aristase" is a pseudonym. *AM*, 27–28.

52. Stefano Antoni, *Why Do So Many Vain Fears Keep You from Frequent and Daily Communion?* (New York: Sentinel, 1923); the Italian appeared in 1904.

53. *RL*, 50.

54. For a biographical sketch of Bishop Louis Gaston de Ségur, see Wendy M. Wright, *Heart Speaks to Heart: The Salesian Tradition* (London: Darton, Longman, and Todd, 2004), 129–34.

55. *RL*, 49–50.

56. *AM*, 98–99.

57. *AM*, 108, 111, 149.

58. Jules Severin, *Vie du père Lintelo de la compagnie de Jésus, apôtre de la Communion quotidienne, membre du bureau des congrès Eucharistiques* (Bruxelles: Librairie de l'action catholique, 1921), 79–80.

59. *LP*, xii.

60. Ferreres, *Decree*, 99–101. Ferreres's translation, oddly, does follow the text in escalating the Communions from "frequentius" to "frequentioris ac etiam quotidianae." The phrase becomes a formula in the controversy.

61. Ferreres, *Decree*, 101.

62. Gennari, "De la Communion," 394.

63. *CEF*, 548.

64. *Decrees of the Council of Trent*, 147.

65. Gennari, "De la Communion," 395.

66. Gennari, "De la Communion," 396–97.

67. Gennari, "De la Communion," 394–95.

68. CEF, 547.

69. Gennari, "De la Communion," 401.

70. Gennari, "De la Communion," 401.

71. Gennari, "De la Communion," 400.

72. Gennari, "De la Communion," 401–2.

73. Gennari, "De la Communion," 402.

74. Gennari, "De la Communion," 413.

75. "Letter from the Sacred Congregation of the Council to the Bishop of Brescia," Ferreres, *Decree*, 150.

76. Gennari, "De la Communion," 413.

77. CEF, 548.

78. François-Xavier Godts, *Réponse au R. P. Couët* (Bruxelles: Albert Dewit, 1905), 6.

79. *RL*, 5.

80. Joseph Kramp, "A Religio-Psychological Attitude Toward the Eucharist," *Orate Fratres* 4 (1930): 514.

81. Francis M. de Zulueta, "Translator's Preface," in *The Eucharistic Triduum: An Aid to Priests in Preaching Frequent and Daily Communion According to the Decrees of H.H. Pius X*, by Jules Lintelo (London: R. & T. Washbourne, 1909), vx.

82. *LP*, 93; *RL*, 19.

83. *LP*, 94.

84. *LP*, 93.

85. *RL*, 18–19.

86. *LP*, 80.

87. CEF, 534.

88. Thomas Patrick Jones, *The Development of the Office of Prefect of Religion at the University of Notre Dame from 1842 to 1952* (Washington, D.C.: Catholic University Press, 1960).

89. Pope Pius XII, *Mediator dei. Acta Apostolicae Sanctae* 39 (1947): 521–95; English version in *The Papal Encyclicals: 1939–1958*, edited by Claudia Carlen (Raleigh, North Carolina: Consortium / McGrath, 1981), 139.

90. Thomas Francis Anglin, *The Eucharistic Fast: An Historical Synopsis and Commentary*, Canon Law Studies, no. 124 (Washington, D.C.: Catholic University Press, 1941), 39.

91. *EH*, 17.

92. *EH*, 17–18.

93. *AM*, 75.

94. Coubé, *Discourses on Weekly Communion*, 10.

95. *AM*, 77.

96. *AM*, 77.

97. *AM*, 77.

98. *AM*, 77.

99. *AM*, 79. *EH*, 18.

100. *AM*, 78.

101. *AM*, 79.

102. *AM*, 79.

103. *AM*, 80.

104. *LP*, 14.

105. *LP*, 13.

106. *LP*, 14.

107. *LP*, 15–16.

108. *LP*, 16.

109. Coubé, *Discourses on Weekly Communion*, 252.

110. *LP*, 35.

111. *LP*, 92.

112. *EH*, 31.

113. *EH*, 32.

114. Meeulenmeester, *Godts, rédemptoriste*, 57.

115. *RL*, 22.

116. Marc Marie Escholier, "Jansen, Cornelius Otto," *Britannica Online*, 1994–1998, http://www.eb.com:180/cgi-bin/g?DocF=micro/300/19.html (accessed 4 June 1998).

117. *EH*, 8.

## Chapter Three

# The Pope of Holy Communion

Our history now turns to Rome. *STS* offers a tale of its own origins; its sketchy narrative demands investigation if we are to perceive the causes of the liturgical shift toward frequent Holy Communion. What motivated Pius X to pursue the campaign for frequent Communion? The prayer intending to spread daily Communion is regarded as a "trial balloon" for the decree on frequent Communion. This chapter analyzes *STS* itself and enumerates the various means Pius X mobilizes to insure that *STS* would not be largely ignored, as had been the formulaic injunctions for frequent Communion for centuries. The four major means for encouraging the victory of the campaign were the Eucharistic triduum, staged mitigation of the fast, establishing lay and clerical societies for this purpose, and the lowering of the age of first Communion.

### FROM BELGIUM TO ROME

The ready sources for the story behind *STS* are three. This Vatican pronouncement points to its own origin, but cryptically. More details appear in articles by J. M. Derély, SJ, and Hector Lemieux, SSS.[1] These reports, written by members of the orders that won the dispute, seem to rely upon the living traditions of their orders, for they are underdocumented.

*STS* provides a sparse frame. The decree alludes to the Lintelo-Godts controversy and this is placed within the much larger, but highly selective, history of the persistent lack of communicating by the faithful. The very recent Roman events dominate this broader history: Pastoral men appealed to Pius for a definitive decision on the dispute in Belgium; the pope desired that the laity be invited to and be able to accept the invitation to communicate frequently; the pope remanded the question to the Sacred Congregation of the

81

Council.[2] The pope's involvement is clear, and this signals that the ultimate decision on frequency of Communion was his.

But who in the Roman Curia funneled the controversy to the pope? What role had Casimiro Cardinal Gennari, the signatory of *STS*? Why was Pius X so hasty? Why did the pope select the Sacred Congregation of the Council to ratify his opinion?

*STS* hints at the impact of the Belgian tempest, if not its true and proper scope. "In our own day the controversy has been continued with increased heat and not without bitterness, so that the minds of confessors and the consciences of the faithful have been disturbed, to the no small detriment of Christian piety and fervor."[3] Decrees seldom admit that they address trifling problems, but that this dispute reached the Vatican and provoked the response that it did may indicate the importance of the dispute to contemporaries. It was so vitriolic and public that the pope himself heard of it. "As it happened, Pius X was keeping an attentive ear close to the controversy. He knew what was going on. And he deplored it with all his heart."[4]

Because Derély and Lemieux sing of their victories, they may, however, overstate the magnitude and rancor of the affair. Hector Lemieux, a Blessed Sacrament father, paints the controversy in this way: "With time, the tone of the controversy grew more violent. Its effects ricocheted from Belgium and France to all over Europe, cutting an ever-wider swath of discontent in the Church. A disturbing restlessness settled in the hearts of well-intentioned Catholics."[5] That *STS* and the Eucharistic movement of which it was the crown have attracted scant scholarly attention does not reprove Lemieux for exaggeration. Still, did the integrated controversies about greater frequency of Holy Communion and the dispositions to receive it really generate so much fanfare?

The size of the controversy in its day may be moot. By analogy, the condemnation of modernism seems to have been quite disproportionate to the issues; indeed, the condemnation may have given greater prominence to the ideas of the accused modernists than they would otherwise have attracted. The results of the condemnation were indisputably dire, especially in America, and this regardless of the size of the original problem, for *Pascendi Domenici Gregis* likely killed theology in the United States for a generation. The consequences, too, of *STS* and the Eucharistic movement were, with respect to the liturgy, immense.

## CASIMIRO CARDINAL GENNARI

Cardinal Gennari links the Belgian controversy to the throne of Peter in two ways. First, Gennari's own scholarly work involved him in the Lintelo-Godts controversy. The publication of an article in the *Annales de T.S. Sacrement* by a priest of the diocese of Namur, a Father Joseph Coppin, was the overture to the dispute, and when this article was published widely in tract form, it outlined approvingly the opinions of Cardinal Gennari.[6]

It is beyond the scope of this book to rehearse the oeuvre of Gennari, but his *Consulatzioni morali-canoniche-liturgiche* included two dissertations of relevance to our issues, "Cons. 39, Circa la confessione delle persone devote e la communione quotidiana" and "Cons. 114, Circa la Communione frequenti ed il decreto 'Quemadmodum.'"[7] Even before the Belgian controversy seethed, Gennari's writings, as appropriated or gainsaid by the controversialists, had invited the pope's interest.

Second, Gennari's position in the Vatican enabled him to advance the cause of daily Communion. Even before the controversy was referred to the Vatican, Gennari had signed the rescript that made the "Prayer for the Propagation of the Pious Custom of Daily Communion" an act of indulgence; he may, of course, have been its actual author. Once the controversy was officially referred to the Sacred Congregation of the Council, Gennari, its prefect, was empowered to resolve the pamphlet dispute as he—and Pius X—saw fit. Finally, the manuscript of *STS* was written by Gennari at the behest of the pope, and the official decree appeared above Gennari's signature.[8] In the entire matter, he served as a factotum of Pius X. Casimiro Gennari helped immensely to transform the liturgical life of the Catholic Church in the twentieth century in three ways—by his publications themselves, by the role of his articles in the Lintelo-Godts controversy, and by his position in the Vatican. It is impossible to know the relative influences of Gennari upon Pope Pius X and vice versa. However, Pius's character, as the antimodernism activities of his papacy show, was not hobbled by passivity.

## POPE PIUS X

What aspects, then, of the life of Giuseppe Sarto, later Pope Pius X, enabled him to embrace frequent, even daily Communion? Once he had ascended to the throne of Peter, what impelled him to challenge a formidable and deep-rooted inertia by promoting frequent Communion for the entire Church?

While he was patriarch of Venice, the future pope declared his membership in the pro-frequent-Communion party by adopting the counsels of Giuseppe Frassinetti, by hosting a Eucharistic congress in 1897, and by having the synod of the patriarchate embrace the notion of frequent Communion in 1898.[9]

Even during his lifetime, Pius X was hailed as "the pope of the Eucharist," and his hagiographers retained the appellation.[10] Perhaps the liturgical revolution of frequent Communion stems largely from the personal piety of the sainted pope. Members of the papal household reported that Pius very frequently visited the Blessed Sacrament, and his demeanor during the Mass, especially when consecrating the host and praying the Lord's Prayer, was devout and edifying.[11] Fernessole summarized the records of the process for the canonization of Pius X. "One is struck by the fervent unanimity with which the witnesses testify to the personal devotion of the pope to the Eucharist. This devotion, moreover, was as simple as it was strong and tender, totally devoid of pretension, of pomposity, and of peculiar externalities."[12] Insofar as the process of the Church for canonization is reliable, this extraordinary personal piety, though derived from hagiography, may be the root of *STS*. Still, devotion to the Eucharist does not automatically equate with frequency of Communion for the laity.

Had the pope merely approved the decree and left its implementation to the flow of history, it might have faded into oblivion and his title, "pope of the Eucharist," might not have prevailed. But Pius X conveyed forcibly and repeatedly, and as directly as papal etiquette at that time allowed, that the will of the supreme pontiff spoke through *STS*, despite its official curial authorship. As his eradication of the modernists showed, Pius pursued his goals with resourceful tenacity. Given the practical ecclesiology of the time, the pope's will, so plainly displayed, demanded gratification and mobilized immense resources. For example, recall how Father Godts, the most ardent and prolific controversialist on behalf of the status quo, capitulated unhesitatingly to the will of the pope upon the publication of *STS*.

As Venetian patriarch, the future pope promoted the Eucharistic movement and he demonstrated a lively personal Eucharistic piety. What did he think about the Eucharist and Communion? His and his surrogates' approbations for the efforts of the proponents of frequent Communion explicitly reveal the play of Pius's mind.

Canon Stefano Antoni and one Abbé Maroni both received gracious recommendations from His Holiness for their writings in favor of frequent Communion very soon after *STS* appeared.[13] Similarly, Pius X lauded Jesuit Father Jules Lintelo and even admitted to the purpose of such praise: to sell more of Lintelo's works and by this means to promote Holy Communion. Cardinal Gennari, writing from Rome on 25 January 1907, reported to Lintelo: "His Holiness accepts your tribute [a gift of books and pamphlets] with the most lively pleasure. He highly commends your Reverence's zeal, and hopes that your works may obtain the widest possible circulation."[14] More effusive praise, though formally more insulated from the pope, is relayed and broadcast by the bishop of Verdun, who attributes it to the cardinal legate, Vincent Vannutelli, at the Eucharistic Congress of Metz (1907). "The

Reverend Father Lintelo was the one whose writings most faithfully reflected the mind and wishes of the Holy Father."[15] And the lauds from the pope continued "in January, 1907, 1909, etc."[16] So, in his activities as patriarch, in his personal devotional life, and in his attitudes toward the Eucharist and Holy Communion, Sarto was and had been for many years a partisan of the Eucharistic movement.

Even these official Vatican pronouncements of sundry sorts deliberately reveal the pope's enthusiastic support for greater use of Communion. If they know anything about changes in the frequency of receiving Holy Communion, most American Roman Catholics glibly credit the general greater frequency of reception to Pope Saint Pius X. Why? First communicants from 1910 until Vatican II learned that Pius X had admitted them to the Eucharistic table at a much younger age than their parents and grandparents. Tons of holy cards and communion certificates testify to the pervasiveness of this attribution.[17] The campaign for frequent Communion, the liturgical movement, and the cause for Pius's canonization all could agree to this "fact" and could use it to their advantage.

Popularizing the nickname "pope of Holy Communion" can largely be credited to Archbishop Edwin V. O'Hara (d. 1956) of Kansas City, who pressed for the canonization of this recent pope. Using all the resources of the media, the cause for Pius's canonization shaped an image of Pius that resonated favorably with the values of American culture. The success, on these terms, of the cause for Pius's canonization gauges, too, how well assimilated American Catholics were by the 1940s. O'Hara's appropriation of the photogenic Pius X for his catechetical expansion parallels how Pius was drafted by both the liturgical movement and the Eucharistic movement for their own agendas.

Astonishingly, Pius's cause for canonization as directed by Vincent O'Hara for an American constituency interpreted his pushing frequent Communion as a manifestation of his sympathies for democracy: "Perhaps his most democratic action was his decision to extend communion to more and more of the Catholic people. Opening the communion rail to more and more men, women, and children was universally hailed as an important breakthrough not only by the theologians of the liturgical movement, but by average Catholics as well."[18] The motivations of Pius in acting with such vigor to restore frequent Communion were quite complex.

Temperamentally, Saint Pius X was decisive, even precipitate, and this allowed him to resolve definitively the Lintelo-Godts controversy—only the latest eruption of disagreements about the use of Holy Communion that had simmered for centuries—with impressive dispatch. Pius's insistence upon the implementation of his various Eucharistic acts reveals a patriarchal, rather than Jacksonian, mentality. Yes, the very pope who was to condone a veritable secret police for the extirpation of modernism exhibits a more autocratic and totalitarian spirit than a democratic one. Saint Pius apparently intervened in several ways with the workings of the curial congregation charged with deciding the controversy to guarantee its conformity with his personal desires. Such an imposition of his will upon a bureaucratic office might strike an American as unconstitutional.

Pius's favoring frequent Communion had been formed by his own pastoral practice as priest and then bishop of Mantua and Venice. This practice is attributable to the Eucharistic movement generally and its literature, particularly the writings of Giuseppe Frassinetti. The political substructure of the Eucharistic movement, as the explicit origins of the Eucharistic congresses indicate, was avowedly antiliberal, antisecular, and antidemocratic. The congressists were nostalgic and conservative; they longed for a Eucharistic reign of Christ in the world that would be realized when Church and state were in an undefined way indistinguishable; an idealization of the Middle Ages gave clues to their usually inexplicit political ideal.[19] This viewpoint, though French and Belgian in the main, accorded quite well with the political situation of the Church in Italy, which had become politically disenfranchised with the loss of the Papal States in 1870. The concordat that settled the political status of the Vatican was concluded in 1929, long after Pius's death, so his political situation was unsettled. Though not the trained diplomat that Leo XIII had been, Pius presumably concurred with the prevailing Vatican view that the reintegration of the Church into political affairs, European but especially Italian, would have been a positive good.


## FREQUENT COMMUNION AND IDEOLOGIES

The political conservatism of the Eucharistic movement cohered with much broader currents of intellectual history, in which the Church disapproved of most intellectual progress during the nineteenth century. The Church regarded intellectual advancement as noxious, not least because it was allied with political liberalism. The collective and pejorative term the Church adopted for the intellectual life of the nineteenth century was "modernism." Pius X condemned modernism with the decree *Lamentabili Sane Exitu* (3 July 1907) and the encyclical *Pascendi Dominici Gregis* (8 September 1907), and he asserted that this phenomenon embodied *all* the ills of the nineteenth century. Modernism, the "heresy of heresies," was a hodgepodge of all the "-isms" of the day—individualism, liberalism, materialism, positivism, rationalism, and secularism—that were, to the Church, baneful. Frequent Communion proved to be double-edged, however, in combating modernism.

On the one hand, frequent Communion cohered explicitly and conveniently with the Church's hostility to rational empiricism. In the promotion of frequent reception of Communion by Pius X's predecessors, opposition to intellectual progress was explicit. As a remedy for "indifferentism and rationalism," Pius IX, for example, in 1856 encouraged the faithful to assist at Mass "as frequently as possible" and "to approach the most holy sacraments of Penance and of the Holy Eucharist."[20] Leo XIII made this agenda more exact in his own frequent Communion encyclical, *MC*. Immediately after describing the miraculous transubstantiation of the bread and wine into Christ's real and present Body and Blood, Leo referred to Eucharistic miracles that also challenged human reason. He summarized the anti-intellectual thrust of the encyclical in these words: "It is plain that by this Sacrament faith is fed, in it the mind finds its nourishment, the objections of rationalists are brought to naught, and abundant light is thrown on the supernatural order."[21] It is unlikely that Pius X was aware that encouraging more frequent use of the Eucharist connected to his antimodernism. Rather, this pope plunged into a campaign for frequent Communion largely as a response to a specific dispute in Belgium. Receiving Communion was, to all these popes, an exercise of faith as well as a public avowal of one's adherence to the faith. To that extent, it intrinsically challenged modernism.

Frequent Communion not only acknowledged, but publicized and made experiential to the masses of the faithful that the Church was subject to historical vicissitudes. How? Typically for an embattled institution, the Church idealized theological stasis; in other words, it claimed always to have adhered faithfully to the teaching of Jesus. Though perhaps originally stimulated by nostalgia or romanticism, evidence of historical development in the Church, especially in the liturgy, accumulated through the sedulous labors of the Benedictine revival. The campaign for the "restoration" of frequent Communion argued mostly from authority—the pope says to do it, so we do it. But as *STS* effected a signal change in Communion practice, it acknowledged the ability, even the necessity, of the Church to change. Thus, with frequent Communion especially, a wedge for destroying the ideology of neo-Thomistic stasis became available to every communicant.

The cause for Pius's canonization spoke with literal accuracy, however, in claiming that his Eucharistic actions were "universally hailed." In so stating, however, the cause misled, because it concealed that any further public discussion about frequency of Communion was strictly forbidden. Apparently, the gag clause of *STS* was much more effective than the condemnation of modernism because Godts's party was, unlike the intellectuals harried by modernism, intrinsically conservative, ultramontane, and docile.

The impression created by the cause for the canonization of Pius X was that compliance with the decree on frequent Communion was instantaneous and universal. The effects of an ultramontane ideology operated in two phases. At first, ultramontanism excited the clergy to insure that *STS* was implemented, and they needed to argue only from the authority of the vicar of Christ. The second phase automatically destroyed the evidence of the first phase, for ultramontanism ideally posited that the word of the pope would be, in itself, efficacious. The faithful, both lay and clerical, of the 1910s and 1920s did not flaunt their noncompliance, and the reason for this noncompliance may have been simple inertia. Nonetheless, the promulgation of a decree, even though obviously highly favored by a pope in ultramontane times, could not be effective immediately. Indeed, the evidence strongly suggests that Communion reception remains rare in particular cultures and regions. The most telling witness in this respect is the second major Eucharistic document of Pius's papacy, *Quam Singulari* (1910).[22] Pius found that to change the deeply imbued sacramental habits of adults was immensely difficult, and so he arranged for children to be formed at a relatively very young age in the frequent reception of Holy Communion.

To attribute frequent Communion to Pius X is correct because his adoption of the program and his sustaining support—which unleashed immense energies to its implementation—did contribute markedly to his goal. To disregard, however, both the vast Eucharistic movement that prepared for Pius's actions and the concerted campaigns that won implementation is faulty, especially with respect to a true appreciation of the nature of development in the Church.

To place the pope in the historical stream of the Eucharistic movement both comments upon the nature of authority in the Church and confirms a pattern for change within the Church and within all large institutions. The first commentators upon *STS* recognized its historical antecedents, but for two reasons these were partially submerged. First, the commentators lived in the era of ultramontanism, in the heavy wake of the decree of papal infallibility by the First Vatican Council. Thus the decree on frequent Communion was placed, in some bizarre effusions, upon the lips not of the vicar of Peter or of Christ, but on the lips of the Sacred Heart of Jesus.[23] Second, their commentaries were also propaganda in favor of frequent Communion, and they consequently reinforced their theme as much as possible in order to achieve its implementation.

As a fruit of the growing acceptance of historical development, commentators in the early twentieth century were able to formulate a model for change in religious behavior. Sometimes, such a model surfaced in the popular press of the Eucharistic movement. For example, Peter Bregenzer's essay in *Emmanuel: Official Monthly of the Priests' Eucharistic League (EPUL)* succinctly described the lesson that history teaches about devotions:

> Great devotions have their genesis as well as their history. . . . At first they are opposed, and after a series of trials they are successful—they merit the approbation and finally the encouragement of ecclesiastical authorities. Finally, if they weather the storms, inevitable to innovations and new devotions, the Holy See takes cognizance of them. The highest authority on earth corrects them if necessary.[24]

This simple model is really a commonplace of the scholarship. As Haquin would have it, more pneumatologically, "The action of the Holy See is a fine example of how the tide of reform, rising from the common folk, at first slowly in accordance with its nature, has been confirmed by the highest authority."[25] Bregenzer, for his part, frames the phenomenon authentically and admits that what is experienced as innovation is simply that, not a restoration. Parallel examples that spring to mind include the histories of the feast of Corpus Christi in the thirteenth century, of the devotion to the Sacred Heart in the seventeenth, and, of course, of frequent Communion in the twentieth.

## THE PRAYER FOR THE PROPAGATION OF THE PIOUS PRACTICE OF DAILY COMMUNION

Seven months before the signing of *STS*, Pius X divulged his pleasure with the Eucharistic movement in general both by selecting the most distinguished members of the College of Cardinals as legates to its congresses and by inviting the International Congress to meet at Rome in 1905.[26] "It was no less a personage than Pope Pius X who selected the Eternal City as the seat of the congress. By convening it within the shadow of Saint Peter's he hoped to give the movement a consecration and prestige such as it had not as yet received, despite the thirty-three papal documents issued in its favor by Pope Leo XIII."[27] In the closing address to the congress, Pius urged the recommendation of frequent Communion by priests to their flocks, especially in reparation for the general ingratitude of humanity for such a gift.

The most influential papal gesture of the Roman International Congress was a simple prayer in Italian that encouraged not just more frequent, but specifically daily, reception of Communion. Because it revealed the pope's attitude toward the dispute raging in Belgium and because it sketched the essentials of *STS*, the prayer figured prominently in the campaign to restore daily Communion to the life of the Church and in the historiography of the campaign. An important explanatory rescript accompanied this "Prayer for the Propagation of the Pious Custom of Daily Communion." Here is a full English translation of the prayer:

> O sweet Jesus, who didst come into the world to give to all souls the life of Thy grace, and who, to preserve and nourish in them this life, hast wished to be their daily food and the daily remedy of their daily weakness, we humbly supplicate Thee, by Thy Heart so inflamed with love for us, to shed upon all souls Thy Divine Spirit, that they who, unhappily, are in mortal sin may be converted to Thee and recover the life of grace that they have lost, and that they who, by Thy help, already live this divine life, may devoutly approach Thy Holy Table every day that they can; so that by means of daily Communion, receiving daily the antidote of their daily venial sins, and feeding daily the life of Thy grace in their soul, and thus purifying themselves always more and more, they may, at last, arrive at the possession of the life of beatitude with Thee! Amen.

The rhetoric of the prayer commands two remarks. First, even its title dubs daily Communion a "pious custom," thus implying an extant though traditional daily use of Communion that patently did not exist in the Church at the turn of the century, except among punctilious priests. More strikingly, the prayer hammers at the notion of *daily* reception of Communion, for the word itself appears once in the title of the prayer and in the English translation seven times. The Italian uses for the same concept the word *quotidiana* six times and *ogni giorno* three times. Such repetition betokens an urgency that permeates a gloss on the prayer: "*Every day*, and not merely every month, every week, three times or six times a week, but *every day*, if they have no real hindrance."[28]

In order to encourage the use of the prayer, Pius enriched it with indulgences. These helped the prayer swiftly become popular the world over.[29] If it was recited once, it was worth three hundred days' indulgence; if the prayer was said daily for a month, and this was conjoined with the standard conditions for the granting of a plenary indulgence—namely, confession, Communion, visit to a public oratory, and prayers for the intentions of the pope—it allowed a plenary indulgence, applicable to the faithful devotee or to one of the souls in purgatory.[30] In themselves, such standard elements of the plenary indulgence encouraged at least monthly Communion, which was relatively frequent at that time. The prayer's theme, lineage, and indulgences made it a natural inclusion in the Eucharistic triduum that was mandated in the wake of *STS*.[31]

Why this telegraphing of a papal opinion? Of course, as merely a prayer it enjoyed no canonical status, but that it expressed the will of the pope himself makes it irresistible to Christians "worthy of the name."[32] In an ultramontane atmosphere, the rescript, presumably written by Cardinal Gennari, also added luster to the prayer, increasing its "power and authority."[33] Those loyal to the pope and the papacy knew, by virtue of this transparent signal, the drift of the pontiff's thought, and they could obediently accommodate themselves to it. Tactically for the campaign, however, the prayer thus resembled a trial balloon, an effort by the pope to anticipate reactions to his forthcoming pronouncement on the frequency of Communion and to secure compliance.

This perception was available even to contemporaries. *EPUL* cautioned its readers, "We do not wish to exaggerate the importance of a simple concession of indulgences, yet might we not consider the above quoted Rescript as a discreet warning of the Holy See, the sign of a wish to see the practice of daily Communion encouraged instead of being made more difficult?"[34]

In light of the prestige of the papacy, such circumspection may seem unnecessary. Four factors likely urged such caution: First, the controversy in Belgium was dangerously public and caustic; an authoritative document could have dreadfully upset the Church in those sectors where first Holy Communion was so enmeshed in the culture. Second, since the disputants were arrayed along the lines of their religious orders, political astuteness required an indirect method. Third, despite the rhetorical sleight of hand, daily Communion was not, in fact, a custom in the sense of "customary, commonplace," and the pastoral experience of Pius X may have braced him for predictable inertia. Along these same lines, when Pius first pronounced upon the liturgy, attempting to restore Gregorian chant in *Tra La Sollecitudini* (1903), the document came from the pope himself as a *motu proprio*, and it caused much ado.[35] Further, the inertia, while not evident, is discernible in some descriptions of Communion practice. Although the pope very significantly ratified frequent Communion, only after nearly fifty years and many consequent changes in the disciplinary practice of the Church—namely, a mitigation of the requirements for fasting before communicating—did the reception of Communion become frequent. Had the decree not mobilized forces of change would this have tarnished the prestige of the papacy? It was already smarting from the loss of its temporal possessions and the simultaneous decline of its political influence throughout Europe. As if in compensation, the papacy became more active in strictly spiritual affairs. A show of incompetence in this proper arena would have gravely wounded the Petrine pride, if not the office itself.

Fourth, the pope monitored the progress of the decree's implementation, as indeed *STS* required. "In their report on the state of their dioceses or institutes they [the gamut of ecclesiastical administrators] should inform the Holy See concerning the execution of the prescriptions therein enacted."[36] That Pius was habitually eager to know the reactions of his flock to his initiatives he had already evinced while patriarch of Venice.[37]

This article of the decree can be interpreted as an admixture, of whatever proportions, of its two main ingredients: Hagiographically, it reflects his pastoral approach, his desire to know well the reactions of his flock to this restoration and the spiritual benefits it occasioned. Bureaucratically, it held the subordinates of Pius, from cardinal archbishops to rural headmasters, accountable for the implementation of frequent, even daily, Communion and spoke this accountability to them with clarity. Motives and strategies aside, that *STS* demanded progress reports shows the pope's own determination to implement frequent Communion.[38]

"The Prayer for the Propagation of the Pious Practice of Daily Communion" disposed the Church to accept and put into effect future papal pronouncements in favor of frequent Communion, not only by revealing the attitude of the pope, but, more importantly and personally, by establishing a means for the inculcation of a new sacramental practice in the mind of each devotee, as well as by painting frequent Communion as a desideratum of the Lord.

The rescript begins with the expression of the desire of the Holy Father, saying, "Our Most Holy Father, having most earnestly at heart that, with the help of Our Lord Jesus Christ, the custom of daily Communion, so salutary and so pleasing to God, should everywhere spread among the Christian people, has deigned" to establish the indulgences. One commentary, in accordance with a consummate exaltation of the pope's vicarship with Christ, said:

> This Rescript affords us positive knowledge of the thought and judgment of His Holiness, Pius X, on the subject of *daily* Communion. It is clearly manifested therein that the Head of the Church, directly assisted from On High in all matters that essentially concern the spiritual conduct of souls, . . . "has sovereignly at heart the desire to see the custom of *daily* Communion spread among the Catholic people: *Cum Ipse maxime cordi.*"[39]

In brief, God wanted daily Communion.

"The Prayer for the Propagation of the Pious Custom of Daily Communion" defines the minimal dispositions for receiving, and does so utterly unambiguously. Thus it epitomizes *STS*. "The only condition for *daily* Communion, apart from that of the state of grace, is to approach 'with devotion.'"[40] The decree for its part specifies simply that the communicant be in the state of grace—that is, free from the guilt of mortal sin through sacramental confession—and that the communicant receive with the right intention. Devotion is tantamount to the appropriate intention. Tesnière comments, "with the thought, the desire to honor God, to thank Him for a benefit, to ask pardon for sins committed, to beg some grace, and above all that of serving Him by the fulfilling of the duties of one's state, by flight from sin, and by the struggle against the passions."[41] These "sins committed" must be venial sins, because any mortal sins must have been addressed in confession.

The two implicit dispositions for receiving Communion daily are likewise the conditions for Communion even only annually at Easter. Most significantly, this heralds the end of the prevalent coordinating of numbers of Communions with the worthiness of the communicant; that is, the end of proportionality. Indeed, while the prayer served as a toe-in-the-ocean and as a means by implementation to encourage ecclesial acceptance of the daily-Communion decree, its real purpose was to settle the controversy by signaling the pope's opinion, if not his resolve, as juridical decrees and a train of inducements would do.

> On his side, Father Couët [of the Fathers of the Blessed Sacrament and one of the principal actors in the controversy] wrote: "The Holy Father wants the attacks against Holy Communion to cease. It was under his inspiration that Cardinal Gennari composed the prayer and drew up the Rescript. The Cardinal told me among other things: 'If they don't understand, and continue their attacks, the Holy Father will take other means.'" The "other means" was the history-making Decree of December 20, 1905.[42]

The prayer and its rescript assume immense importance, then, in the campaign for frequent Communion.

## SACRA TRIDENTINA SYNODUS (STS)

A commentary on the decree begins with the basics, such as its title and authorship. The decree is entitled *DECRETUM de Dispositionibus Requisitis ad Frequentem et Quotidianam Communionem Eucharisticam Sumendam. DE QUOTIDIANA SS. EUCHARISTIAE SUMPTIONE. Sacra Tridentina Synodus.*[43] The heart of the decree, as was the heart of the dispute between Fathers Godts and Lintelo, is to specify the dispositions for Holy Communion, especially frequent and even daily reception. The titling of Vatican documents conventionally relies upon the first words of the first sentence that appear in the title lines, and so this decree is universally referred to as *Sacra Tridentina Synodus*. Remarkably, this opening makes the decree seem to depend immediately upon the Council of Trent.

On several counts, this makes sense. First and most generally, the official Church, throughout the centuries from Trent until the Second Vatican Council, considered Trent more authoritative than the more recent First Vatican Council.[44] Second and consequently, Godts and Lintelo each claimed for himself the lineage of Trent.

The issuing bureau was the Sacred Congregation of the Council, whose original mandate to interpret the actions of the Council of Trent grants this particular congregation jurisdiction over the Lintelo-Godts controversy, given the Tridentine terms of their dispute. *STS* is signed by the prefect of the congregation, Cardinal Vincent, bishop of Palestrina, and the secretary, Cajetan de Lai. A desire for continuity with Pope Leo XIII's very recent encyclical on frequent Communion provides another reason to cite this text of Trent, for he had used the same in *MC*. "It has always been the desire of the Church that at every Mass some of the faithful should be present and should communicate."[45] An additional reason for such seeming reliance upon Trent is that the terms of the decree, so innovative with respect to the living practice around 1900, must for the sake of consistency with the antimodernism of Pius X be painted as a restoration. "Trent" in the title offers this camouflage of conservatism up front.

The desires of the pope actually determine the provisions of the decree. So much did Pius X support daily and frequent Communion, and so clearly did he signal this support, that his involvement in the campaign for frequent Communion virtually places the pen that wrote the decree in his hand. "The Pope himself, as desirous as any for the spread of the practice of frequent and daily Communion among the faithful, entrusted the business to the S.C. of the Council, which after mature deliberation formulated its decisions. These the Pope confirmed, and ordered their publication, and they form the disciplinary part of the decree."[46] The "mature deliberation," uncharacteristically expeditious for the disinterested workings of a sacred congregation, consumed four days! This speed also confirms papal intervention.

But the decree was issued by the Sacred Congregation of the Council and was not a *motu proprio* of Pius X. Given the structure of the Vatican bureaus at the time, this was the appropriate body handling all questions about the sacraments and thus, in this case, for settling the Belgian dispute. As its title indicates, the Congregation of the Council's charter was to insure the "accurate application of the Council's [i.e., Trent's] decrees."[47] Why does *STS* report, as if exceptional, that Pius X placed the issue before the proper congregation? In commenting upon what was usually a routine matter of the bureaucracy, the decree is able to iterate the pope's involvement in the case. Later, the document states explicitly that Pius has ratified its contents.

The decree consists of an explanatory section and a disciplinary section.[48] It begins, and begins to explain itself, by providing an excerpt from the Council of Trent on the ideal of the Eucharist: "The holy Council wishes indeed that at each Mass the faithful who are present should communicate not only by spiritual desire, but sacramentally, by the actual reception of the Eucharist."[49] Already in its first sentence, *STS* resorts to proof texting.

The remainder of the text of Trent indicates that the council "does not condemn as private and illicit" those Masses at which none of the attending faithful communicate.[50] The original purpose of this chapter, then, was to answer objections of the Protestant reformers that the Mass, celebrated privately with only the priest communicating, was aberrant. Trent does this by asserting that all Masses are communal in character, "partly because the people communicate spiritually and partly also because they are celebrated by a public minister of the Church, not for himself only but for all the faithful who belong to the body of Christ."[51] So, Trent wants, or says *in this context* that it wants, the faithful to receive Communion whenever they assist at Mass. This wish of Trent was not granted, and Communion as rare persisted. This monograph tries to establish that the thorough implementation of Vatican pronouncements can be explained historically only by consideration of factors outside the church; a purely theological explanation must defer to the Holy Spirit.

Even getting the faithful to comply with the obligation for Sunday worship has for centuries been a challenge for the clergy. The Council of Agde in the sixth century legislated Sunday Mass attendance, and the pertinent canon of the Code of 1917 traces its lineage to the Decretal of Gratian in the middle of the twelfth century.[52] Obligations of the law imply that a behavior is neglected. Leo XIII observed this principle in *MC* when he addressed the requirement for Easter Communion imposed by the Fourth Lateran Council in 1215.[53] The evidence is convincing that, from Trent through the pontificate of Pius X, the majority of the faithful were not attending Mass even weekly, much less daily. The distribution of Communion outside of Mass, except for viaticum, largely followed upon *STS*. Given these realities, how ambitious is the leap to *daily* Communion already promised in the title of *STS*!

The decree immediately argued by assertion that Trent "declares plainly enough the wish of Christ that all Christians should be daily nourished by this heavenly banquet."[54] That Christ himself wishes all Christians to receive Communion every day is asserted as if self-evident. This notion seems rooted in an axiomatic identification of the documents of Trent and the will of Christ. Given the practice of the Church since Trent, it must have been the case that Christ's will in this regard had been unflaggingly frustrated.

*STS* then attempted to bolster its declaration of dominical mandate to communicate daily by citing the classic Eucharistic promise of John 6: "This is the bread that has come down from heaven; not as your fathers ate the manna, and died. He who eats this bread shall live forever." According to the decree, the disciples then understood that since the form of the sacrament is bread, and since its type is manna, and since both bread and manna are to be eaten daily, the "Christian soul might daily partake of this heavenly bread."[55] The decree further justifies its ambition by explaining that Fathers of the Church had equated the phrase "our daily bread" in the Lord's Prayer to "the eucharistic bread which ought to be our daily food."[56]

Recall that *MC* also hinged on the understanding of the Eucharist as food, and so *STS* remains connected in this other way with the recent teachings of Pius's immediate predecessor. *STS* was "part of the plan of general revival of piety which the Sovereign Pontiff indicated in his first Encyclical as his chief aim—*restaurare* [*sic*] *omnia in Christo*."[57] The pontificate of Pius X embraced a very active and thorough conservatism, or at least such an appearance. Scriptural attestations of daily "breaking of bread" that are interpreted precritically as Eucharistic passages and the declination model of Church history, where all since the apostolic age is loss of religious faith, contribute mightily to the hopefulness of *STS* in calling for frequent, but better yet daily, Communion.

While alluding to the controversy that precipitated its utterance, the decree proposed that the actual end of the Eucharist is twofold—purgation from venial sins and prevention of mortal sins. This end is to be had ultimately and solely through the eating of Communion. Communion does not exist to reward virtue, even as the Eucharist does not exist for its own honor through devotions. The decree then contrasted the frequent reception of the Eucharist during the primitive and patristic eras of the Church with reception during subsequent ages—that is, the Middle Ages through the nineteenth century— when piety was cold and Jansenism especially made the issue of frequency of Communion disputable.[58] Previous anti-Jansenist pronouncements from the magisterium have not succeeded, the decree continues, for Jansenism has proved too virulent and the question of the proper dispositions for Communion has persisted, even to the present.

This rarity of Communion, this distortion of piety, is largely blamed upon Jansenism, represented famously by Antoine Arnauld's *De la fréquente Communion*. This shunts the document to the immediate occasion of this decree, the Belgian dispute between Lintelo and Godts. "Pastors of souls" brought the controversy to the pope, who referred it to the Congregation of the Council, which in four days of "sedulous" examination produced the second component of the decree, its discipline.

The narrative and explanatory section of the decree well deserved both complement and analysis. The disciplinary section speaks so forthrightly that most commentaries upon its terms were mere dilations and iterations.[59] "This decree is so luminous that any explanation would be useless, and its importance can escape no one."[60] Because it prunes away the flourishes, this excerpt from a manual of moral theology published in 1908, satisfactory enough to be in its fourth edition by 1918, is an epitome of the practical consequences of *STS*. The summary sensibly appears in a section of the manual about the dispositions of the soul for receiving Communion within a chapter on the subject of the Eucharist as a sacrament; another large section of this manual, not to the purpose, treats the sacrificial nature of the Eucharist.

> The old controversy about frequent communion was finally settled by the decree of Pius X, December 20, 1905. The mind of the Church on the question is therein clearly expressed. The decree says in effect: Let frequent and daily communion, a practice which is very much desired by Christ our Lord and by the Catholic Church, be open to all the faithful of whatever rank and condition they be, so that it may not be refused to any one who is in the state of grace, and who approaches the Holy Table with a good and upright intention. The good intention consists in a desire to fulfil the divine will, to be more closely united with God, and by that divine remedy to fight against one's weakness and defects, and not to approach out of routine or vanity, or worldly motives. Venial sin is not an obstacle to daily communion, although it is in the highest degree becoming that daily communicants should be free from all fully deliberate venial sin. The sacraments, it is true, produce their effect *ex opere operato*, and yet because they produce greater effect in those who are better disposed, therefore care must be taken to make proper preparation for holy communion and due thanksgiving afterward. The confessor's advice should be asked in order that daily communion may be practised with more prudence and with greater fruit, but the confessor should not prohibit daily communion to anyone who is in the state of grace and who approaches with an upright intention. Parish priests, confessors, and preachers should frequently exhort the faithful to the practice of daily communion, according to the approved teaching of the Roman Catechism, or the Catechism of the Council of Trent.[61]

*STS*'s disciplinary section begs for three amplifications: First, with respect to the crux of the contention between Godts and Lintelo, the decree observes that a fruit of receiving Communion frequently will be the gradual elimination not only of venial sin, but also of "affection thereto."[62]

Second, religious institutes and orders were singled out for two explicit reasons; a covert, strategic reason also applies: First, many of the extant rules and ordinances of nonclerical religious actually specified certain days for receiving Communion, and these specifications now were universally reduced to mere recommendations before the authority of *STS*. *Quemadmodum* (*QMM*) of fifteen years prior had moved in this direction but was particularly emphatic of the role of the confessor in determining access to Communion. While the terms of the decree apply to all of the faithful, religious by virtue of their state in life were considered prone to adopt the terms of the decree; already, religious communicated much more frequently than the laity, often by rule.[63] Here the emphasis of the decree upon daily Communion as an end manifests itself. Rules and customs that specified several days a week for receiving Communion both were encouraging Communion of much greater frequency than that of the laity in general and had been formulated with this enhancement of Eucharistic practice in mind. After the promulgation of *STS*, *frequent* means in essence *daily*, and communicating several times in the week did not attain to this "restored" ideal. These concerns led the decree to require that its own text be read aloud in all religious houses once a year, during the octave of the feast of Corpus Christi. The strategic reason for addressing religious at such length is that religious, since they were controlled by ecclesiastical authorities, could form a veritable army of daily communicants who could draw the laity to frequent Communion by their example.

Third, note that the confessor's approval for receiving daily is still recommended and that the practice of the preparation and thanksgiving for Holy Communion is to be observed. Both of these provisions of *STS* seem to have disappeared quickly in areas, such as in the United States, where increasing the numbers of Holy Communions became an overriding goal.

## THE EUCHARISTIC TRIDUUM

Even as the "Prayer for the Propagation of the Pious Custom of Daily Communion" tilled the soil for *STS*, a number of papal actions continually kept the idea of more Communions on the agenda. The decree included some mechanisms for the persistence of the issue, for example, the mandated reporting of ecclesiastics on the progress of the decree to the Roman pontiff. Indeed, the sheer volume of implemental and hortative documentation subsequent to *STS* provokes this rhetorical astonishment, "Did ever such a series of Documents appear on one subject and for one and the same purpose, emanating from the Holy See in so short a period of time?"[64]

One curial document moved the campaign for frequent Communion from the realm of personal prayer, where the "Prayer for the Propagation" originally applied, to the realm of an annual diocesan triduum "for the purpose of promoting frequent Communion."[65] Technically this document was a letter from the Congregation of Indulgences and Relics, signed by Cardinal Serafino Cretoni (d. 1909) and dated 10 April 1907, but the letter professed to convey what Pius X "earnestly desired"—that the graces obtainable through the continuing spread of frequent, and even daily, Communion "increase."[66] The triduum unfolded thus: It was to occur at each cathedral on the Friday, Saturday, and Sunday following the feast of Corpus Christi. All churches responsible for the care of souls, however, should as a minimum have followed the plan for the Sunday of the triduum.

The service for each of the three days consisted of three parts: The program began with preaching, "especially upon the dispositions of soul needed for its [Communion's] due reception." Immediately after the sermon, the Blessed Sacrament was to be exposed and the "Prayer for the Propagation" was then to be recited by the congregation. Note that this prayer recapitulated the matter of the sermon in that it specified that venial sin was both remedied and prevented by Communion. Then a standard hymn for honoring the exposed Eucharist, "Tantum Ergo, Sacramentum," was sung, and this in turn was followed by Benediction. Sunday's program additionally encompasses the morning Mass. The letter recommended that the sermon elaborate upon the mystery of the Eucharist, as the Gospel lesson for that day (Luke 14:16–24) readily allowed; in reality, this parable of the unattended banquet proves most serviceable for a pro-Communion homily. Then, the letter continues, "the faithful will receive Communion in a body."[67] This seems to be a prescription for a "general Communion," jargon that often occurs in the literature of the campaign. Sunday afternoon's exercises were to follow the framework of Friday and Saturday, but supplemented by the addition of a "Te Deum" before the singing of the "Tantum Ergo, Sacramentum." All participants in these services merited indulgences of suitable richness.

To what extent was this letter observed by ordinaries and pastors throughout the world? Reasons to believe that the letter met with considerable compliance include the following: It expresses a very specific desire of Pius X in ultramontane times, and this desire for a Eucharistic triduum both signals and is a component of an overarching campaign in favor of daily and frequent Communion. Derély implies that the spread of the "Pious Custom" prayer followed from the popularity of the triduum.[68] Duhr simply asserts that the annual triduum "contributed powerfully" to the spread of the message of frequent Communion.[69] If book sales are any indication, Lintelo's book, *The Eucharistic Triduum: An Aid to Priests in Preaching Frequent and Daily Communion According to the Decrees of H.H. Pius X*, entered a second edition in French after only a few months and was speedily translated into English.[70] *STS* did oblige clerics and prelates to promote its teaching. The letter, while nonjuridical and only expressing the desires of the pope, in fact provided a papally sanctioned and public method for fulfilling this obligation of *STS*. That is, bishops and priests did not need to contrive their own means to further the cause of daily Communion.

In addition, the triduum was a mainstay of the Priests' Communion League, whose raison d'être was the implementation of the decree; its other standard for promoting frequent Communion was pamphleteering.[71] Incidentally, the charter for the Priests' Communion League further detailed the content of the triduum; this shows that the Vatican privileged the triduum for propagating *STS*.

This indulgenced triduum was subsequent to the decree and could thus seek overtly to guarantee compliance. Many of the psychological benefits to the campaign were augmented by the paraliturgical quality of the triduum, for the triduum deployed social pressures for the spread of frequent communion.

## MITIGATIONS OF THE FAST

Another very important class of actions to encourage more Communion was the modification of pre-Communion fasting for the infirm. Issued both by the Sacred Congregation of the Council (7 December 1906) and by the Sacred Congregation of the Sacraments (23 December 1912), these mitigations garnered considerable attention in the atmosphere of legalism and conservatism that then characterized the Church and with regard to the Jansenistic notions of worthiness and purity as qualifications for Holy Communion.[72] Truly, these were the very first official and authoritative relaxations of the fast for ordinary Holy Communion in history.[73] Canonists justly connect these relaxations to the program of Pius X articulated in *STS*. For example, Stadler reports,

> Shortly after the issuance of the Decree . . . there was raised the question of modifying the general law of fasting before Holy Communion in favor of the sick. . . . In the resulting decree, *Post Editum* [7 December 1906], . . . Pope Pius granted a concession whereby the sick who had been confined to bed for a month and whose state of sickness furnished no hope of a speedy recovery could be allowed to receive Holy Communion, though they had found it necessary to take some liquid food beforehand.[74]

*Post Editum* was the first wedge in the relaxation of the Eucharistic fast. But the code of canon law of 1917 still insisted upon the "natural" fast from midnight as a general rule for communicants.[75]

The apostolic constitution *Christus Dominus* (1953) heralded "the most far-reaching changes in the law of the eucharistic Fast since Apostolic times."[76] Its provisions allowed that, before communicating, water might be drunk at any time, all other liquids except alcohol might be drunk up until one hour prior, and food might be eaten until three hours prior. The ramifications of this change were immensely beneficial to the campaign.

In fact, *Christus Dominus* reveals that nearly fifty years after *STS*, daily Communion for all Catholics remained unrealized. Pius XII, who came to the throne of Peter twenty-five years after the death of Saint Pius X, admitted his motivation in the text. "In issuing this decree, We trust that We will be able to contribute much to the increase of the Eucharistic piety, and so more effectively move and inspire all to participate at the Table of Angels, to the certain increase of the glory of God, and of the holiness of the Mystical Body of Jesus Christ."[77] The strictness of the fast—not scrupulosity about ethical purity or debates about dispositions to receive—was blocking frequent Communion decisively.

Immediately upon a further modification in 1957, with the promulgation of *Sacram Communionem*, orders for hosts from one of the largest suppliers in the Midwest of the United States increased 45 percent "overnight."[78]

The total recodification of canon law was initiated by Pius X, but this project was not completed until 1917 in the pontificate of Benedict XV. Naturally, the relevant canon summarizes the provisions of *STS*. One commentary on the code reads simply, "The faithful should be admonished according to the decrees of the Holy See to receive the eucharistic bread frequently, and even daily, and that those who assist at Holy Mass should not only communicate spiritually, but be prepared to receive in reality our Lord in the holy Eucharist. (C. 863)."[79] The same code limited the distribution of Holy Communion to the times of day when Mass was allowed to be celebrated, encouraged frequent visits to the Blessed Sacrament, and insisted upon churches being left unlocked for a few hours per day to accommodate visitors.[80] It also limited exposition of the Blessed Sacrament in the ostensorium to the octave of Corpus Christi; outside of this time, the permission of the ordinary for exposition was necessary.[81]

The exceptionally speedy formation of social aggregations to promote more Communions reveals an urgent pope. For example, seven months after *STS* the cardinal vicar of Rome approved the erection of a diocesan Priests' Communion League.[82] This local confraternity was "honored with a Brief" and "favored with great privileges" within a fortnight, and, only four months later in a bureaucratic move of unprecedented dispatch, it was raised to an archconfraternity, an "Archiassociation Primaria" with the power to franchise internationally.[83] This priestly archconfraternity, one only of a host of similar and often overlapping organizations, existed precisely and explicitly to carry *STS*, particularly by clarifying and disseminating a correct interpretation of the decree by the clergy. "The Sacerdotal League for Communion is opportune because it protests against a false interpretation, alas! too common, which some would put upon the Decree *Sacra Tridentina Synodus*."[84]

The Holy See energetically anticipated and exploded objections to the campaign of the Eucharistic movement for frequent Holy Communion. Because the decree itself forbids even discussing the twin issues of the dispositions necessary for admission to Communion and frequency, opposition to the decree itself never surfaced in print. The decree's success in silencing all debate testifies to the efficacious power of the papacy in those ultramontane times.

Real objections to the *motu proprio*, *STS*, are mediated in print only by the pro-frequent-Communion press; these are often legalistic in strategy. These include that it is not a "pontifical enactment" signed by the Holy Father and that the restoration it enjoins is of such moment that an encyclical rather than a decree would be the proper vehicle.[85] *MC* is one encyclical that answers the "legal" objection of disproportionality and feebleness. In other words, a papal edict by Pope Leo XIII had already unequivocally exhorted the faithful to more frequent reception of Communion.

The second "legalistic" argument is answered less legalistically than politically. The veritable stream of Vatican pronouncements that interpreted and enforced *STS*, however, parried the objection that the decree was not pontifical by shouting with unmistakable enthusiasm that the pope supported the restoration of daily Communion wholeheartedly.

The theologically more interesting objections targeted frequent and daily Communion itself. Proponents of frequent Communion labeled such objections by the broad category offered by *MC*, and the phrase became standard: "Prejudices and vain fears" generated opposition to greater use of Holy Communion, often under the euphemistic umbrella of "false interpretations." The standard translation of the phrase "prejudices and vain fears" deprives Leo of his vigor, but it benefits the campaign rhetorically and politically: It hints at the experiential nature of the opposition, and thus grants the opponents some historical lineage and some exculpation.[86]

A third objection to frequent Communion is the complaint that the terms were impractical.[87] The literature hints at two elements of this impracticability. First, in light of the weight of centuries of contrary custom and habit, frequent Communion would not, in the foreseeable future, return to the life of the Church. "The Pope [seems to be] pursuing a chimera."[88] Rarity of Communion did not exist in isolation. It was coherent with ritual practices, emphatic of the doctrine of the Real Presence, that maintained a strict but consoling distance between the physical presence of the God-made-Man on the altar and the faithful. One such ritual practice was fasting, a way of purifying the sinful human being in preparation for encounter with the Divine, but an array of taboos and pomps emphasized the transcendence of the sacrament. In this ethos, such a revolutionary restoration in piety was, to opponents, unimaginable. Indeed, Pius's pose as a conservative and "restorer" acts fairly effectually against this lack of imagination; he trumps the silent opponents by claiming that his own program is most conservative, dating back to the will of Christ clearly articulated to the apostles. In an ultramontane climate, too, the pope's faith in the ability of the papacy to effect change in liturgical practice and piety seems, historically, to have been well placed, given the mitigated success of the campaign.

More significant are objections that hinge upon the worthiness of the communicant. These are variously named:

> For example, our unworthiness, our backwardness in virtue, our ill-tamed passions, lapses into grievous sin, fear lest some may be led to receive sacrilegiously, a dread of evils commonly expressed by those very vague terms "want of reverence" and "over-familiarity," the danger of carelessness in preparation and thanksgiving, diminution of devotion in receiving, or, what is so constantly mistaken for this, mere dulness of the emotions and lack of sensible experiences, such as must almost inevitably result at time from habitual Communion, or any other daily religious exercise, daily celebration of Holy Mass not excepted, as priests must candidly admit.[89]

The objections devolve to a fear of routinization and the consequent extinction of emotions appropriate to the awesomeness of the Real Presence in the individual soul. This resistance to the decree was met in two principal ways.

The first counterattack relied unabashedly and solely on the authority of the pope. "We Catholics depend for our safe religious guidance, not upon any private teacher or teachers, however learned or however saintly, but upon the Divinely assisted leading of the See of Peter."[90] That the will of the pope, and not just some curial commission, is in favor of daily Communion and that the pope is serious enough and interested enough continually and variously to bolster more Communion suffices to motivate priests and laity alike to accept the "restoration."

The second counterattack demanded distinguishing between human experiences, including the highly formalized preparation for and thanksgiving after receiving Communion, and the operation of the sacrament. In this approach, human experiences are demoted but the operations of the sacraments, their real spiritual benefits, are exalted. If the communicant did not know a welling of emotions upon receiving Holy Communion, that did not imply that the Communion was sacrilegious or defective. This welling of emotions was deliberately conditioned, of course, by the elaborate and festive practice of first Holy Communion. Faith in the sacrament and in its operations as described by the Church assured the communicant, if she was within the window of eligibility, that she benefited from the sacrament.

Here, too, appears a crux of the debate about the frequency of receiving. Conservative opponents of frequent Communion observed that Communion received very seldom, but with immense emotional and ritual ado, was experienced by the communicant as immensely beneficial.[91] Would not daily Communion eliminate this experience and its correlative valuing of the sacrament?

The argument against this stance acknowledged the complex interactions between emotions and routine but consigned them to irrelevancy with respect to the Thomistic notions of sacramental efficacy.

Another expression of this same issue speaks theologically. The regnant and Thomistic dogma of sacramentality examined the relationship between the experience of the recipient and the action of Jesus in the sacrament: Because the sacraments worked *ex opere operato*, they did not depend upon the dispositions or experiences of the receiver, so long as the reception was licit. In light of the magnitude of the personal sacramental encounter with the Real Presence of Jesus, one's own preparation for the encounter should, of course, be heroic. But the point of *STS* was to specify the minimally acceptable conditions under which a person may receive, and these were simply two. The communicant must be free from mortal sin and must be properly motivated by the love of God. Receiving itself then admits the Real Presence of the Lord into the soul and body of the recipient, and the union with God draws the recipient along a path of spiritual and moral progress.

The second impracticability attributed to the decree by the opposition was its swelling of the ranks, not only of frequent communicants, but also of frequent penitents. This garnered considerable attention in the literature. Communion traditionally and actually had always been tied to confession; the specifications for many indulgences required the linking of the two sacraments. If these conditions prevailed, logic dictated that greater use of Communion would necessitate many more confessions. *STS*, if swiftly and successfully implemented, would have *all* Catholics receive Communion daily, and this would have immured confessors in their boxes, for *all* Catholics would be confessing beforehand.

To forestall this problem and the opposition which it fueled, the Congregation of Indulgences issued a decree on 14 February 1906. This decree reiterated the indult from the time of Pope Clement XIII (d. 1769) which conceded that those who habituated penance and Communion were not strictly obliged to confess weekly in order to qualify for indulgences.[92] In short, this clarification declared "that those who practice daily or quasi-daily Communion gain the indulgences without being bound to a confession so regular and so frequent," even if this had been stated in the proper rescript.[93]

## CHILDREN AND PRECOCIOUS
## FIRST HOLY COMMUNION

As is normal with any significant pronouncement from the Vatican, quibbles arose about *STS*, and these were answered by the Congregation of the Council with the approval of the pope. One important question worried the relationship between first Holy Communion and frequent Communion. The Sacred Congregation of the Council issued *De Communione Puerorum* (13 September 1906) to declare that even children just admitted to Communion should be invited to continue receiving frequently.[94]

This decision apparently did not settle the matter, and so *QS* continued the trend toward more Communion. This document proved highly effective. The essence of the decree was to reduce the age of first admission to the Holy Table. Generally, the age of first Communion had been around twelve to fourteen, and *QS* lowered the age to about seven, the age of reason. While he was patriarch of Venice, the future Pope Pius X had often admitted to Communion much younger children than was the general custom, so long as they could avow that the Blessed Sacrament was the Body of Christ.[95] That Pius adopted this strategy for fostering more Communion is unsurprising. By effectively reducing the age for first Communion, this decree, however, threatened the French sacramental-catechetical system. In this milieu, its upshot was to disconnect three aspects of first Holy Communion—the rite of passage to adulthood (secular and also familial), the completion of religious instruction (catechetical), and admission to full communion in the Church through the completion of initiation (sacramental). The episcopate of France viewed *QS* as a serious enervation of the Church at a critical moment in its conflict with liberalism, with anticlericalism, and with secularism, for the extant arrangement of religious instruction and sacramental preparation had seemed effective.

Appropriately, *QS* has attracted immense scholarly attention, particularly in France. But in the broader history of the use of Communion, its being seen as overshadowing *STS* seems a common error. For example, Antonio Nieri judges the twin pillars of the reinvigoration of Eucharistic piety to be *MC* and *QS*. He devalues *STS* by failing to account adequately for its ambition—daily Communion.[96] This devaluation follows from placing the papal documents only in the environment of papal documents and not in their wider unfolding—of both sources and implementation. *STS* thus becomes a mere derivative or redundant decree. On the other hand, Linda Gaupin sees the integrality of *QS* to the "general Eucharistic and liturgical reforms that Pius X endeavored to initiate during his pontificate."[97] From the point of view of the Eucharistic movement and the campaigns for frequent Communion, the document *STS* is absolutely pivotal. It defines the dispositions necessary for receiving Communion; it specifies that *frequent* means daily; it indicates the ardor which impelled the pope himself to embrace daily Communion. This decree touches to the quick the purpose of the Eucharist and thereby reveals a shift in attitude toward the sacraments and toward the relationship between this world and the transcendent.

*QS*, which is merely disciplinary, does signal a new and ultimately most successful strategy of Pius X for the implementation of more frequency of Communion in the face of continued resistance.[98] Even Jules Lintelo admits that habits do not die without a struggle. He wrote, "But, it must be granted, many are as yet the situations in which habits of life and prejudices are such that frequent Communion is particularly difficult."[99] Adults, formed in and habituated to annual Communion, despite the vigorous promotion of the pope's wishes, did not accede; children, formed by the formidable Catholic pedagogical establishment to regard frequent reception as the norm, would not only use the sacrament frequently but would be agents for encouraging the greater use of Communion by adults.[100] The success of the campaign for frequent Communion was won not by changing the ingrained habits and attitudes of adults but by training children to a new sacramental praxis.

## NOTES

1. J. M. Derély, "Les décrets eucharistiques du bienheureux Pie X," *Nouvelle revue theologique* 9 (1951); Hector Lemieux, "Life or Death," *EPUL*, special centenary edition (October 1956).

2. *STS*, 13.

3. *STS*, 13.

4. Lemieux, "Life or Death," 504.

5. Lemieux, "Life or Death," 503.

6. Derély, "Les décrets eucharistiques," 900–1.

7. Casimiro Gennari, *Consultazioni morali-canoniche-liturgiche su casi e materie svariate che specialmente riguardano i tempi nostri* (Rome: Monitore Ecclesiastico, 1902), 186–92 and 582–615.

8. Lemieux," "Life or Death," 505.

9. Duhr, 1285. Fernessole, *Pie X: Essai historique*, 2:57. Antonio Nieri, "Esperiense e riforme liturgiche," in *Le radici venete di San Pio X*, edited by Silvio Tramontin (Brescia: Morcelliana, 1987), 58.

10. "Thank God, we have lived to see the Pope of Daily Holy Communion—the dawn of blessed Eucharistic days." E. M. Bachman, "Frequent and Daily Communion: Read Before the Eucharistic Congress of Pittsburgh, October 15, 1907," *EPUL* 14 (1908): 2. "Pope of the Eucharist" is a more inclusive epithet that obviously encompasses the idea of frequent reception of Holy Communion. Carlo M. Poletti, "Eucharistic Congress of the Priests' Eucharistic League in Rome," *EPUL* 19 (1913): 84.

11. Fernessole, *Pie X: Essai historique*, 2:55–56.

12. Fernessole, *Pie X: Essai historique*, 2:55–56.

13. Derély, "Les décrets eucharistiques," 907; and Stefano Antoni, *Why Do So Many Vain Fears Keep You from Frequent and Daily Communion?* (New York: Sentinel, 1923), i.

14. Casimir Gennari, "Approbation of the Author's Eucharistic Tracts from His Eminence Cardinal Gennari, on Behalf of His Holiness Pius X," in *ET*, v.

15. *ET*, vi.

16. Derély, "Les décrets eucharistiques," 907.

17. Steven M. Avella, "'Cara America': Sources and Images of American Catholic Devotion to St. Pius X" (typewritten document), 37.

18. Avella, "Cara America," 35.

19. *Congressist*, although lacking in euphony, was the argot in American English to label a participant at a Eucharistic congress.

20. Stadler, *Synopsis and Commentary*, 34.

21. *MC*, 502.

22. Sacred Congregation of the Sacraments, *Quam Singulari. Acta Apostolicae Sedis* 2 (1910): 577–83, edited by R. Kevin Seasoltz, *The New Liturgy: A Documentation, 1903–1965* (New York: Herder & Herder, 1966), 17–22.

23. "In the twentieth century, Pope Pius the Tenth reigning, the lips of Our Blessed Lord again moved, and from His Sacred Heart the same teaching [of Trent] is renewed." J.A. McN., "A Plea for Daily Communion," *EPUL* 15 (1909): 86.

24. Peter M. Bregenzer, "The Devotion to the Eucharistic Heart," *EPUL* 29 (1931): 161.

25. André Haquin, "Le mouvement eucharistique et les décrets de s.Pie X," in *Dom Lambert Beauduin et le renouveau liturgique*, recherches et synthèses, section d'histoire, 1, preface by Olivier Rousseau (Gembloux: J. Duculot, 1970), 60.

26. Fernessole, *Pie X: Essai historique*, 2:59.

27. Schwertner, *Eucharistic Renaissance*, 238.

28. Albert Tesnière, "Commentary on the Prayer for the Spread of Daily Communion," *EPUL* 11 (1905): 201.

29. Derély, "Les décrets eucharistiques," 901.

30. Casimir Gennari, "Rescript on the Prayer for the Pious Custom of Daily Communion," *EPUL* 11, no. 9 (1905): 203–4.

31. Derély, "Les décrets eucharistiques," 901.

32. Albert Tesnière, "Commentary on the Rescript [on the Prayer for the Pious Custom of Daily Communion]," *EPUL* 11 (1905): 204.

33. Tesnière, "Commentary on the Prayer," 199.

34. Untitled and anonymous reference to the *Revue théologique française* (October 1905): n.p., in "The Priests' Communion League," *EPUL* 13 (1907): 283.

35. Literally, "by one's own initiative." A *motu proprio* is a "papal decree or legislative document issued by the Sovereign Pontiff at his own initiative rather than in response to a request." *Dictionary of Ecclesiastical Latin*.

36. *STS*, 15.

37. Nieri, "Esperiense e riforme liturgiche," 58.

38. Lemieux calls the pope's strategy in using the prayer and its rescript a "ground-softening," for it allowed the pope to "show his hand" while at the same time not committing him to the cause of frequent Communion. Lemieux, "Life or Death," 504.

39. Tesnière, "Commentary on the Rescript," 204.

40. Tesnière, "Commentary on the Prayer," 202.

41. Tesnière, "Commentary on the Prayer," 202.

42. Lemieux, "Life or Death," 504.

43. *STS*, 400.

44. Joseph A. Komonchak, "Modernity and the Construction of Roman Catholicism," typewritten document provided to the author in 1996; published version appeared in *Cristianesimo nella storia* 18 (1997).

45. *MC*, 505.

46. Ferreres, *Decree*, 21.

47. B. Sause, "Council, Congregation of the," *NCE*.

48. Ferreres, *Decree*, 18.

49. Ferreres, *Decree*, 24.

50. *Decrees of the Council of Trent*, 147.

51. *Decrees of the Council of Trent*, 147.

52. W. J. Sherzer, "Sunday," and M. Herron, "Sunday and Holiday Observance," *NCE*.

53. *MC*, 505.

54. *STS*, 11.

55. *STS*, 11.

56. *STS*, 11.

57. Joseph Heuser, "The Holy Father's Wish Regarding Daily Communion," *American Ecclesiastical Review* (July 1906): 61. The actual word is *instaurare*, which is invariably translated as *restore*.

58. *STS*, 12.

59. The primary example of this form of commentary is Petrus Bastien's *De Frequenti Quotidianaque Communione ad Normam Decreti "Sacra Tridentina Synodus"* (Rome: Desclée, Lefebvre et Socii, 1907).

60. "The Decree on Daily Communion," *EPUL* 12 (July 1906): 149, extracted from *La revue theologique française*, n.v. (March 1906): n.p.

61. Thomas Slater, *A Manual of Moral Theology for English-Speaking Countries*, annotated by Michael Martin (New York: Benziger, 1908), 108–9.

62. *STS*, 14.

63. "It is obvious that such persons [religious] are more likely to have the due dispositions for frequent and daily Communion." Ferreres, *Decree*, 135.

64. "The Priests' Communion League, Read at the Eucharistic Meeting of Metz," *EPUL* 13 (1907): 287.

65. Sacred Congregation of Indulgences, "Yearly Triduum of Prayer for the Purpose of Promoting Frequent Communion," in *ET*, 16.

66. Sacred Congregation of Indulgences, "Yearly Triduum," in *ET*, 19.

67. This entire paragraph summarizes and cites this document, "Yearly Triduum," in *ET*, 16–19.

68. Derély, "Les décrets eucharistiques," 901.

69. Duhr, 1287.

70. Zulueta, "Translator's Preface," xxii.

71. Pietro Respighi, "Instruction Given to the Members of the Priests' Eucharistic League, for the Propagation of the Pious Practice of Daily Communion, and Approved by Pius X," in *ET*, 23.

72. Fernessole, *Pie X: Essai historique*, 2:74–75.

73. "Ordinary" Holy Communion excludes the cases of viaticum, or reception of Communion immediately before death, and cases in which the reserved hosts were consumed to prevent desecration.

74. Stadler, *Historical Synopsis and Commentary*, 64.

75. Stanislaus Woywod, *The New Canon Law: A Commentary and Summary of the New Code of Canon Law*, preface by Philip Bernardini, third edition, revised (New York: Joseph F. Wagner, 1918), 172.

76. Pope Pius XII, *Christus Dominus, Acta Apostolicae Sanctae* 45 (1953): n.p., translated by John Ford, in James Ruddy, *The Apostolic Constitution "Christus Dominus": Text, Translation and Commentary, with Short Annotations on the Motu Proprio "Sacram Communionem,"* Catholic University of America Canon Law Studies, no. 390 (Washington, D.C.: Catholic University Press, 1957), vii.

77. Pius XII, *Christus Dominus*, 15.

78. M. Demetria Newman, "Some Interesting Memories of Sr. M. Demetria Newman Regarding A[ltar] B[read]" (typewritten document), transcription, Altar Bread / Oral History, Archives of the Benedictine Sisters of the Perpetual Adoration, Clyde, Missouri.

79. Woywod, *New Canon Law*, 173.

80. Woywod, *New Canon Law*, 174 and 260–61.

81. Woywod, *New Canon Law*, 261.

82. Jules Lintelo, "The Preacher's and Confessor's Influence in Promoting Frequent Communion," *EPUL* 13 (1907): 190.

83. "The Priests' Communion League," 279. Duhr, 1287.

84. "The Priests' Communion League," 280.

85. "The Priests' Communion League," 280.

86. The text actually reads, "Itaque praeiudicatae adversantium opiniones, inanes multorum timores, speciosae abstinendi causae penitus tollendae." *MC*, 653.

87. "The Priests' Communion League," 280.

88. *ET*, 27.

89. Zulueta, "Translator's Preface," x.

90. Zulueta, "Translator's Preface," xi.

91. Emil Springer, *Haben wir Priester noch Vorurteile gegen die häufige und tägliche Kommunion der Gläubigen?* (Paderborn: Bonifacius, 1910), 7ff.

92. Duhr, 1287; Ferreres, *Decree*, 107–8.

93. "The Priests' Communion League," 284.

94. Derély, "Les décrets eucharistiques: 903–4; Zulueta, "Translator's Preface," ix.

95. Fernessole, *Pie X: Essai historique*, 2:74ff.

96. Nieri, "Esperiense e riforme liturgiche," 56–58; Some proponents of frequent Communion concede, when discussing *STS*, that *MC* went "largely unnoticed." They

also, like Nieri, consider *STS* merely an implementation of *MC.* "The Priests' Communion League," 287.

97. Gaupin, "First Eucharist and the Shape of Catechesis," 176.

98. Derély and Fernessole both perceive the subordination of *QS* to *STS,* but do not elaborate upon it. Derély, "Les décrets eucharistiques," 903, and Fernessole, *Pie X: Essai historique,* 2:75ff.

99. Lintelo, "The Preacher's and Confessor's Influence," 197.

100. Sarah C. Burnett, "A Timely Pamphlet on Daily Communion," *Fortnightly Review* 22 (1915): 561, mentioned the resistance of some parents to their pastors' encouraging frequent Communion among children.

*Chapter Four*

# American Journals and Associations for Frequent Communion

This chapter mines the two Eucharistic periodicals that were the official organs of the campaign in the United States—*Emmanuel: Official Monthly of the Priests' Eucharistic League* (*EPUL*) and the *Sentinel of the Blessed Sacrament* (*SSac*). The former is the official publication of the Priests' Eucharistic League (PEL) and is still published by the Blessed Sacrament Fathers; the latter was the organ of the People's Eucharistic League (PPL). Together they orchestrated the campaign for greater Eucharistic devotion, including greater frequency of Holy Communion. As they were popularized, they could manifest its characteristics. Spontaneous and diffuse phenomena such as the Communion breakfasts provide very little usable documentation of the campaign. Thus these periodicals serve as the best historical witnesses. Fortunately, these Eucharistic magazines were quite embedded in their sponsoring organizations. How was Eucharistic devotion promoted by these organizations and in the pages of these two periodicals? Because the periodicals reported abundantly, if redundantly, the limited tactics for encouraging frequent Communion, some detailed examples will impart a sense both of the penchant for founding frequent Communion clubs and of propagandizing, in print, for a massive shift in the devotional life of the American Catholic Church.

## CATHOLIC JOURNALISM

It seems judicious to begin by placing *EPUL* and *SSac* in context to avoid overstating their influence. What was Catholic periodical literature in the period? How did these two Eucharistic periodicals fare in this market? These questions give a sense of the scope of the campaign for frequent Holy Communion. What proportion of other forms of Catholic publishing,

111

especially books, concerned Eucharistia—the devotion to and use of the Eucharist?

Willging and Hatzfeld's *Catholic Serials* (*CS*), measuring seven and three-quarter inches of shelf space of mimeographed reports in two series totaling fifteen volumes, reveals quite a profusion of Catholic periodical production in the entire expanse of the nineteenth century.[1] Of the total of 1,396 serials, 70 percent used English exclusively, 8 percent were bilingual in Irish and English, 11.5 percent were in German, and nearly 10 percent were in French. Basque, Hungarian, Arabic, and Ukrainian were used exclusively by one periodical each.[2] In the 1890s, when both *EPUL* and *SSac* commenced, periodicals in English were booming; fully 47 percent appeared in this decade alone, while only 25 percent had seen the light in the 1880s. German and French publications saw only modest increases, and this reflected the tapering of immigration and the mastering of English by these groups. Most serials published weekly, but nearly 31 percent were monthlies—at least according to their own plans, for *CS* strove for completeness by including even the ephemeral.

*CS* ranks by explicitness of Catholicity in three categories: Catholic by "purpose," by "attitude," and by "national tradition."[3] Those that are Catholic by purpose are further segregated into "official," "religious," and "inofficial."[4] The bibliography also classifies by type, such as newspaper and magazine, and by subject, running from agriculture to temperance. General magazines and family issues total forty-eight; "religious, devotional" constitute sixty-six.[5] These categories may mislead in attempting to apply some form to the amorphousness of the data. In other words, here categorizations are fuzzy.

Each entry in *CS* provides dates of operation, various titles under which a single periodical appeared, piggyback and daughter publications, locations of offices and plants, editors, summary descriptions of the contents, and so forth. Circumspection is advisable in using this resource. As Willging himself writes, "It should be clearly noted that the compiler regards these articles as preliminary rather than definitive and the emphasis is on bibliography and format rather than contents of the publications. We request users to furnish us with corrections."[6] In the concluding volume, he again cautions that there are "certainly many mistakes in details."[7] Still, *CS* is our only recourse to sense the place of these Eucharistic periodicals in the Catholic landscape.

How did the two Eucharistic journals fare in the market of Catholic religious periodicals? Data for the circulation of periodicals are derived from the standard of the advertising business, the *American Newspaper and Annual Directory*.[8] Most of the following data are from 1924, because this year is least plagued with gaps. The first three examples belong in *CS*'s category of "devotional" and are of particular interest because they represent the most popular devotions with which the Eucharistic movement needed to contend.

> *Ave Maria* was started by the founder of the University of Notre Dame, Edward Sorin, CSC; it has always been published there and been controlled by the Congregation of Holy Cross.[9] Established in 1865, it is one of the oldest Catholic periodicals of national distribution, and it prospered sufficiently in its early days to support a retirement home for religious of the congregation. One editor, Daniel E. Hudson, also a priest of the Holy Cross order, served from 1874 until 1929. That this weekly magazine allied itself with the *Messenger of the Sacred Heart* and *L'echo de France* in 1868 in the vending of joint subscriptions indicates a cooperation that precludes conscious competition among American Catholic periodicals. *Ave Maria*'s aim was indicated in the subtitle: "To the honor of the Mother of God"; it intended to be "the means of advancing the cause of religion by promoting devotion to our Blessed Lady." From 1935 on it was called a "family paper" or a "Catholic home weekly." It contained a great variety of matter, being rich in fiction, poetry, articles on religious problems, documents and pastorals, brief essays, editorials, anecdotes, clerical obituaries, and book reviews; there was a "Children's Department" and occasionally a music sheet. From 1892 forward a literary supplement appeared for some time. The periodical was praised as "the most satisfactory of all religious magazines of the age," known throughout the states and abroad as a scholarly literary publication providing wholesome, educational, and entertaining reading for the whole family. Msgr. Ellis in his *Guide to American Catholic History* has cited its value as a source for devotional history.

In 1923, it achieved a circulation of thirty-eight thousand, and its annual subscription was $2.50. The titles on its tables of contents for that same year indicate that neither the Blessed Sacrament nor Holy Communion merited attention.

Also of Marian emphasis and sponsored by the Dominicans since 1891, *Rosary* circulated fifty-nine thousand copies and cost $3.00 for a subscription.[10] This "devotional family magazine" declared as its primary purpose "to spread the devotion of Our Lady of the Rosary in literature, history, dogma, poetry, art, and song."[11] It editorialized on contemporary events and also, besides reviewing books, reviewed on a regular basis many nonreligious magazines.[12] In a very tenuous sense, it competed with *Ave Maria, Catholic World,* and *Donahoe's Magazine,* but upon the completion of its first full volume, *Ave Maria* "congratulated" *Rosary*.[13] Editorship remained in the hands of Dominicans, and many of the contributors were also Friars Preachers, often from other lands; the laity also contributed.[14] In the course of its history, it seems to have evolved into a bulletin of an association, the "Rosary Confraternity" (1921) and later the "Official National Rosary Society Magazine."[15]

The giant of these three devotional periodicals is the *Messenger of the Sacred Heart*, which printed 303,117 copies each month. It has always been supervised by the Society of Jesus and its purpose was to "control" the Apostleship of Prayer; in the United States it was established in 1866, and in 1913 editions of the *Messenger* were appearing in thirty countries and in presumably at least as many languages.[16] Supplemental publications included *The Pilgrim of Our Lady*, *Little Pilgrim*, and *Apostleship of Prayer*.[17] "Its content consisted for years of the explanation of the need for joining the devotion, to give the means to do it and the examples of saints who had received the fruits of it by prayer, in the sacraments, with honoring the Cross, for themselves and others; intentions for prayers are always suggested."[18] In 1885, it expanded its explicit aims, adding the "literary" to its devotional purpose, and it also defined itself as the "official organ of the Prayer-League."[19] With respect to Eucharistic promotion, in 1913 each month included a page or two under the title "Eucharistic Propaganda."

These thoroughly Catholic magazines, as their names indicate, each cultivated among the faithful a certain emphasis in devotional life. Several factors prevented these tightly focused magazines from becoming outrightly exclusive or overtly competitive in their emphases. First, the periodicals' sources were almost totally derivative of European matter. They all eventually incorporated more homegrown material but still excerpted from a wide variety of usually unacknowledged sources; they were omnivorous. As the publications became more established, this dependency declined. For example, the *Messenger* "was a translation into English from the French original; slowly some original matter was added, then more, until besides its remaining connection with headquarters and the international aim to support the devotion to the Sacred Heart, the MSH [*sic*] had become an American publication."[20] Their content was therefore Catholic, at least so far as was determined by their range of sources.

By thus compiling, the magazines could provide many diverse handholds for their American readers who, as immigrants, had brought many distinctive configurations of pieties with them. Once invited by the comfortably familiar in a publication, the reader would be influenced by the particular agenda of, for example, the devotion to the Sacred Heart. But while the magazines tried to exalt their own devotions, their purpose, as a group and in the context of the United States in the late nineteenth and early twentieth century, was unitary: to maintain the Catholicity of their readership in the hostile, Protestant environment.

It was to be expected that this rising success [of the Church,] increasingly apparent after 1880, would draw down upon the Church the ire of its enemies.

... The new wave of bigotry crystallized in the American Protective Association founded at Clinton, Iowa, in March, 1887, by Henry F. Bowers, and six associates, and for the next decade every corner of America rang with cries of warning against the Church of Rome.[21]

The special devotions that these magazines favored were officially approved, and the priestly editors would have been schooled in their exact relations to the fundamentals of the faith; consequently, they were careful neither to become inordinate in their peculiar pieties nor to deform Catholic devotional life. At the same time, as we shall see in the particular case of the Eucharistic movement, all devotions, though not disparaged, could be whittled into shapes that allowed the privileged piety of the editor and of his religious order to prosper.

To subscribe was often to join some pious union, but these institutions varied greatly in degree of commitment, administrative structure, eligibility, and the like. As to accessibility, all of the preceding would have been available to both lay and clergy membership, as well as subscribers.

The fourth example is, according to Willging and Hatzfeld, not "devotional" but rather fraternal, and so presumably coordinated with a more structured and much more institutional association. This magazine, which appeared under very slightly different titles—*Columbiad* and *Columbia*—was founded by leaders of the Knights of Columbus in 1892, but it was anticipated by local chapters' bulletins as early as 1867 and became the official organ of the Knights "only in 1903."[22] It had truly served as a society newsletter until that date; it then expanded its contents to "matter of general literary interest."[23] In fact, by 1925 it was disclaiming its fraternal roots and boasting the largest circulation in the world; *CS* classifies it as "Catholic by attitude."[24] Its circulation, more than double that of the *Messenger*, was 770,000; its subscription price was $1.00 per year, but it was free to members.[25] Priests were able to join the Knights, but the organization was lay in nature. The role of the Knights of Columbus in encouraging frequent Holy Communion, especially by means of the Communion breakfast, will be examined below.

Finally, for the sake of comparison with *EPUL*, which did limit itself to clerical readership, consider the *American Ecclesiastical Review*. The *Review* was published not by a religious order, but rather by an individual priest of the archdiocese of Philadelphia, Herman J. Heuser (d. 1933).[26] Except for a five-year interruption, he edited it from its founding in 1889 until 1929. The magazine was not devotional, but rather "ecclesiastical or professional."[27] In the very first volume Heuser implied that his project was for the intellectual edification of the clergy, for "priests should always remain men of books."[28] The *Review* often employed faculty of the Catholic University of America, many of whom were Europeans; Heuser solicited contributions of great breadth and

> thus the *Review* became a storehouse of learned articles on theology, canon law, liturgy and church history, carrying out the general legislation of the Church and the specific interpretations of the Baltimore councils. Some problems of the time that received regular treatment were temperance, secret societies, diocesan statutes, "casus morales," education. . . . Social reformation also was an important subject.[29]

The *Review* also occasionally published homiletical aids. In 1923, it raised its rate to $4.00 per year, and its circulation was twenty-two thousand. In the same year, it published eleven articles that evidently touch upon the Eucharist, but the titles indicate that these were legal rather than pastoral or theological. No titles revealed interest in or opposition to frequent Communion.

These five periodicals—three devotional, one fraternal, and one clerical—provide some context for *EPUL* and *SSac*.


## THE EUCHARISTIC MAGAZINES

The circulation of the Eucharistic magazines in 1923 was, for the sacerdotal *EPUL*, 10,263, and for the laical *SSac*, 20,963. The reverend members of the PEL paid $1.00 per year for membership and the subscription to *EPUL*; the laypeople paid $2.00 for *SSac*.[30] The circulation of *EPUL* remained nearly constant for the next ten years; it recorded a readership of 11,876 in 1932. In contrast, the organ of the PPL declined by almost 23 percent in the same period; its circulation in 1932 was 15,164. Both *EPUL* and *SSac* remained quite modest in their circulation.

*SSac* specified its devotional purpose, describing itself by means of a subtitle as "devoted to the Honor of the Holy Eucharist."[31] Its content showed the immense breadth of the terms *devote* and *honor*, for it included "stories, some of them serials, devotional poems, sketches of religious instruction, legends, editorial notes, 'humor,' a 'Children's Home' section, and book notices." After 1928, it acquired the readership of the "Nocturnal Adoration Society."[32] In 1923, titles in the table of contents indicate that eight articles dealt with the Eucharist per se; this figure excluded the Holy Hour, which was centered upon the Real Presence, and also meetings of Eucharistic associations, which numbered ten. Only one title indicated a concern specifically for frequency of Communion.

What markets did the Eucharistic publications attain? The *Catholic Press Directory*, first published in 1923, estimated the Roman Catholic clerical population of the United States at 22,545 and the total Catholic population at 20,103,761, thus *EPUL* was reaching nearly 46 percent of priests.

The circulation data do not necessarily indicate absolute penetration of the clerical market. Many rectories housed more than one priest, and presumably some priests shared their periodicals. For example, the Archdiocese of Cincinnati listed 191 placements for its active clergy in 1922.[33] Most of these placements, a total of 66 percent, were single-man parishes. But a clear majority of priests—56 percent—shared their domiciles. Of joint-tenant clergy, nearly 60 percent shared with only one other, and nearly 9 percent lived in groups of five or more. However, the larger groupings were invariably regular priests.

Most readers of *SSac* were probably laity because *EPUL* fulfilled the Eucharistic appetite of the clergy. Indeed, this segregation of readerships had been intended from the very beginning of *EPUL*, and the Blessed Sacrament Priests presumably continued this policy. Father Bede Maler, OSB, the business manager of the nascent *EPUL*, granted a subscription to a laywoman with obvious reluctance.[34] *SSac* reached approximately 0.1 percent of the American Catholic populace, while the *Messenger of the Sacred Heart* was read by approximately 1.5 percent. Lay periodical calculations should be multiplied by a factor greater than for clerical periodicals, given typical domiciles and sharing among neighbors.

Simply to correlate circulation data with the prevalence of a particular devotion would oversimplify. A general principle of historical research about religion, however, applies. A social historian of religion is continually faced with an ultimately intractable problem of evidence. One can, with some difficulty, observe and even measure religious practice, the external forms of religious behavior. There remains, however, the nagging doubt as to whether such external forms bear much in relation to inner experience.[35] The particular circumstances of *SSac* and *EPUL* allow some deeper analysis and some tentative observations.

First, consider the decline in subscriptions to *SSac*. If a simple correlation were postulated as Gibson's axiom might propose, this would indicate a fading popularity of Eucharistic devotionalism. But through this period the liturgical and devotional practices of Catholic laity centered increasingly upon the Blessed Sacrament. Franciscan Father Chinnici has declared, "Emerging from the devotional revival in the second half of the nineteenth century, the eucharistic movement was the most vital spiritual movement of the first fifty years of twentieth-century American Catholicism."[36] Thus the decline in circulation of the Eucharistic periodicals more likely indicates such broad acceptance of the Eucharistic piety that it no longer required the periodicals. The credibility of such an assessment might be enhanced by comparative studies with other movements, such as the Blue Army of Fatima, the Lay Retreat movement, and so on. Still, the fruits of the Eucharistic movement, both in the liturgical movement and in the devotional taxonomy of American Roman Catholics after the Second Vatican Council, confirm Chinnici's judgment.

*EPUL* and *SSac* sought to reshape Catholic devotional life by placing the Eucharist in the center. Remember that the few other specifically devotional magazines in the sampling above—*Ave Maria, Rosary, Messenger of the Sacred Heart*—did not claim such ambitious goals. Admittedly, all at first aimed to further their own brands of prayer, of veneration, of devotional practices. Insofar as all the devotions promoted by these magazines were licit and worthy, they all referred, by some chain or mechanism, to the essentials of Catholicism, both dogma and practice. As one priest friend of John Henry Cardinal Newman explained,

> They [Protestants and infidels] forget that what is commonly believed or prac-ticed among Catholics is an indication of the mind of the Church, since she tolerates or authorizes it. The devotions to the Church are the legitimate conse-quences of her doctrines, and a contempt for them shows that the doctrines have no hold on the mind that despises them.[37]

And so it is improper to postulate simplistically dualistic relationships. For example, the Jesuit periodical, the *Messenger*, promoted, in a word, the Sa-cred Heart of Jesus. But to depict the Sacred Heart in opposition to Eucharis-tic devotion would be wrong.[38] Sacred Heart devotion, basically a retrieval of the doctrine of the love of Christ for humanity and a corrective to obsessive fear of God, entailed a fresh articulation of the bases of Catholic faith and urged upon enrollees a distinctive set of devotional practices.[39] These were not, taken individually, at odds with Catholic piety generally; the devotions form, however, a distinctive configuration that marked the subscriber to the *Messenger* as a member of this special Apostolate of Prayer. A subscriber would be encouraged prayerfully to make "a daily offering of one's prayers, good works, and suffering" as actions of reparation for the general disregard of Jesus in the world.[40] The "apostle" was to make a Holy Hour once per month. He would recite at least a decade of the rosary daily for the intentions of the pope. Most importantly for our concerns, he would receive Commu-nion "monthly or weekly," either of which was extraordinarily frequently in those days. This spirituality of the *Messenger* indeed lent an impetus to both the Eucharistic movement and its gradually emerging "restoration" of frequent Communion.

Does any resource provide a yet wider view of the entirety of Catholic literature, including books? Can the relative position of the Eucharistic move-ment in the Catholic universe of devotions be corroborated from this additional resource? Walter Romig's *The Guide to Catholic Literature* included not only books, in the generous sense of the term, but also their reviews and independent articles in most general Catholic periodicals. The volume for the years 1888 to 1940 discovers 112 titles treating Eucharistic devotion and fully 146 concerning Marian devotion.[41] Some of these titles are duplicated, because devotions do not parse so easily. For example, Saint Alphonsus Liguori's *Visits to the Blessed Sacrament and to the Blessed Virgin*, since the devotions are directed to both Jesus in the Blessed Sacrament and Mary, appears under two categories, "Eucharistic Devotions" and "Marian Devotions." The category "Holy Communion" includes eight separate works and authors.[42] "Frequent Communion" names only four authors, and the total of their works on the subject reckons to thirteen, of which eleven works are by Father Francis M. de Zulueta, SJ (d. 1937).[43] Rosary devotions comprised twenty-four titles.[44] These figures plead for the vitality of the Eucharistic movement.

This investigation of the American campaign for frequent Holy Communion relies upon *EPUL* and *SSac* because the periodicals report in detail the activities of the associations that they served, the PEL and the PPL. The advantage of this approach is that the magazines were discrete institutions that both took as their mission the promotion of Eucharistia—of which frequent Communion was preeminent—and so this first detailed archival investigation into the movement must take account of them. These, like most American Catholic periodicals, "digest" information from a wide variety of sources, and they depict the strategy, eventually successful, of placing Holy Communion in the center of American Catholic devotional practices.

The fiftieth anniversary edition of *EPUL* observed that the Eucharistic movement unfolded in America smoothly, with no single year "a picture of striking accomplishments."[45] The editor admitted that the movement rapidly accomplished much, and he credited this progress to the hierarchy, teachers, and priests.[46] The editor downplayed the role of the magazine, almost isolating it from the League: "It was *Emmanuel's* most enviable privilege to pioneer in the field of the eucharistic press in North America as the monthly organ of the Priests' Eucharistic League. . . . In the late nineties as well as in the early part of the present century, the League provided the greatest single impetus to the eucharistic movement in this country."[47] Because the activity of the League centered in the Eucharistic congresses and the local and regional meetings these inspired, this article emphasized those, in a false opposition to the matter in *EPUL*.

But this reliance upon the two magazines admittedly poses disadvantages. Both periodicals, for virtually their entire histories, were controlled by the Fathers of the Blessed Sacrament. The determinative mission of this order, founded in France by Saint Pierre-Julien Eymard, was evident in its customary salutation, "Adveniat regnum tuum Eucharisticum!" (May your Eucharistic kingdom come!). This phrase augments the Vulgate's Pater Noster, which reads simply, "Adveniat regnum tuum." The goals of the periodicals and the order were identical—promotion of all manner of devotion to the Blessed Sacrament. These propagandistic magazines unflaggingly painted a rosy picture. Thus, reliance upon these periodicals must be tempered with other publications and with some data from outside of the timeframe from 1894 to 1926.

In addition, while they appear to be virtual archives of the Eucharistic movement in the United States, this is a false impression. As published accounts of the events of the Eucharistic movement and, even more so, as propaganda for the enhancement of Eucharistic piety, these periodicals are likely tendentious. For example, one account of the founding of the PEL suppresses the fact that Archbishop William H. Elder of Cincinnati had been in attendance at the first organizational meeting of the league. Still, because the popularization of frequent Communion is the main focus of this book, the popularizing press serves as a reasonable witness.

Much of the material that appears in *EPUL* was penned by secular priests who belonged to the PEL. So, while the Blessed Sacrament Fathers edited the magazine, they encouraged the "reverend fathers" of the secular clergy to contribute. Even from its inception in 1895, before it was remanded to the Fathers of the Blessed Sacrament, *EPUL* solicited contributions from the members of the PEL. Some standard features were penned by diocesan clergy. For example, William G. Lallou (d. 1973), a priest from Philadelphia, wrote to correct rubrical solecisms in a column called "Liturgy." An example more indicative of the faithfulness of the Fathers of the Blessed Sacrament to their secondary mission of nurturing all priests in their vocations is the authorship of the monthly "Subjects for Adoration" by both diocesan priests and members of other orders. The "Adoration" was a prayer method invented by Saint Eymard, but the order did not retain prerogatives for elaborating upon this technique. For many years, a second priest of the Archdiocese of Philadelphia, Father Joseph Louis J. Kirlin (d. 1926), wrote these meditative pieces.

Perhaps the vested interests of these two magazines in magnifying their own successes distort the picture of American Catholic devotional life in the late nineteenth and early twentieth centuries. On the other hand, the Eucharistic movement and its campaign for frequent Communion patently succeeded, insofar as American Catholics who attend Mass nowadays usually communicate. Still, the one scholarly article on the Eucharistic movement in the United States places frequent Communion squarely in the forefront of devotional activities.[48]

The final drawback in relying upon these two periodicals is that they were virtually exclusively in English. Does not the limitation to English-language periodicals distort the picture of Catholic Eucharistic piety in this era, when immigrants constituted so much of the "American" Catholic Church? The two English-language periodicals sifted by this history enjoy unimpeachable status as official organs of the two official organizations of Eucharistic devotions. Typical to the genre, these official periodicals largely drew upon European publications. As *SSac* and *EPUL* refract these sources, the official organs collected and publicized matter presumably very similar to what other "immigrant" periodicals featured. Even as the immigrants were being Americanized, the Eucharistic movement in the United States recognized that the Eucharist, as a sacrament that transcended national and ethnic loyalties, could expedite the Americanization of the Catholic Church.

## DEFINING THE PRIESTS' EUCHARISTIC LEAGUE

The proliferation of national and international Eucharistic societies among the laity occurred to a smaller extent among priests as well. The nomenclature of these societies became quite confusing, however, since their ends overlapped. At the first organizational meeting of the League in Covington, Kentucky, Bishop Camillus Maes proposed that the name of the association be "Priests Eucharistic League in place of *'Confraternitas Sacerdotum Adoratorum—Prêtres Adorateurs'*—Priest Adorers."[49] Bede Maler mistook the official Latin name of the group, for its statutes read thus, "Statuta Associationis Sacerdotum Adoratorum seu Aggregationis Sacerdotalis Congregationi Ssmi. Sacramenti a R. P. Eymard Institutæ."[50] The earliest enrollees in the United States had joined an organization headquartered in Paris, and this may explain why *EPUL* persisted in referring to members as *adorers*, a cognate from French. When Father Maler was soliciting the bishops of the United States to support the first establishment of the Blessed Sacrament Fathers here, he encountered a xenophobia that urged him to delay their arrival by several years.[51] Perhaps the name proffered by Maes's sounded more American and would have thus improved recruiting.

The imprecisions that marred the explanations even of contemporaries in sorting out the various aggregations may indicate, however, the vitality of the thrust to restore frequent Holy Communion. Zulueta, the translator from the French, attempted a clarification in a footnote in Jesuit Father Jules Lintelo's *The Eucharistic Triduum*:

> The league for priests here referred to [i.e., "The Priests' Eucharistic League for the Propagation of The Pious Practice of Daily Communion, and Approved by Pius X"] is the one established at San Claudio, Rome, July 27, 1906, by the au-

thority of the then Cardinal Vicar—Cardinal Respighi—under the title of "Lega Sacerdotale Eucharistica," a distinct organization from that of "The Priest Adorers" (*Prêtres Adorateurs*). But as the latter body came to be called in America "The Eucharistic League," in England, in order to save confusion, it has become the practice to refer to the "Lega Sacerdotale" as "Priests' Communion League," or "Priests' Daily Communion League."[52]

In the United States, both aggregations of priests were administered by the Fathers of the Blessed Sacrament. In fact, in 1909 one priest, Father Emile Poirier, SSS (d. 1953), directed the two. The older group, officially in the United States called the Priests' Eucharistic League, descends indubitably from Saint Pierre-Julien. Pope Leo XIII approved this group, and it was "canonically erected at Rome on the 16th day of January, 1887, by His Eminence Cardinal Parrocchi, Vicar-General of His Holiness; and its constititutions were definitely approved."[53] Its title, both in French and Latin, reveals the league's primary end: to encourage the priestly practice of Adoration before the Blessed Sacrament for one hour per week. This group, reflecting its founder, admittedly encouraged frequent Communion among the laity; however, pushing more frequent reception became a priority only gradually but did not replace its foundational concern—the personal sanctification of both secular and religious priests through the Adoration. The greater frequency of Communion among one's parishioners was to be the fruit of the enhanced holiness of the priest through his dedicated and pious relationship to the Blessed Sacrament. Henceforth, Eymard's association of *prêtres-adorateurs* will be called the Priests' Eucharistic League (PEL).

The younger institution, whose Latin title is Sacerdotale Eucharisticum Foedus, was founded six months after the promulgation of *Sacra Tridentina Synodus*.[54] "Immediately, to show his keen interest in the matter, Pope Pius [X] suppressed the three years' delay *ad experimentum*, to which all such associations are subjected. On the third day he raised it to an *Archassociatio Primaria*."[55] The single priority of this archassociation was unequivocal: "to spread, by all means within the power of priestly zeal, the doctrine taught by the Decree of 20th of December, 1905, and promote its practice."[56] In other words, "the paramount aim of the Communion Leaguer, as such, is to inculcate, in season and out of season" the frequent reception of Holy Communion by the faithful.[57]

The story of the magazine *EPUL* is thoroughly interwoven with the story of the PEL. Father Kirlin, in a demonstration of what may best be characterized as pious fervor, depicted Jesus himself as the organizer. "The Priests' Eucharistic League was founded by Our Lord in the Upper Chamber of Jerusalem the night before He died."[58] The league's own narrative of creation begins at

Saint Meinrad's Abbey, a Benedictine monastery in southern Indiana. It had suffered a devastating fire and, in its acute financial need, began a bimonthly mailing for benefactors, both past and prospective.[59] A monk, Bede Maler, OSB (d. 1936), who would eventually and justly be called the "patriarch of the Eucharistic Movement" in America, was the editor.[60] Its success led to a grander project, a fundraising magazine for all Benedictine monasteries in the United States, and Maler edited this too, beginning in 1888. The subject matter of this circular, *Sankt Benedikts-Panier*, was culled largely from European periodicals, and Maler happened upon the statutes of the PEL in a magazine called *Hirtentaesche*.[61] He and several other priests from Saint Meinrad's joined the league in 1890. These were not the first American clerics to subscribe, but at the request of the General Direction of the league in Paris—that is, the Blessed Sacrament Fathers—Saint Meinrad's became the center for the administration of the league in the United States in 1891.[62]

Archbishop Elder and Fathers William Cluse, Joseph A. Blenke, Henry Brinkmeyer, and Bede Maler convened at the invitation of Bishop Camillus P. Maes to organize the league in the United States at the latter's home in Covington, Kentucky, on 7 March 1894.[63] This birthday meeting of PEL in the United States recognized straightaway the importance of establishing a publication in order to promote the growth and health of the league.[64]

The ideas for both a league and an integral, official magazine certainly subsisted in the American culture of the late nineteenth century. The formation of and participation in fraternal associations in the United States peaked in the late nineteenth century, and all manner of associations relied upon newsletters to establish and maintain identity. As Maler recalled, the founders considered some sort of publication essential to the success of the association. The name *Emmanuel* derived from a German periodical for the laity and dedicated to Eucharist themes, and the literal meaning of "Emmanuel," "God-with-us," proclaimed to the priestly readership the Eucharistic doctrine of the Real Presence of the Body of Christ in the Blessed Sacrament. Henry Brinkmeyer, rector of Saint Gregory's Seminary in the Archdiocese of Cincinnati, was commissioned to present the project of the magazine at the first convention of the league, to be held at the University of Notre Dame in August 1894.

At this gathering, attended by six bishops and 150 priests, three noteworthy events gave birth to *EPUL*.[65] First, at an organizational meeting of the diocesan directors of the league, the editorship of the newsletter was urged upon Father Bede.[66] He was the natural choice because he had founded and was editing the lay-oriented German-language Eucharistic magazine of Saint Meinrad's Monastery, *Paradiesesfrüchte*.[67] Saint Meinrad's simply could not handle the publication of an additional periodical, so Maler declined.[68]

Then, two papers were presented to the convention at large. Edward A. Bush, vicar general of the Diocese of Pittsburgh, in a talk entitled "Means of Propagating the League," sketched an array of means for promoting it. He daringly urged recruitment of seminarians, even though they were not priests; he recommended Eucharistic meetings in abundance and in variety, including specifically the annual diocesan retreat; he proposed splitting the hour of Adoration into two half-hour segments; and he urged the founding of a magazine or newsletter in Latin.[69] Bush observed that many professions benefited from magazines dedicated to their interests and reasoned that Latin would aid in uniting the American priests, many of whom were immigrants; it also would distance the American Eucharistic League from the "nationalistic" leagues in Europe.[70]

Henry Brinkmeyer, delegated by the founding committee of the league to do so, read a paper entitled "The Establishment of a Eucharistic Monthly." He declared that the magazine was not only necessary because of the centrality of the Blessed Sacrament in the life of both priest and Church, but its creation was also a "duty" of the league. He proposed its two general functions: It would help maintain a fervent faith among priests, and it would unify them both in prayers for each other and in conveying practical suggestions for their work, particularly in centering all their work ever more in the Blessed Sacrament.[71] The contents, being largely practical, would come from two sources—submissions by the priest-subscribers, reporting their own experiences in promoting Eucharistia, and the business of the association itself, "its object and constitutional activity," which took place through all sorts of meetings.[72] According to Brinkmeyer, the magazine would automatically sustain and even expand the PEL because it would concern itself with its operations. "The nature of the League, its spirit, its rules and regulations, its manifold advantages—all these offer constant topics for discussion among the associates, and for those whose co-operation they would invite to the grand work."[73] Regular features would delve into topics—moral, liturgical, dogmatic—"briefly and entertainingly."[74] Brinkmeyer asserted that books were forbidding and "dead," while a magazine would be beneficially repetitious and "pithy." Presumed objections were defused: What would fill the pages? "A superabundance of matter would suggest itself to the editor of such a journal calculated to render the paper edifying, instructive, and interesting."[75] Could the magazine support itself? Who would edit it? He believed that it would succeed financially and requested that the fathers of the Congregation of Holy Cross and Notre Dame University establish a center for the league and publish *EPUL*. Notre Dame avoided the task. Did Notre Dame anticipate no benefit in exalting Eucharistic devotion and thus undermining its own, highly successful *Ave Maria*?

So the responsibility for editing the magazine fell to Bishop Camillus Maes. In the periodical's debut, Bishop Maes formally and courteously accepted the post. "In assuming editorial control of EMMANUEL, we consider neither the labor we bestow nor the shortcomings of which we are conscious. We work for a God who has a right to be better known among his own that he may be better received and loved."[76] The significance of this particular contribution to the Eucharistic movement was duly noted by Maes's eulogist. "For a number of years he reserved to himself the editing of the official organ of the League, 'Emmanuel,' taking up with his cheerful alacrity this important work, though already burdened by the exacting demands of his own great office."[77] In fact, Maes edited it until 1904, and in 1905 the magazine became the particular ministry of the Fathers of the Blessed Sacrament.[78]

Its lay complement, *Sentinel of the Blessed Sacrament* (*SSac*), does not boast such a clear account of its birth. *SSac* did, like *EPUL*, entwine itself with its sponsoring organization, the PPL. Although not credited by the quasi-official histories of this lay league, Father Jeremiah Foley (d. 1931) of Saint Louis, Missouri, urged the establishment in each parish of "the Association of Lay-Adorers" at the First National Eucharistic Congress, convened in Washington, D.C., in October 1895. He demonstrated a knowledge of its French connection to the analogous priestly organization and their heritage in Saint Eymard, but the fundamental piety of Foley's proposed lay organization was a full and continuous hour of Adoration every month.[79]

Eventually, however, this association sprouted not along the Mississippi but in the East, and under a different name—People's Eucharistic League (PPL). It was "formally organized on November 30, 1896, as a general association with the cathedral at New York as the Head Center for the United States."[80] The credit for establishing this coalition of parochial groups implicitly belongs to Eliza O'Brien Lummis (d. 1915), who animated also the Nocturnal Adoration, organized the men's "Corpus Christi reunion," and founded the Catholic Theatre movement.[81] "The PPL was the outcome of a simple association formed in 1895 at St. Francis Xavier's Church, New York. The Association met with great success, and after a little while rules similar to those which now govern the general body were formulated for it."[82] The name of the instigator of the initial cell, at Saint Francis Xavier's, remains unknown. Saint Francis Xavier Parish is staffed by Jesuits, an order that has a reputation for long encouraging frequent reception of Holy Communion.

One account, presented at the Eucharistic Congress in Philadelphia, implies that the PPL descended directly from Saint Pierre-Julien. "It represents, to a considerable extent, the Guard of Honor of the Blessed Sacrament, established by Pere Eymard."[83] The language of this account seems deliberately to equivocate, not perhaps to conceal the facts of the origin, but rather to gild the lineage by an ex-post-facto alliance with Eymard and his order.

As was the case with the clerical organizations, the various Eucharistic devotional associations for the laity were inchoate at the turn of the century, and even contemporaries erred in sketching their names, requirements, and histories.[84] The simple association of New York City's parish of Saint Francis Xavier may have been founded under a different title, such as "The Eucharistic Society," as O'Brien implies,[85] and clearly was established independently from any affiliation with the Fathers of the Blessed Sacrament, but great similarity to Eymard's vision allowed for a speedy incorporation of this parochial group into the broader and more resourceful movement.[86] A "simple association" in a parish was hardly an archconfraternity, *prima primaria*. By a letter dated 4 June 1897, the New York group was approved for inclusion in the lay company of the Blessed Sacrament Fathers' ministry. The assistant superior general of this order, Father Albert Tesnière, reported that his superior general "aggregates the associates of the various Guards of Honor of that city [New York] to the arch-association directed by the congregation, and renders them participants in all the merits, prayers, and indulgences of the congregation of the aggregate members in the whole world."[87] This notwithstanding, the New York initiative planned to submit its own charter to Rome for approval.[88] The kernel of the PPL then spread to five parishes, including the cathedral, by 1897, and a general assembly was held there in January. As a substitute for numerous other aids to meditation and to unite the various parochial groups, the magazine *SSac* was judged necessary.[89]

The governance of PPL cohered with the prevailing ecclesiology. Power flowed downward through the hierarchy, clearly and strictly defined, to the laity. PPL "was governed by a Protector [the archbishop of New York], General Director, and Local Directors in each of the different centres [usually parishes]."[90] This clerical leadership was seconded by lay leaders, namely, a "General President, a General Vice-President, a General Secretary, and a Board of Central Control." These latter with the democratic titles were all laywomen.[91] Because the PPL functioned as an auxiliary to the PEL, because it was not self-governing, and because the laity and the clergy were separate classes, *Ssac* did not solicit members' contributions. Its pages included devotional poems on Eucharistic themes written by laypeople, but most of the matter came from clerical and religious pens. Clerical authors exhorted readers to perform the monthly and obligatory hour of Adoration to which they had committed themselves by virtue of their membership in the PPL and to receive Communion frequently. Proceedings of the conventions of the PEL, including papers, were reported summarily in *SSac*. Eliza O'Brien Lummis, who was general president in 1900, edited the bulletin at first, but once the

Blessed Sacrament Fathers were established in New York, one of them, Arthur Letellier, SSS, assumed this office.[92] His name appeared on the title page of the magazine as late as 1920.

The two "organs" were aimed at propagating and maintaining associations. That the associations were both leagues betokens their administrative and practical dovetailing. Both associations and magazines for most of their lives were controlled by the Fathers of the Blessed Sacrament. The PEL functioned truly as an association—it had meetings, elected officers, collected dues, and so forth. The PPL was in essence merely a term for the readership of the periodical *SSac*; of course, as laity interested in Eucharistia, these subscribers were mobilized to assist at the functions of the priestly association. For both, the overarching goal was to spread the Eucharistic Kingdom of Christ.

Because the readerships differed in character, the content of the magazines also differed. For example, *EPUL* routinely advertised *SSac* because the priestly readership of the former, by definition leaders of their parishes, could effectively augment the circulation of the latter. It made no sense for *SSac* to advertise its "sister" publication *EPUL* because laity were excluded from subscribing. *EPUL*, although for priests, published very little in Latin, while *SSac* scrupulously stuck to the English language. *EPUL* strove to meet the general interests of the parish priest: It disseminated papal decrees and commented upon them, discussed fine points of liturgical celebration, and, most importantly and copiously, provided practical advice for the furtherance of Eucharistic devotions, including frequent reception of Communion.

*SSac* addressed the religious concerns of the laity: It proffered, explained, and meditated upon the liturgical calendar and illuminated monthly devotional themes, and presented both vignettes of Catholic personages and travelogues. It answered with exactitude intricate questions from readers about the earning of indulgences. The magazine served as a bulletin board for the cause for canonization of Father Pierre-Julien Eymard. Often, it retailed the patently miraculous. Father Francis Xavier Lasance puffed the magazine in these words:

> Not only do we find what we naturally expect in a periodical devoted to the interests of the Blessed Sacrament, choice matter in relation to the Holy Eucharist, but we are also regaled regularly with a variety of articles, pertaining not only to asceticism and hagiography, but also to general literature, art, poetry, history, biography, travel, notable events, and topics of current interest.[93]

This description attempted to downplay the Eucharistic thrust of the magazine, while, in fact, *SSac* milled most of its matter with a Eucharistic grindstone. For example, the travelogues that appeared in the 1926 volume were categorized in the general index as "The Eucharist in Many Lands."[94] When the magazine discussed popular, even dominant devotions of the era, such as the rosary and the Sacred Heart of Jesus, it massaged these devotions so that they became Eucharistic, and it thus prepared the way for the Eucharist to establish hegemony over all Catholic pieties.

Naturally, both magazines encouraged prayer; in particular, they facilitated the Adoration, a pious practice required of both lay and clerical leaguers. The laity were to perform the Adoration monthly. Priests not only committed themselves to its weekly observance, but also to the monthly submission of reports on their observance of the Adoration. These were called *libelli* and also and less formally "Tickets of Adoration."

Although the Adoration may have been disjunct from the Mass in time, it centered upon it. First, the Adoration was to be performed, if at all possible, in the presence of the Blessed Sacrament, reserved. Second, the Adoration employed the four classical modalities of prayer—adoring, thanking, expressing sorrow for sins, and requesting—to divide the hour into quarters.[95]

> Jesus, the august Priest and Victim on Calvary, offered the Sacrifice of the Cross to His Eternal Father as an act of Adoration, Thanksgiving, Reparation, and Petition, in the name of the whole human family. The Holy Sacrifice of the Mass, a continuation of Golgotha's oblation, has the same four-fold end and purpose. The Mass, the most sublime of all prayers, should be the chief devotion of every Catholic heart.[96]

The Adorations for the laity described in *SSac* at times consist of a program of sacramental education. In 1917, for example, Father A. Joseph Chauvin, SSS, wrote a series whose topics filled the entire calendar year. Their titles were "The Memorial of the Sacrifice of the Cross," "The Mass a Continuation of the Sacrifice of the Cross," "The Application of the Sacrifice of the Cross," "The Liturgy of the Mass—the Church," "The Liturgy of the Mass—the Altar," and "The Liturgy of the Mass—Sacred Vessels and Vestments."[97] Notice that each topic ran for two monthly issues, presumably because the material was trimmed to fit within one hour's Adoration.

These "Subjects for Adoration" for the laity that focus upon the Mass were theologically progressive as well as regressive. They might explain that the Mass was offered by the entire Church, not just by the priest, and that the devotees could and should unite themselves with the Masses that were transpiring someplace in the world. Chauvin tells the readers to join, during the Adoration, with "all the priests who are at this moment celebrating and offering to God the adoration of Jesus."[98] Thus each Adoration is at one with the perfect adoration that Jesus performed in his passion. Identification with the priest-celebrant and ownership of the Mass is also encouraged in the petition section of the Adoration. "O Jesus, my benevolent High Priest, grant that henceforth the celebration of the Sacred Mysteries be no longer in my eyes the affairs of the priest alone, the Mass his alone,—but that by *'my concurrence,'* it may become *'my celebration,'* it may be *'my affair, my Mass, my Sacrifice'"* (italics in original).[99] This sort of involvement of the laity in the enactment of the Mass, though purely spiritual, does point in the same direction as does the liturgical movement—toward ownership of the Mass.

On the regressive side, the interpretations of the ceremonies of the Mass smacked of the medieval in their allegorizing. The rubrics needed basic description, too, because many of the actions of the priest were invisible to the congregation. "At the breaking of the Host, the Church allows us to contemplate on the Cross the Body that was torn under the stripes of flagellation, under the points of the nails and the thorns. . . . Again, she desires to represent at the same time the breaking of the bread that Christ Himself made at the Last Supper."[100] Attention to the sufferings of Jesus fits into the prayer mode, "thanksgiving," because the devotee should feel grateful for the salvific actions of Our Lord.

The next fifteen minutes of the Adoration were dedicated to "reparation," or the examination of one's own life. In this particular series, Chauvin made reparation into a critique of one's own behavior, even etiquette, at Holy Mass. The lay adorer asked himself, "Am I exact in observing all the ceremonies prescribed for me by Holy Church when assisting at Mass?" and "How do I profit by the instructions of the Sacred Liturgy? Do I try to imbibe the liturgical spirit?"[101] But more importantly for our theme, the Adoration also promoted frequent and even liturgically "correct" Holy Communion. The adorer asked, "Am I persuaded that the best way to participate in the fruits of the Sacrifice is to communicate in the Divine Victim and in preference immediately after the Communion of the Celebrant?"[102] The "petition" segment of the Adoration likewise focused upon the Mass itself, rather than upon the particular and pressing needs of the adorer. "Ask the benevolent High Priest to give you great esteem for the ceremonies of the Mass," Chauvin advises.[103]

While the four modalities of prayer were not of his devising, Saint Pierre-Julien Eymard's contributions of other elements of the Adoration were significant. The prayer was allocated entirely to the mystery of the Real Presence of Jesus Christ in the sacrament of the altar. Second, he organized and systematized the Adoration by insisting upon the *full* hour of prayer, by making it essential to the Eucharistic associations he founded, and by instituting the *libelli*.

The monthly column that was an aid to this Adoration for the priests usually divided itself into four sections, corresponding to these classic modes of prayer. That the Adoration was directed by the doctrine of the Real Presence was enacted, ritually, by the adorer's proximity to the tabernacle.[104] From this contemplation of the tabernacle would come an enrichment of the faith because the tabernacle pointed to the "Eucharistic veil," which in turn referred to Jesus, then to his Heart, and finally to the love of this Heart.[105]

Because the Adoration lasted by obligation one hour exactly, and because of the overlapping of pious practices and devotions in the foment of the Eucharistic movement, the Adoration gradually and in practice became indistinguishable from the Holy Hour. This latter method was credited to Saint Margaret-Mary Alacoque in the apparitions of the Sacred Heart. Because the Adoration was to be done in the church building and while the devotee was oriented toward the tabernacle, it overlapped considerably with the idea of the Visit to the Blessed Sacrament.

The clearest evidence of the blurring of the Adoration and the Sacred Heart devotions comes from the pages of *EPUL*. For example, at the convention of the PEL in 1919, one committee insisted upon calling the Adoration by its official name, "The *Priestly* Hour of Adoration" (emphasis added), but at the same time urged the greater use of the Holy Hour in the parish and for the laity, and further urged that the priest's Adoration be completed at the public Holy Hour "wherever possible. The value of this practice to priest and people cannot be overestimated."[106]

Of course, because *EPUL* was reserved to the priests, the contents of its column "Subjects for Adoration" often treated particular needs of the clergy. For example, in 1911 a series of six "Subjects" discussed "priestly virtue."[107] On the other hand, the Adoration could serve as a preparation for Communion for the priest.[108]

The Adoration, exhibiting immense variety as performed by both layperson and cleric, generated much discussion in the popular Catholic press. For example, Father Frederick Faber (d. 1863) was cited on the topic of the Visit, specifically, but this was then applied by *SSac* to the Adoration. "The ways of visiting the Blessed Sacrament must be as various as the souls of men," said Faber. "In a word, there is no best way to spend the hour." Father Francis Reilly summarizes the point in quoting Faber about the Adoration, saying, "Each one makes it in the most natural way, and this is the best way for him."[109] *SSac* argues that the Adoration, irrespective of how it is done, will be beneficial.

One treatment of the Adoration recommended that it conclude with some form of the Visit to the Blessed Sacrament and that it be punctuated by "acts" of faith, hope, and love. This article even provides one such prayer: "Jesus, Jesus, Jesus, I believe in Thee, I hope in Thee, I love Thee with all my heart! I desire Thee, my sweet Saviour truly present in the Blessed Sacrament, come into my heart!"[110] Here is one pithy directive for the Adoration.

*Adoration*—Make an act of faith in the Real Presence, or read such an act from your prayer book. Acknowledge who Our Blessed Lord is, and who you are. Recite the Litany of the Sacred Heart slowly, pondering on each of Our Lord's titles and applying it to His life in the Blessed Sacrament.

*Thanksgiving*—Thank Our Lord for the grace of knowing His Real Presence, for the favor of your present visit, for anything He may have recently done for you. If you have been to Communion in the morning, do not fail to express your gratitude. You might, also, go over the Litany of the Sacred Heart once more! This time in thanksgiving.

*Reparation*—Read an act of reparation from your prayer book. Make an act of contrition for your own shortcomings since your last adoration. Recall what you promised Our Lord. Seek out the cause of your failures. Find out why the wishes of the Sacred Heart have met but faint echoes in your own heart, and resolve that in the future you will make more earnest efforts to meet these wishes.

*Prayer*—As intentions to be prayed for during the last quarter of an hour, you have, in the first place, the interests of Jesus. Father Faber thinks touchiness about the interests of Our Lord a happy sign in our spiritual life. Then come your own needs and those of relatives, friends, and benefactors. You must never forget the souls in purgatory. . . . Finally, say five Our Fathers and five Hail Marys for the intention of the Holy Father, to gain the Indulgences attached to the hour of adoration.[111]

Some entries in *EPUL* indicate that the entire hour should be communal; this could apply regularly to the laity in the parish, but for the clergy it especially applied when they were gathered for Eucharistic meetings.[112] In such circumstances as this common prayer, the entire hour could be preached, and some authors recommended series of sermons, presumably for the benefit of the laity.[113] Descriptions of the more usual Adoration for the priest give the impression that it was soothing and solitary meditation: "What a blessed relief to go apart into the church, shut the door on all the vexatious things that trouble us, and be alone with Our Lord! To sink on our knees with a sigh of relief, for a sweet converse with our understanding Friend. To lay before Him our problems, our hopes, and our plans."[114]

For the laity the hour of Adoration may have been solitary, but the Adoration was sometimes organized into bands of twelve persons, each of which was supervised by a "zelator," whose function was to "inquire if the members were faithful to their hour and make known to the Secretary any change of hour or residence, through the medium of a box placed in the church for this purpose."[115] Thus the layperson was made accountable for her Adoration, not by means of *libelli* but through the monitoring of the zelator.

Theoretically, *EPUL* had no need to urge that its own clerical readers receive Communion frequently because priests were obliged to communicate in fulfilling the rubrics of the Mass. On rare occasions the priests were reminded of their duty to say Mass every day. The members of the sacerdotal league received innumerable encouragements, both exhortative and practical, to increase the frequency with which their parishioners received Communion. Sometimes the worth of the priest's ministry was pegged to the number of communicants. *SSac* spoke directly to its readership with urgent appeals to receive Communion often.

PEL operated as a loose fraternal organization, self-governed under statutes, the heart of which were written by Saint Eymard. As the newsletter of the society, *EPUL* reported the activities of its members insofar as they fostered the Eucharistic reign of Christ—congresses, conventions at various administrative levels, proceedings, and sermons at these gatherings. The newsletter reported meticulously the deaths of members of the league and systematically assigned the offering of Masses for the deceased of the league. Within each month's number, leaguers are asked to pray for a list of intentions.

In contrast, PPL, while formally allied to the PEL through supervision of both leagues by the Fathers of the Blessed Sacrament and encouraged to participate in various functions of the Eucharistic movement, did not function as a self-governing society. Consequently, *SSac* provided no record of resolutions and policies, except as determined by its "Direction," the Fathers of the Blessed Sacrament.

## NOTES

1. Eugene P. Willging and Herta Hatzfeld, *Catholic Serials of the Nineteenth Century in the United States: A Descriptive Bibliography and Union List*, 15 volumes (Washington: Catholic, 1968); henceforth, *CS*.

2. *CS*, 15:68.

3. *CS*, 15:69.

4. *CS*, 15:69.

5. *CS*, 15:69.

6. *CS*, 4:iii.

7. *CS*, 15:iv. A pertinent solecism is *CS*'s statement that *SSac* was "founded, published, and edited by the *Fathers of the Blessed Sacrament* and was the organ of the People's Eucharistic League, which was founded in 1897."

8. *American Newspaper Annual and Directory*, 1924 edition.

9. *CS*, 4:25. All the information and the direct quotation in this paragraph come from *CS*.

10. *CS*, 14:136.

11. *CS*, 14:136–37.

12. *CS*, 14:137.

13. *CS*, 14:137. *CS*, 14:138.

14. *CS*, 14:137.

15. *CS*, 14:137.

16. *CS* notes that the Franciscans in Cincinnati published a German-language American edition, called *Der Sendbote des göttlichen Herzens Jesu*, under the auspices of the Jesuit-directed Apostleship of Prayer. *CS*, 11:70. John J. Wynne, "Apostleship of Prayer," *Catholic Encyclopedia*.

17. *CS*, 14:99.

18. *CS*, 11:71.

19. *CS*, 11:71.

20. *CS*, 11:70.

21. John Tracy Ellis, *American Catholicism*, 2nd revised edition (Chicago: University of Chicago Press, 1969), 108–9.

22. *CS*, 10:35.

23. *CS*, 10:35.

24. *CS*, 10:35.

25. *CS*, 1:33.

26. *CS*, 5:12.

27. *CS*, 5:12.

28. *CS*, 5:14.

29. *CS*, 5:14.

30. Average income for the United States in 1924 was $2,196; a loaf of bread cost nine cents, and a gallon of milk fifty-four cents. *1924: Pages of Time: A Nostalgia News Report* (Goodlettsville, Tennessee: Interactive, n.d.).

31. *CS*, 5:14.

32. *CS*, 14:146.

33. *The Official Catholic Directory*, 1922 edition, 65–71.

34. Bede Maler, Personal Records and Papers, Box 16, 1894–1903, Priests Eucharistic League—Correspondence, 1894–1903, Press Book 6, pp. 710–22, Saint Meinrad Archabbey Archives, Saint Meinrad, Indiana, to "Madam," unnamed woman, 3 May 1895, carbon copy of autograph letter.

35. Ralph Gibson, *French Catholicism*, 158.

36. Chinnici, "The Eucharist, Symbol of the Church," 146.

37. Dalgairns, *Devotion to the Heart of Jesus*, 62–63.

38. Often this polarizing of positions seems to have been rooted in "political" factors, such as rivalry between religious orders. For example, Maurice Festugière and Lambert Beauduin, two Benedictines, engaged in a "battle royal" with Jesuits who took great umbrage at the former's book, *La Liturgie catholique, essai de synthèse* (1913), which seemed to the Jesuits to denigrate their Apostleship of Prayer. Sonya A. Quitslund, *Beauduin: A Prophet Vindicated* (New York: Newman, 1973), 28.

39. Gibson, *French Catholicism*, 252.

40. John J. Wynne, "Apostleship of Prayer," *Catholic Encyclopedia*.

41. Actually the number treating Eucharistic devotion represents a larger number of individual works because authors with several in a given category may be listed only once or twice. For instance, Zulueta's name appears twice under "Frequent

Communion," but under Zulueta's name-entry, eleven titles refer to this topic substantially. Walter Romig, *The Guide to Catholic Literature* (Detroit: Walter Romig, 1940–1968), 1:415 and 1229. Romig, *Guide to Catholic Literature*, 1:755–57.

42. Romig, *Guide to Catholic Literature*, 1:530 and 912.

43. Romig, *Guide to Catholic Literature*, 1:415 and 1229.

44. Romig, *Guide to Catholic Literature*, 1:993.

45. "Fifty Years of Eucharistic Service," *EPUL* 51 (January 1945): 1.

46. "Fifty Years," 2.

47. "Fifty Years," 2–3.

48. Chinnici, "Eucharist," 146.

49. Bede Maler, "The Jubilee—Convention of the Priests' Eucharistic League in the US: 1894–1919," *EPUL* 25 (1919): 250.

50. "Statuta Associationis Sacerdotum Adoratorum seu Aggregationis Sacerdotalis Congregationi Ssmi. Sacramenti a R. P. Eymard Institutæ," *EPUL* 1 (1895): 5.

51. Vincent Wagner to Father Petre, 3 June 1897, carbon copy of autographed letter signed in Maler, Bede (1876–1937), Personal Records and Papers, Box 16, 1894–1903, Priests' Eucharistic League—Correspondence, 1894–1903, Press Book 6, Saint Meinrad Archabbey Archives, Saint Meinrad, Indiana, 522.

52. *ET*, 20n1.

53. "Supplement to the May Number of 'Emmanuel,'" *EPUL* 8 (1902): s. 1.

54. Thomas N. Taylor, "The Priests' Communion League for the Promotion of Daily Communion," in *Report of the Nineteenth Eucharistic Congress, Held at Westminster from 9th to 13th September, 1908* (London: Sands, 1909), 267.

55. Taylor, "Promotion of Daily Communion," 267.

56. Taylor, "Promotion of Daily Communion," 279.

57. Taylor, "Promotion of Daily Communion," 267.

58. Kirlin, Joseph L. J. "The Priests' Eucharistic League—Its Nature and Purpose," *EPUL* 32 (1926): 235.

59. "The Story of the Eucharistic Movement in the United States," *EPUL* 2 (1896): 49–52. *CS*, 4:35.

60. "A Retrospect of the Eucharistic Convention," *EPUL* 25 (1919): 410.

61. Tentler states, without documentation, that PEL was founded in Germany in 1879. The connection, then, between the German origins and the French direction is puzzling. Leslie Woodcock Tentler, *Seasons of Grace: A History of the Catholic Archdiocese of Detroit*, foreword by Edmund Cardinal Szoka (Detroit: Wayne State University Press, 1990), 170; Albert Kleber, *History of St. Meinrad Archabbey* (Saint Meinrad, Indiana: Grail, 1954), 390.

62. Even before Maler joined, two American bishops, Louis de Goesbriand (d. 1899) of Burlington, Vermont, and John C. Neraz (d. 1894) of San Antonio had enrolled. "The Story," 50. A few individual priests, probably familiar with the league from their seminary days in Europe, were also members, and the Sulpician Fathers may have been promoters of the league at the seminary in Baltimore. Fintan Mundwiler, "History and Present Status of the Eucharistic League in the United States," *American Ecclesiastical Review* n.s. 1, 11, no. 5 (November 1894): 329.

63. Camillus P. Maes, "The First Convention of the Eucharistic League in the United States," *American Ecclesiastical Review*, n.s. 1, 11, no. 5 (November 1894): 338.

64. Maler, "The Jubilee—Convention," 254–55.

65. Chinnici, "Eucharist," 147.

66. Maler, "The Jubilee—Convention," 255.

67. This title is collective for the several publications of several purposes, all initiated by Dom Bede and subjected to various alliances, supplements, and the like. See *CS*, 4:33–36. *Sankt Benedikts-Panier* was the official organ of "the Devotion and the Fraternity of the Holy Face," headquartered at Tours. This magazine claimed to be a "weapon against irreverence, swearing and desecration of the Sunday"—and so overlapped with the specialization of the Holy Name Society. *CS*, 4:35.

68. Maler, "The Jubilee—Convention," 255.

69. E. Bush, "Means of Propagating the League," *American Ecclesiastical Review*, n.s. 1, 11, no. 5 (November 1894): 351.

70. Bush, "Means of Propagating the League," 351.

71. Henry Brinkmeyer, "The Establishment of a Eucharistic Monthly," *American Ecclesiastical Review*, n.s. 1, 11, no. 5 (November 1894): 353.

72. Brinkmeyer, "Establishment of a Eucharistic," 353.

73. Brinkmeyer, "Establishment of a Eucharistic," 353.

74. Brinkmeyer, "Establishment of a Eucharistic," 353.

75. Brinkmeyer, "Establishment of a Eucharistic," 353–54.

76. Camillus P. Maes, "Salve, Adoratores," *EPUL* 1 (1895): 3.

77. "Bishop Maes and the Eucharistic League," *EPUL* (1917): 217.

78. E. J. Baumann, "Maes, Camillus Paul," *New Catholic Encyclopedia*.

79. J. F. Foley, "How to Promote Devotion to the Blessed Sacrament among the People," in *Eucharistic Conferences: The Papers Presented at the First American Eucharistic Congress, Washington, D.C., October, 1895* (New York: Catholic Book Exchange, 1896), 112–13.

80. "The People's Eucharistic League," *EPUL* 4 (1898): 57.

81. "In Memoriam [Eliza O'Brien Lummis]," *SSac* (1916): 150.

82. Michael J. Lavelle and Eliza O'Brien Lummis, "The People's Eucharistic League," *EPUL* 6 (1900): 36.

83. Lavelle and Lummis, "The People's Eucharistic League," 34.

84. Lay organizations included "the confraternities of the Blessed Sacrament, the Tabernacle Societies, the Associations of Nocturnal Adoration, of Communion of Reparation, the People's Eucharistic League, the Eucharistic League for Seminaries, the League of the Sacred Heart, the Apostleship of Prayer, etc." O.S.B., "Organization of the Eucharistic Movement: A Proposition Submitted to the Eucharistic Convention of Philadelphia, 1899," *EPUL* 5 (1899): 222. The confusion of contemporaries surfaces in the writing of the Reverend Thomas O'Brien, for one example. His paper at the New York Eucharistic Congress, meeting for three days in September 1904, asserted that the Confraternity of the Blessed Sacrament, "one of the oldest," was founded in Rome at the Dominican Church of the Minerva and was approved by the

pope in 1539; later he stated that the confraternity was founded by Saint Pierre-Julien Eymard. Thomas O'Brien, "Eucharistic Confraternities and the People's Eucharistic League," *EPUL* 11 (1905): 127–28.

85. O'Brien, "Eucharistic Confraternities," 131.

86. O'Brien, "Eucharistic Confraternities," 131. "The celebration of the feast of Corpus Christi at the cathedral, but six months after the formal organization of the Eucharistic League, marked the affiliation of the New York association to the work of Saint Eymard." "The People's Eucharistic League," 58.

87. "Second Report of the People's Eucharistic League," *EPUL* 4 (1898): 206.

88. "The People's Eucharistic League," 60.

89. Lavelle and Lummis, "The People's Eucharistic League," 36–37.

90. Lavelle and Lummis, "The People's Eucharistic League," 36–37.

91. "Second Report of the People's Eucharistic League," 205.

92. The archives of the Archdiocese of New York do not possess any of these original bulletins.

93. Emile Poirier, "Eucharistic Periodicals and Publications," *SSac* 21 (1918): 461–62.

94. "General Index," *SSac* 29 (1926): 792.

95. James French, "The Hours' Adoration," *EPUL* 15 (1909): 9.

96. "Archconfraternity of the Blessed Sacrament, or the People's Eucharistic League," *SSac* 19 (1916): 500.

97. "General Index," *SSac* 20 (1917): 3.

98. A. Joseph Chauvin, "Subject of Adoration: The Liturgy of the Mass—The Prayers," *SSac* 21 (1918): 58.

99. A. Joseph Chauvin, "Subject of Adoration: The Liturgy of the Mass—Its Ceremonies," *SSac* 21 (1918): 246.

100. Chauvin, "Ceremonies," 172.

101. Chauvin, "Ceremonies," 244–45.

102. Chauvin, "Ceremonies," 246. Exactly when the frequent Communions were to occur was a persistent issue between the liturgical movement and the Eucharistic movement. See chapter 7.

103. Chauvin, "Ceremonies," 247.

104. French, "The Hours' Adoration," 8.

105. French, "The Hours' Adoration," 4–5.

106. V.F.K. [*sic*], "A Retrospect of the Eucharistic Convention [at Notre Dame, Indiana]," *EPUL* 25 (1919): 401. See also John Henry Nawn, "The People's Eucharistic League," *EPUL* 31 (1925): 47.

107. "How to Erect New Centres of the People's Eucharistic League," *EPUL* 17 (1911): 206.

108. "The Priests' Eucharistic League—Its Nature and Purpose," *EPUL* 32 (1926): 236.

109. A.J.V. [*sic*], "Archconfraternity of the Blessed Sacrament, or People's Eucharistic League: What It Is and How to Join It," *SSac* 24 (1921): 371.

110. "Spiritual Communion," *SSac* 14 (1911): 75.

111. A.J.V., "Archconfraternity of the Blessed Sacrament," 371–72.

112. "Editor's Notes," *EPUL* 32 (1926): 279; and "History and Present Status of the PEL in the United States," *EPUL* 32 (1926): 249.

113. "The Third Eucharistic Diocesan Congress of Rome," *EPUL* 27 (1921): 258ff.; Charles F. Curran, "Sermon Plans for the Weekly Adoration Hour," *EPUL* 43 (1937): 246.

114. "The Priests' Eucharistic League—Its Nature and Purpose," *EPUL* 32 (1926): 237.

115. "The People's Eucharistic League: Philadelphia Report," *EPUL* 6 (1900): 40–41.

## Chapter Five

# Promotion of and Opposition to Frequent Communion

*EPUL* detailed techniques with which the priests could promote frequent Communion among the laity. These pastoral efforts were usually reported in detail at myriad clerical Eucharistic conferences and conventions at all levels—diocesan, metropolitan, national, international. "Papers" constituted much of the programs of these meetings, but they were hardly academic. Lacking both the proper substance and style, they rather preached the very concept of frequent Communion and then proposed schemes for securing the compliance of the laity in this "restoration" of the earliest practice of the Church. These mostly similar schemes overwhelmingly were firsthand accounts of success by the presenters.

*EPUL* provides a spotty record of these many meetings. *Ssac* seconded the efforts of *EPUL*, but less with proceedings and papers, and more with anecdotes about the fruits of frequent Communion, sententious encouragements for it, tales of the miracles of Communion and the Blessed Sacrament, and so forth. *Ssac* tried to persuade the laity, its audience, directly.

*EPUL*'s editorial emphasis on promoting frequent Communion seems to have cycled through the years from 1905 through 1926. Calls for and discussions of the benefits of frequent Communion numbered six in 1905, as if in anticipation of *STS*. Twin peaks of the upland trend that ran to 1916 occurred in 1907 and 1909; the average number of articles appearing in each volume from 1905 to 1916 was nearly seven. The late teens and early twenties form the valley, with an average of only one article per year. The mid-twenties witness a topical resurgence—1925 tallied five articles and 1926 tallied six.[1] Presumably because of firsthand knowledge of the rates of receptions of Communion, the priest-editors of these magazines and the organizers of the meetings about the Eucharist saw progress and then a decline in the frequency of reception; they all then redoubled their efforts in the 1920s.

An initial burst of fervor often accompanies a major change in ritual policy, as it did with the vernacularization of the rites in the early 1960s. A subsequent period of consolidation lacks the thrill of novelty and innovation, and so can be perceived as retrogression. Joseph Kramp, SJ (d. 1940), saw a relative decline in the frequency of reception as evidence that devotions connected with communicating actually discouraged receiving and so were "exaggerated and unnatural."[2] According to him, greater frequency of Communion clashed with devotional practices among Catholics in the nineteenth century that were rooted in and suited to God's fearsomeness. He wrote, "Are the prevailing communion devotions of the faithful psychologically possible? Can the soul be depressed by a clear consciousness of its nothingness and at the same moment be elevated to the heights of intensest love and devotion?"[3]

## MEETINGS TO PROMOTE
## FREQUENT HOLY COMMUNION

To detail the varieties—and possibly to discern an evolutionary pattern—of the monster meetings of the Eucharistic movement lies beyond our scope. Rallies and conventions and congresses were made possible by the expansion of the railroad, and such events in support of all manner of causes were a distinctive mark of the late nineteenth and early twentieth centuries. For instance, the editor of *Ssac* quoted approvingly the plan for the promotion of Marian devotion.

> Mass meetings and public assemblies are the order of the day. . . . They are dear to the heart of the times—rallies, congresses, conventions—how they stir public interest, rouse enthusiasm, bring like-minded people closer together! The sight of a great concourse of folk, gathered for a single purpose, stirs the blood and warms the heart. Why should not this great means of stimulating interest and stirring zeal be used to glorify the Mother of God, and spread devotion to her name?[4]

As this quotation reveals, the Eucharistic movement stood not alone in utilizing congresses and other vast gatherings; pilgrimages, as well as Gregorian and Marian congresses, also involved large assemblages of people.[5] Large-scale meetings characterized the founding of political movements, and even of the Catholic and antiliberal parties of Belgium.[6] Meetings of all dimensions became the first and preeminent means of promoting the Eucharistic Kingdom of Christ.

The first International Eucharistic Congress in Lille in 1881 set a pattern for the two basic components, worship and colloquy. Worship was both liturgical and devotional; significantly, these categories would have been anachronistic to the congressists. Liturgically, Masses abounded—pontifical, requiem, and "communion"; but the Divine Office absented itself from the program. Eucharistic, popular devotions, such as the Holy Hour, served as a staple. Some rituals seem to have been composed for the congresses, and they grew in elaboration and grandeur over the years. The most remarkable example of this was the ceremonial welcome of the Papal Legate.[7] But the final procession and Benediction, though drawn from ancient and accepted Catholic customs, was unquestionably the climax of the meetings. Its preeminence was clear in the organization of the thirteenth chapter of the official report of the Twenty-Eighth International Eucharistic Congress of Chicago, 1926; the chapter, "The Eucharistic Procession," described the entire concluding day of the congress and subordinated the Mass to the procession. The epigraph to the chapter summarized it:

> GREATEST Single Day's Migration in Chicago History—How the Crowds Travelled—Many Spent Preceding Night in the Open—Description of People Arriving on Grounds—800,000 Persons Present—Preparations Made for the Mass—A Beautiful Setting—The Prelates Take Their Places, Escorting Papal Legate—Officers of the Mass—Sermon by Cardinal Hayes—Devotion Overcomes Discomfort—Recreation While Awaiting Hour of Procession—The Order of Participants—People Line Roadway Around Lake—Greeting to Units Changes to Devotion as Blessed Sacrament Approaches—Cardinal Bonzano Carries Ostensorium—Thunder Rolls, Rain and Hail Fall—Procession Does Not Falter—Sun Shines Again—Devotion Increases—Benediction at Cross—Recessional—The Rush Homeward—A Miracle of Transportation—Explanation of Congestion—Pageantry of Procession—The Floats—Repairing Damage to the Grounds.[8]

The concluding procession conveyed, and was meant to convey, the political strength of the Catholic Church. While its description included vignettes of piety, the procession was a parade in essence and experience. Its route at Chicago was three miles long. Lay participants formed three divisions:

> Division number two, led by De LaSalle band, included the Knights of Columbus float, "Columbus bringing Faith to America;" the Slovak unit; the Slovenian unit and the boys' band of Visitation parish, Garfield Blvd., Chicago. Following was the Father Marquette float, "Marquette Bringing Faith to Chicago;" the Holy Name Society; the Croatian Unit; the Belgian Unit; the Hungarian Unit.[9]

The laity prepared the way for the clerical contingent, and this, too, manifested the hierarchical nature of the Church:

> The Clergy and prelates were arranged in the following order: Priests—(a) Members of religious orders; (b) secular clergy. 1. Vested in Cassock and

surplice. 2. In vestments. Monsignori. Abbots—(a) Mitred abbots, bishops, archbishops, papal attendants to Cardinals, Cardinals, attendants to legate, Papal Legate carrying the Blessed Sacrament, with bearers of the Canopy.[10]

The ultimate presence of the Blessed Sacrament in the monstrance and under the canopy did not preclude festivity. "Because of the length there is a long wait as the different units pass, each acknowledged in turn by faithful, interested friends. Due recognition is given to all representatives by the spectators who are strung out into ribbons of humanity."[11] The mood did grow solemn as the Blessed Sacrament approached a particular section of spectators:

> A hush comes over the faithful as the sound of a tinkling bell reaches their ears, indicating the nearer approach of the Papal Legate, bearing the Blessed Sacrament. All kneel devoutly as Cardinal Bonzano comes into view through the double line of Knights of Columbus standing at attention, bearing aloft the silver Ostensorium. His eyes fixed, his lips moved in prayer, his steps measured. Acolytes strewed roses in his path. Before him the Censors moved rhythmically.[12]

By far this was the most magnificent of closing ceremonies for an American Eucharistic gathering and aptly proportionate to the scale of the first international congress in the United States. Virtually all Eucharistic conferences, even small, local, and specifically clerical meetings, concluded with processional displays simultaneously of faith in the Blessed Sacrament and of Catholic clout.

Worship at these Eucharistic meetings was structurally identical to practices available in parishes, but magnified and ennobled. Worship by the sacerdotal fraternity contributed integrally to one main purpose of the Priests' Eucharistic League (PEL) as articulated in Bishop Maes's introductory letter to the first edition of *EPUL*, the "sanctification of the priesthood."[13] A significant element of the public prayer at meetings of the reverend leaguers was the solidarity the priests enjoyed in the ritual actions. For instance, several commentators note the thrill felt by all the priests encircling the altar and reciting the Pater Noster with arms extended, cruciformly, during these meetings.[14] One element of Saint Pierre-Julien Eymard's original mission was to boost the morale of the secular priests and thus to stanch departures from the priesthood.

## PRESENTATIONS AT THE MEETINGS AND IN PRINT

The pragmatic papers on encouraging frequent Communion of the laity reveal the theological underpinnings and pastoral attitudes of the members of the

PEL, and they form a considerable amount of the material that both edified the leaguers at meetings and then appeared in *EPUL*. The copious matter is most expeditiously described first with respect to the role of the priest in encouraging frequent Communion. These papers addressed, through an overly zealous interpretation of *STS*, the theological issue of the necessity of frequent Communion; they also imagined the reluctance and even the objections of the clergy, and preempted them. The priestly promoters' techniques for multiplying the numbers of Communions and communicants were elaborated and, at some meetings, even subjected to robust criticism. These techniques included adjusting the schedule of Masses; persistence, both in preaching and in counseling in the confessional; instituting a Eucharistic triduum annually; and, most importantly, social organization.

*EPUL*, as the in-house organ for the PEL, could not have retained any opposition to the very idea of frequent, even daily, Holy Communion. Papers at conferences generally argued by declaration, and they only needed to declare that Pius X said two things: that the laity should communicate frequently, even daily, and that the priests were obliged to encourage this "restoration" of sacramental practice. Elaborations of this argument simply glossed *STS*. Loyalty to the Holy Father was gauged by one's promotion of frequent Communion. The exact application of *STS* seems to have been worked out not in individual commentaries but in vigorous exchanges. For example, one extremist, Father L. F. Schlathoelter of Troy, Missouri, tried to argue not only that frequent Communion was advisable or beneficial, but that it was also absolutely necessary for salvation.[15] While the ideal of frequent Communion was publicly unassailable by virtue of its issuance by the Vatican and clear support from the pope, such an extremity of interpretation was quickly and cogently dismissed.[16]

## OPPOSITION TO FREQUENT COMMUNION

In the Catholic ethos of the time, explicit resistance in print to *STS* was inconceivable. Expansively apply the hermeneutical principle that laws only exist if the crimes they proscribe do, in fact, occur. In the context of liturgical scholarship, Paul Bradshaw states the principle in this way: "Regulations provide excellent evidence for what was actually happening in local congregations, not by what is decreed should be done but by what is either directly prohibited or indirectly implied should cease to be done."[17] The vast amount of literature on ways of promoting frequent Communion indicates two things. First, the immemorial custom of infrequent Communion was vigorously resisting change even among priests. Second, while this may simply be attributed to the inertia of custom and habit, an inherent conservatism, the crusaders for the implementation of *STS* articulated "theological" excuses for the resistance. Papers addressed the proper zeal for promoting frequent Communion and tried to disable the putative bars against promoting it. The alleged objections, scrupulously absent from the literature, were not even addressed by the proponents, and all were lumped into the ignominious category of "prejudices."

The persistence of obstacles to such a profound change in liturgical and devotional practice as frequent Communion is well witnessed in the literature. Zulueta, the translator of Father Lintelo, summarized the "vain fears":

> Many difficulties and misgivings—there is question here only of religious, spiritual, or ascetical ones—may occur, and evidently do occur, to clerical and lay minds. For example, our unworthiness, our backwardness in virtue, our ill-tamed passions, lapses into grievous sin, fear lest some may be led to receive sacrilegiously, a dread of evils commonly expressed by those very vague terms, "want of reverence" and "overfamiliarity," the danger of carelessness in preparation and thanksgiving, diminution of devotion in receiving, or, what is constantly mistaken for this, mere dulness of the emotions and lack of sensible experiences, such as must almost inevitably result from habitual Communion, or any other daily religious exercise, daily celebrations of Holy Mass not excepted, as priests may candidly admit.[18]

Zulueta so described the misgivings of those who were resisting frequent Communion so as to preclude genuinely theological or spiritual qualms; typically, the proponents effectively curtailed discussion. The linchpin of the "restoration" of frequent and even daily Communion was that the pope willed it for all Catholics, and if the pope willed it, so did Christ. Books on the topic, which were often serialized or excerpted in *EPUL* and *Ssac*, used John 6 as a proof text to support this intention. To guarantee that frequent Communion was not seen as an innovation, these authors then ran through all of church history: The Fathers of the Church always advocated frequent Communion. The Middle Ages had much less need for Communion because the Church was so holy then, and the Protestants and Jansenists, for opposite reasons, denigrated the Blessed Sacrament. The saints and notables of the Counter-Reformation who advised frequent Communion were likewise marshaled to support Pope Pius X's program.

The self-accusation of unworthiness was countered by pointing out that the Blessed Mother, too, was unworthy of such intimate, physical contact with God, but that the love of God, in Christ, willed this contact. Better to do the will of God than to cling to one's unworthiness. Correlatively, the legal terms of *STS* that required only freedom from mortal sin before communicating were trumpeted incessantly. The answers to the prejudice that frequent Communion would cause a decline in the sense of "fervor" usually mobilized two elements. The first answer highlighted two aspects: Frequent communion would generally be accompanied by adequate preparation and thanksgiving to sustain fervor. Communion itself, properly understood, was an excellent preparation and thanksgiving for subsequent Communions. The second, a theoretical or theological answer, relied upon the dogma of Catholic sacramental theology: While one's dispositions for a sacrament might exert some effect, the action of Christ in the sacrament, *ex opere operato*, by virtue of the divine will, must benefit the soul.[19]

The literature also took into account the practical and broader sacramental context of receiving. Two issues attracted the most attention: The first was the need to break the bond between Communion and confession. The second was that ecclesial legislation insisted upon both penance and the reception of Communion at Easter; thus, a link had been forged and a pattern of sacramental praxis been established for centuries.

The origins of a virtual indissolubility of always going to confession immediately before going to Communion in the lived sacramental system of the Church presents an issue too complex for exhaustive treatment here. Suffice it to observe that an emphasis upon the Real Presence of the Redeemer, God and man, in the sacramental species—that is, an emphasis upon the utterly transcendent within the sacramental Body and Blood—gave rise to worries about impurity and unworthiness on the part of the communicant.

Indeed, it is in the context of connections between the Eucharist and penance that we meet the most common putative objection of the clergy to implementation of the decrees of Pius X. Given the status quo of sacramental practice, the expansion of Communions, ceteris paribus, might have generated an exponential growth in the numbers of penitents and hence an unbearable increase in the allocation of pastoral energies to the confessional.

The pontiff himself seems to have met this issue head on in the issuance, very shortly after the promulgation of *STS*, of an instruction on plenary indulgences. Plenary indulgences could be had by the fulfilling of codified sets of pious practices, but most usually the indulgences required confession, Communion, and prayers for the intentions of the pope. While the sets could vary widely, the subset of confession, Communion, and prayers for the pope became a norm, and so was abbreviated in briefs on indulgences simply as the "usual conditions." The earning of these plenary indulgences seems to have been foremost in the minds of many of the American faithful, who followed the prescriptions for the indulgences meticulously.[20] With the promulgation of *STS*, Communion reception was to become more frequent, but the earning of plenary indulgences obligated the use of the sacrament of penance as well. One salubrious effect of Holy Communion was the prevention of sin. If one was a daily communicant, therefore, one had virtually no need of penance—generally and ideally speaking—because sin was only a remote and rare occurrence. However, even the pious daily communicants wanted to earn indulgences, which were applicable, via reparation, to the poor souls in purgatory; and, for this rich indulgence, one was obligated to confess. To reduce the anticipated demands upon confessors, as they would be inundated by devotional penitents, Rome spoke:

> The Sacred Congregation of Indulgences declared, February 14, 1906, that those who receive Communion daily, or nearly so, can gain plenary indulgences without being bound to confess regularly every week, or every fortnight, or even every month. By this ordinance, the Sovereign Pontiff has wished to emphasize the practical character of the decree [*STS*], and to remove all obstacles to its most thorough application.[21]

This decision had as its ultimate end, of course, the encouragement of frequent Communion by all the laity.

*EPUL*, both in independent articles and in the papers presented at Eucharistic meetings, addressed the alarmist prediction of too many penitents in two ways. First, *STS* specified that the only required disposition for communicating was that a person be free of mortal sin. Venial sins themselves were expunged by receiving Communion; thus, Holy Communion was often styled a "remedy." Second, and logically developed from the papal decree, the anticipated explosive increase of confession duty was denied flatly. Rather than spending more time in the confessional, the priest whose parish implemented frequent Communion would actually spend less. But, to encourage frequent Communion, priests should be more available, and on days and at times more convenient to the laity.[22] Pope Pius X himself advised the faithful, "Do not spare your priests; go to Confession; keep them in the Confessional. Go to Holy Communion until their arms drop from weariness."[23] A large reduction of time spent hearing confessions would result, logically, from Pius's teaching. Thus the strongest objection to frequent Communion among the clergy was not only debunked, but reversed.

But one element of American Catholicism, its Irish roots, may well have impeded the campaigns for frequent Communion, the most prominent aspect of the broader Eucharistic movement. Irish American Catholicism may be tainted, through properly Irish Catholicism, with infamous Jansenism.

How Irish was the American Roman Catholic Church in the nineteenth century? The massive emigration of the Irish to the United States because of the potato famine of 1848 began their dominance of the Catholic Church in

America. "The midcentury Irish emigration created the first large, sustained membership growth spurt of the American Catholic Church, and Ireland's efforts to provide for the spiritual needs of its emigrants laid the groundwork for the long dominance of Irish Americans in the American clergy and hierarchy."[24] As the Catholic Church in Ireland identified itself with Irish nationalism and became institutionally vibrant under the leadership of Paul Cardinal Cullen (d. 1878), it was able to send many priests from its surplus to the United States. Between 1842 and 1890, All Hallows (the Irish seminary for the foreign missions) sent more than six hundred priests to the United States; six of these became bishops, and one a cardinal.[25] One handy gauge of the influence of the Irish and Irish Americans in the American Roman Catholic Church is membership in the episcopal college. "From the 1850s through the 1880s, the Irish, including native priests of Irish descent, accounted for roughly half the consecrations, rising to 60 percent in the 1890s and to 75 percent by the early 1900s . . . despite the fact that Germans by that time accounted for at least a quarter of American Catholics."[26] From the realm of the popular comes this evidence of the dominance of the Irish in the Catholic Church: Being Catholic cohered with being Irish, at least in conflicts over popular devotions from the old country. Robert Orsi details this in the drawn-out conflict over the local Italian festival in New York's Harlem around the turn of the century.[27] Although this evidence is suggestive, its diversity supports what stands unquestioned in the historiography: that the Irish dominated the American Roman Catholic Church.

Was the character, then, of Irish American Roman Catholicism Jansenistic? It depends upon the operative definition of *Jansenism*, a word so resistant to clarification. One writer conflates rigorism and Jansenism and sexual repression.

> Irish rigorism is conventionally attributed to Jansenism imported from Europe by French-trained Irish priests. There is some truth to the story, but it is far too simple an explanation. There was a French influence at Maynooth, the most important Irish seminary, but it tended toward an anti-Vatican nationalistic stance that placed the faculty and Cullen at swords' point for much of his tenure. Cullen's rigorist party, as often as not, were recruited from the Irish College in Rome, which he controlled. The fact that Protestants preached the same rigorist sexual doctrine points to local sources for Irish attitudes.[28]

Problems and questions abound in this citation. Maynooth was founded in the late eighteenth century, and Jansenism had been officially dead since the late seventeenth. Insofar as Jansenism allied itself with Gallicanism, it, too, would have been "anti-Vatican and nationalistic."

The point is that historians doubt the simple formulation of Jansenism flowing from France to Ireland. That the Irish middle class was sexually restrained seems indisputable; the causes of such restraint are not so clear.

> One must be very cautious in applying the term "Jansenistic" to the severe and anxious strain which undoubtedly developed in Irish middle-class Catholic spirituality in the eighteenth century. It is true that a severe and anxious spirituality was now the dominant characteristic of French Jansenism, and it is likewise true that by far the greater number of the Irish clergy now received their theological formation in France, but the Irish institutions there had a record of opposition to Jansenism, and while the clergy undoubtedly returned with some Gallican leanings, the Jansenist strain must have been slight.[29]

Once again, the concept of Jansenism when applied in Ireland pertains in large measure to sexual mores and not to frequency of recourse to the sacrament of the Eucharist. If not derived from French Jansenism, this Irish pessimism may derive from the influence of English spiritual writers such as Challoner, and Irish culture, even from pre-Christian roots, predisposes to such pessimism.[30] Indeed, Jansenism, too, qualifies as pessimistic about human nature, as its doctrine of the paucity of souls that would be saved shows. Irrespective of the source of this pessimism, insofar as it results in profound self-conceptions of unworthiness, it would deter frequent Holy Communion so long as Communion was understood as reward for piety and virtue. This metaphor of "reward" was easily and generally inferred from the prevailing advice of the moral theologians to regulate frequency of Communion according to dispositions and benefits of the individual souls.

## PIOUS ASSOCIATIONS FOR FREQUENT COMMUNION

The PEL swam in an ocean of American fraternalism. The period between the Civil War and 1900 was the "Golden Age" of associations: 20 to 40 percent of the male population of the United States was involved in some sort of lodge—prototypically, the Masons—and they created in the lives of most Americans a "massive presence."[31] A pervasive principle was, in order to accomplish any goal, associate. The Eucharistic movement partook of this ethos and thus won compliance with the papal thrust for more, and more frequent, Holy Communion. "Organization is the watchword of the day, in politics, in business, in religion; and we have most illustrious examples of it in our Eucharistic Congresses, in the 'Priests' Eucharistic League,' in the 'People's Eucharistic League,' and many kindred spiritual organizations."[32] An avalanche of papers by members of the PEL urged that local clubs be formed that would take as their mission both general devotion to the Eucharist and more frequent reception of it. Within these various associations, Communion of ever-increasing frequency was at least encouraged but more often required. The more precisely oriented frequent-Communion societies were highly recommended to priests for the benefit of young people, especially as a means of exerting peer pressure to counteract the weight of old-fashioned and parental practice of Communion only at Easter. Sacerdos, who contributed many articles to *EPUL*, wrote, "The formation of circles whose members promise a certain number of Communions every week, the times of Lent and Advent, the months of the Sacred Heart of Our Lady, and St. Joseph, the feast of some favorite saint, the forming of spiritual bouquets—all these are practices in the treasure-chest of the apostle of daily Communion for children."[33] As with the clerical associations, a confusing plethora of organizations for the laity witnesses the vitality of the Eucharistic movement.

The second reason for forming associations to increase the frequency of Communion was the awareness that social pressure not to communicate was formidable. This had been evident in the times of Ignatius Loyola, when Communion, if frequently received, was done in secret, and it persisted into the twentieth century. "A daily Communicant was a marked man or more often woman, marked either as presumptuous or as a sacrilegious hypocrite."[34]

Let us study the case of just one such association called the Frequent Communion Guild. Because Father Francis Cassilly, SJ (d. 1938), of Chicago, was specifically invited to the Eucharistic Congress of Cincinnati (1911) to disseminate the Frequent Communion Guild, his association seems in some sense exemplary—at least to one founder and eventually the official protector of the league, Bishop Camillus Maes. Cassilly reported great success in organizing "guards of honor" for the Eucharist. The success was measurable by the spontaneous spread of the local club from one boys' college to many other educational institutions, and more importantly by the number of Communions received. Cassilly reported, "In a day college, where the total number of Communions, registered by an association of 240 members during the first month of its existence, was 800, it rose during the last month to 2,480, giving an average of more than ten Communions for each member.[35] Cassilly did not claim, however, initiative for the founding of the guard; he modestly reported that he "somehow" became "closely connected" with it.[36] Father Michael Hoferer, SJ (d. 1947), of Saint Ignatius College, Chicago, seems to have been the initiator.[37] Though unnamed in Cassilly's account, Hoferer preached and taught vigorously the principles of *STS*, but this strategy resulted only in a short surge of Communions.

Cassilly believed that the fundamental concept of association, initially so successful in the controlled environment of a college of boys, could yet be applied universally, and so he moved to expand and even thought to secure approval from the pope. According to Cassilly, the advantage of the guard, in contrast to the PEL, was that his group focused exclusively on reception of the Blessed Sacrament while the latter demanded "hours of adoration and visits of the Blessed Sacrament, but did not require frequent Communion."[38]

An account in *EPUL*, from Cassilly's address to the Eucharistic Congress in Cincinnati, omitted an explanation of how the name changed, but more significantly omitted the organizational origins of the guard/guild. The new name did match its avowed purpose and scope—the implementation of *STS*.[39] "It should be noted that this name [Frequent Communion Guild] was adopted at the above-mentioned conference as more appropriate and specific."[40] Cassilly did not provide in his account the original format of the club or its institutional setting, for the unnamed Hoferer had actually been attempting to implement *STS* within a junior sodality, of which he was director.[41]

Early twentieth-century sodalities were constituted into "sections," which adopted particular programs of action and spheres of influence.[42] Hoferer's "guard of honor" was actually a "Eucharistic section" of the junior sodality. This section comprised those sodalists who "pledged to do what the Holy Father had urged upon all students in Catholic schools. Concrete results were at once secured. The boys had committed themselves to a definite plan of action, and they proceeded to carry it out."[43] The guard of honor may have originally been, or was at other sites, a cadre of exemplary students who escorted the Blessed Sacrament in the annual procession of Corpus Christi.[44] As *STS* exerted its influence, the guard evolved into a society for receiving Communion, even as the Eucharistic piety of the church evolved from devotional to sacramental.

Within the guild, rank was earned straightforwardly. To enroll, a lad pledged to communicate once per week, but a holder of the third degree needed to communicate daily.[45] The origins of the guild could have enslaved it to elitism, since, as part of the sodality, it was already exclusively prestigious in three ways. First, the sodality required certain devotional activities for membership; indeed, one requirement of membership in the sodality, at least in places where sodality membership accompanied *first* Communion, was a pledge for monthly Communion, quite pious in those days and an anticipation of *STS*.[46] Second, membership was pleasing to teachers and administrators; sodalists must have ingratiated themselves to these authorities to be enrolled. Third, and this in reference to the guard/guild particularly, the names and ranks of members of the Eucharistic section were especially advertised—this an addition to the badge that all sodalists wore. Fortunately, the egalitarianism of *STS* motivated a recasting of the sodality:

It was evident to all [at the meeting of directors of the guard in June 1911] that the plan of organization must not be exclusive, that it must be the practical working expression of our Holy Father's decree on frequent Communion, and that it must have no limits not indicated in the decree itself. It was recognized likewise that the work could in nowise be restricted to Sodality membership, and that, if the Greater Glory of God is to be consulted, it must spread as an independent organization to schools, establishments and places of every kind where no Sodality exists, or can exist.[47]

Priests, either in schools or in parishes, usually initiated these clubs for driving up numbers of Communions. For one contrastive example, however, consider a similar organization under the aegis of the Fathers of the Blessed Sacrament. These official promoters of Eucharistia advertised in 1917 for applicants to "The Association of the Knights of the Blessed Sacrament."[48] Its overarching purpose, as explained to the clerical readers of *EPUL*, was to foster Catholicism and "an ardent love for Jesus Christ in the Most Blessed Sacrament."[49] Thus, it is not totally dedicated to frequent Communion. In a contemporaneous edition of *Ssac*, the purposes of the organization are listed. These included the Eucharistic emphasis but added the association's preventative power. The association existed "to foster in youthful hearts the spirit of our holy religion and an ardent love for Jesus Christ in that Treasure and Glory of our time-honored Church, the Blessed Sacrament of the Altar; . . . To shield them [the knights] from the numerous and subtle dangers that crop up on every side."[50]

The frontispiece of this particular issue featured the uniformed members of the association at the parish staffed by the Blessed Sacrament Fathers in New York City, with brass band. It served young men, ages eleven to seventeen, and seemed to provide a pious association for those too young yet for membership in the Holy Name Society.[51] Knights were likened to "bodyguards," as if to undermine notions that practicing the faith was girlish.[52] Only five years later, *EPUL* informed its readership of the existence of "The Knights and Handmaids of the Blessed Sacrament," which has been "recently inaugurated." However, that the title of this later notice reads simply "Knights of the Blessed Sacrament" suggests descent from "The Association of the Knights of the Blessed Sacrament" of the 1917 notice. While the membership of the 1922 association was open to religious and priests, its original purpose was to assist the laity; it was not so limited as had been the 1917 group in age range or sex, for it included, "ladies, young ladies, men and young men."[53] Its avowed purpose lacked the very specific articulation of Cassilly's Frequent Communion Guild, for it broadened that somewhat in comprising "a Crusade to promote frequent Communion *and* the chivalrous service of Our Lord in the Blessed Sacrament" (emphasis added).[54] "Chivalrous service" seems to have encompassed various devotions, such as marching on the feast of Corpus Christi and even dressing in prerevolutionary livery. Again, *chivalry* denotes noble virility.

Sometimes a bold scheme, ostensibly and solely targeted to the promotion of more and more frequent Communion, was dignified with the title "sodality," even though it did not subscribe to the structure of the true sodality. F. A. Purcell's paper at the International Eucharistic Congress in Amsterdam (1924) minimized the social-organizational elements, even though he wanted to retain the title "sodality." In this respect, his idea was similar to the PEL. His proposal also illustrated another category of "papers" presented at Eucharistic meetings—namely, those which sought to increase compliance with *STS* by outlining logistics. What adjustments in a parish would encourage more frequent Communion?

His solution was twofold. First, he urged that confession be more available. Then he suggested that, to manage the harvest of communicants from this innovation, the parish be regimented into four squads that were assigned to communicate on specified Sundays of the month. Again, for ease of administration and supervision, the squads were segregated into men, women, boys, and girls. Each squad was dignified with the title *sodality*.[55] To call such squads sodalities impoverished real ones, for the only function of the squads was boasting about the number of communicants, as this information was both recorded and publicized. To attain satisfactory numbers, each squad was subdivided into platoons, headed by sergeants who monitored both attendance at Mass and Communion reception. Purcell vaguely allowed for the possibility of inserting this scheme into extant clubs, associations, and the like. As if all the moral and spiritual good of such a scheme were insufficient motivation, he presented a fiscal motive to the reverend pastors:

> Let the parish priest who is worrying over his parish debt concentrate upon the frequent Communion of his people and his temporal embarrassments will vanish like the mist before the rising sun. . . . It is important to foster the spiritual ideal even from a selfish, material motive, for the more devout our people are, the more they will give toward the support of the church.[56]

Purcell established the explicit aim of these "sodalities" as the increasing of frequent Communion, and he subscribed to the transformative power of more frequent Communion for the good of the world, especially in the quelling of concupiscence.

Historical cataclysms also helped to specialize aggregations that promoted Eucharistia. One such organization grafted both an antiquarianism and an interest in international peace onto a Eucharistic stock. In the early 1920s an attempt was made to organize a Eucharistic Peace Crusade. Recruiting for this group relied upon discerning the cause of the First World War in the failure of the nations of Europe to acknowledge the Real Presence of Christ in the Blessed Sacrament, as the Eucharistic Congress at Lourdes (1914) had pleaded. It further enlisted all crusaders in the actions of the pending Eucharistic Congress in Rome, a congress that would emphasize, at the behest of the pope, that Jesus was the King of Peace. However, this aggregation was largely mystical, for membership was immediate upon the recital of the following pledge while the aspirant oriented himself to the tabernacle:

> Jesus, King of Peace, really present in the Blessed Sacrament, I want to be one of Your Crusaders. I now form the intention of offering up my Masses, Communions, and Adorations for Your Triumph at the International Eucharistic Congress in Rome in May, 1922. O Mary, my good Mother, Queen of Peace and Lady of the Most Blessed Sacrament, help me to be a loyal Crusader.[57]

Besides the spiritual fruits of this crusadership, one's participation in the Roman International Eucharistic Congress of 1922 was affected not only by preparatory prayer but also by the symbolic offering by the pope of all the paper records of all the members' offerings—of Masses, Communions, and Adorations—for peace. There is no way to validate these reports. The form for recording one's contributions was printed in the advertising section of *Ssac*; subsequent treatment of the legal niceties of rendering these accounts shows that the Fathers of the Blessed Sacrament who ran the crusade put great stock in this accounting. An obvious parallel may be drawn to the *libelli* demanded of the priests in PEL. Published reports listed numbers of Masses, Communions, and Adorations offered for the success of the Roman Congress, in three categories—men, women, and children.[58] Note that this aggregation differed significantly from Cassilly's, especially in promoting three pieties—Masses, reception of Communion, and visits to the Blessed Sacrament that consisted in Adoration—and in guaranteeing the privacy of the member.

Examples of these sorts of associations abound, but their essential similarities obviate any further elaboration.[59] Documentation of the actual extent of these societies, and similar, unreported ones, is lacking. Even the advertisements for some of these clubs carefully distinguished them from other Eucharistic clubs. For example, the report of the Eucharistic Crusade for Peace, in light of this abundance of aggregations, distances itself from the French "Eucharistic Crusade for Children," "The Knights and Handmaids of the Blessed Sacrament," and the "Eucharistic Army."[60] Yet another group, the "League of Little Communicants," tried to organize first communicants immediately upon this rite of passage to adulthood into *frequent* communicants so that declination from the sacrament would be forestalled. Its trappings—ribbons, badges, and so forth—resemble those of Cassilly's Frequent Communion Guild to a remarkable extent.

The obscuring of the origins of Cassilly's Frequent Communion Guild in the junior sodality points to a fundamental strategic question posed to the Eucharistic movement in particular and to the institutional church in general: Should organizations be founded exclusively for the enactment of *STS*? Or should extant organizations expand their activities to push more frequent reception by their members? Or is appropriate action found somewhere along a continuum between these positions? Father Purcell, at Amsterdam, allowed his Communion squads to subsist within already extant clubs only with reluctance. F. George Dineen, writing more than ten years after the promulgation of *STS*, lamented that very narrowly targeted organizations had not been more widely established. "If this conclusion [for Communion Guilds separate from the Sodality] had later been carried into effect rather than an effort to subordinate Communion organizations to other associations, the cause of frequent Communion would have profited much more from organization than it has."[61] The philosophy of the sodality was diametrically opposed:

> It is a great mistake, and one too commonly made by zealous people, always to try to meet new needs by organizing a new society. As new needs are constantly increasing, the result would be such a multiplicity of societies that after a while we should hardly have enough Catholics left even to furnish officers for them all. . . . In this connection, the formation of sections in the Sodalities commends itself especially to prudent organizers. . . . Under the banner of the Blessed Virgin, call for volunteers from the Sodality, and form a section which can take charge of the [new] work as long as it is needed, without any fuss or formality, under its own simple officers, president, secretary, and treasurer. Then, when the need for the work is over, the section may disband and allow its members to go on to some new and needed form of activity.[62]

Generally, papers in *EPUL* propose the latter course, urging the enlistment of extant associations in the campaign for frequent Communion. This would involve broadening the focus of such immensely influential and popular groups as the Knights of Columbus and the Holy Name Society.

Communion breakfasts in the promotion of frequent reception of Holy Communion deserve mention, but their impact is immensely difficult to determine. Even before *STS*, these were becoming strong traditions, if not institutions, but because they were not of the essence of any one organization, either parish or Eucharistic league, no reliable and comprehensive record exists. Still, by analogy with the other movements under discussion here, one could posit a significance for the Communion breakfast movement if for no other reason than the role they played in moving toward more frequent reception. Because the Knights of Columbus claim credit for inventing them in the 1890s, and because the Knights are the predominant Catholic fraternal and benevolent society in the United States, and because Father Arthur Riley, in his preliminary work in the 1940s for a history of the Knights, did attend to this movement, we rely largely upon his papers for these few observations.

Membership in the Knights was restricted to men judged to be "practical Catholics," and this included, according to the Kansas State Council, "living up to the laws of the Church, particularly in regard to attendance at Mass, reception of the Sacraments."[63] Indeed, in the first decade of the twentieth century, the Kansas Council resolved that all members document their fulfill-ment of their Easter duty to their local chapter's secretary. Given that a season of Communion breakfasts early in the spring is presumed by an editorial in the *Tablet*, a periodical of the Knights, one might surmise that breakfasts were invented to encourage the making of the Easter duty. More generally, breakfasts addressed the problem of religious tepidity among males. As a his-tory of Louisiana Knighthood says, "The prevalent attitude among so many [was] that religion and religious practices were for women—men did not go in for such activities."[64]

A claim to the honor of devising the Communion breakfast captures its two essential features, reception of the sacrament en masse and a breakfast afterward:

> It is believed that the first corporate Communion and Breakfast held in the United States was held by the members of Morning Star Council [No. 294, Brooklyn, New York, instituted January 9, 1898] on May 28th, 1898. Mass was celebrated at 8:00 A.M. in St. Paul's Church, Congress and Court Streets, Brooklyn, N.Y. Breakfast followed in the rear of a bakery store across the street from the Church at Warren and Court Streets.[65]

"Corporate Communion" presumably occurred with some show of solidar-ity, such as sitting together and processing as a group, and wearing a badge of membership. The priests were doubtless involved in the planning so that they would not be embarrassed by the extraordinary number of communi-cants. Breakfast literally broke the required fast from midnight and provided an occasion for socializing. Often, as the breakfast concluded a lecture or two was given, and after this the whole day might be spent in organized de-votions. Another breakfast day required a "half hour period of adoration be-fore the Blessed Sacrament, dividing the membership into equal numbers led by a captain to recite a set series of prayers."[66] This all-day event ended with Benediction, a common feature of Catholic piety in those days. The claim to having invented the Communion breakfast predates *STS* by nearly ten years; a similar backdating is mentioned explicitly in the history of the Knights of

Columbus in Louisiana.[67] These could corroborate the grassroots nature of this significant change in Catholic sacramental practice—more and more frequent reception of Holy Communion. That the Communion breakfast followed so closely upon the founding of the local chapter may have been quite typical, for this was also reported in the history of the Knights in Kansas.[68]

About thirty years after the Communion breakfast was invented, it may have been losing some of its primary focus. The *Tablet* editorial implies that the after-breakfast speakers could be far too numerous (twenty or thirty!) and even too political, and a short notice in *Columbia*, the Knights' official magazine, denounces as indecorous entertainment that was often included in breakfast programs.[69]

Beginning in the last decade of the nineteenth century, the Knights were encouraging their members to communicate with frequency, and this can be attributed to the Eucharistic movement. In addition to the Communion breakfast, the Knights encouraged the "general Communion" of their membership in many ways. For example, the State Council of Oklahoma resolved in 1913 that all local chapters should communicate as a unit on Easter and Christmas, and they reported in the same year that four local chapters were communicating as a group twice a year, three were doing so three times a year, two were doing so four times annually, and one was receiving monthly.[70] Perhaps an indication of the efficacy of the Knights in changing Catholic sacramental practice is found in their own claims: "In 1902, parish records show only 7,000 Holy Communions for the year, including men, women, and children, besides Sisters. But by 1912, the number had jumped up to 17,150 and in 1917, the report shows 23,461. The order [of Knights] is not to be credited solely for this remarkable change."[71] By 1933, the Knights were not just urging the Easter duty upon their members, for, after an avalanche of similar resolutions from a number of state delegations, the national convention passed the following: "RESOLVED. That State Deputies be urged to designate a Sunday within the Easter period, which shall be known as the Annual Communion Sunday of the Knights of Columbus, and that subordinate councils arrange for a general communion to which their members and other Catholic laymen shall be invited."[72] The Knights, by inviting and encouraging all laymen to fulfill the Easter duty in their company, were also recruiting. Eight years later the Supreme Council was urging quarterly general Communions upon the state councils.[73] At the same convention, a sermon at the opening pontifical Mass was defining a "practical Catholic" not merely as one who made his Easter duty, but as one who makes "frequent use of the sacraments."[74] This change in defining a Catholic layman, which occurred in less than fifty years, indicates the success of the campaign for frequent, even daily, Holy Communion.

Another instance of expanding the functions of an already extant group is that of the Holy Name Society of Chicago. Its mobilization during the International Eucharistic Congress apparently stirred controversy, judging by the protracted defense of its official function during the congress. This controversy about the appropriateness of relying upon a group that was not patently Eucharistic may have a basis in politics, broadly construed, including the concept of "turf."[75] But, in the long term, adding a devotional practice or making one more frequent did not seem to threaten identities because the practice of more-frequent Holy Communion was a universal imperative of the pontiff. As frequent Communion progressed, observers praised the strategy of expanding the ends of existing organizations.

> Wonderful, indeed, is the army of the faithful that give expression of their devotedness in the reception of the sacraments. Under the banner of our sodalities, our leagues and societies, our unions and third orders, our congregations and confraternities, the love of God is fostered and developed and His Eucharistic Presence is appreciated in a manner that is astonishing to the unbeliever and consoling to those who have at heart the honor of the Eucharistic Christ and the salvation of immortal souls.[76]

If an organization expanded its distinctive profile of pieties in order to accommodate a devotion that the highest authority of the Church had promulgated, the organization would impress the hierarchy with its loyalty and compliance.

On the other hand, to establish an organization specifically and exclusively for the newly and officially emphasized devotion did manifest the power of that authority. Founders of these very tightly focused, daily-Communion clubs responded with celerity to these demands and did so not only in response to the authority, but also within a system that rewarded them.

The discourse of these specific organizations serves as a privileged locus for their theology. The very nature of pious clubs was to differentiate their special subsets of believers from the rest of the faithful. The objective of the association was, however, to make themselves special delicately, without vitiating the Catholicity of the membership. The identity of a Holy Namer was, therefore, both an avoidance of, and a struggle against, blasphemy; the former on a personal level, and the latter on the social. An apostle of prayer in the Jesuit association cultivated devotion to the Sacred Heart of Jesus; a sodalist emphasized in his or her devotional life the Blessed Virgin Mary; a member of the Blue Army of Fatima honored the Blessed Virgin in a yet more particular way, in her apparition of 1917. No particularistic organization could deny other devotions and retain its Catholicity, but neither could the nature of one club be to promote an entire vast array of pieties. By their nature, devotional associations were obliged to choose and limit. Not to do so would explode the very purpose of the organization. An augmentation, however, of the practices and values of a particular organization might not fatally undermine the identity of the group. This is especially true if the expansion reaffirms the loyalty of any particular group to its parental institution.

Because Pius X insisted upon frequency of Communion for all, and because of the ultramontane model of the ecclesiastical polity, no pious association as an institution dared to resist his impetus. The identity of the organization, in part defined by the particular practices of its members, also needed linkage with the entire Church, and so the clubs rather easily accommodated and encouraged the frequent Communion devotion. Even as English, the language of the colonizers, served to unify such nations as India and the Philippines, so did the implementation of greater frequency serve to consolidate numerous pious associations in an overarching loyalty to the Roman Church. Further, the success of each association in implementing more and more frequent Holy Communions, often reported statistically, accorded it prestige.

## NOTES

1. These data derive from the indexes of the volumes. Volumes 12 and 20, which lacked indexes, were not surveyed.

2. Joseph Kramp, "Why Frequent Communion Is Declining," *Fortnightly Review* 29 (1922): 381. Kramp was a native of the Rhineland in modern Germany, and so presumably was addressing German liturgical realities; the editor of the *Fortnightly Review*, Arthur Preus, did not contrast the conditions in Kramp's practice with that of the United States.

3. Kramp, "Why Frequent," 381.

4. "A Practical Suggestion for Sodalities," *Ssac* (1916): 496.

5. "International Gregorian Congress," *Ssac* (1920): 331–33.

6. E. H. Kossman, *The Low Countries, 1780–1940*, Oxford History of Modern Europe (Oxford: Clarendon, 1978), 247.

7. An entire chapter of the commemorative volume for Chicago's international congress is allocated to the reception of the papal legate, Cardinal Bonzano. Cornelius Francis Donovan, *The Story of the Twenty-Eighth International Eucharistic Congress Held at Chicago, Illinois, United States of America, from June 20–24, 1926* (Chicago: Eucharistic Congress Committee, 1927), 73–83.

8. Donovan, *Twenty-Eighth International Eucharistic Congress*, 227.

9. Donovan, *Twenty-Eighth International Eucharistic Congress*, 240–42.

10. Donovan, *Twenty-Eighth International Eucharistic Congress*, 242.

11. Donovan, *Twenty-Eighth International Eucharistic Congress*, 242.

12. Donovan, *Twenty-Eighth International Eucharistic Congress*, 242–43.

13. Camillus Maes, "Salvete, Adoratores," *EPUL* 1 (1895): 1.

14. "Philadelphia Regional Convention," *EPUL* 26 (1920): 246; and "Retrospect of the Eucharistic Convention," 407.

15. L. F. Schlathoelter, "Frequent Communion is Necessary for Salvation," *EPUL* 21 (1915): 369.

16. Father Joseph MacCarthy responded to Schlathoelter, "It is well to bear in mind that *the Saintly Pius X has not made frequent Communion any the more obligatory than it was before he issued his famous decrees.*" Joseph MacCarthy, "Is Frequent Communion Necessary for Salvation?" *EPUL* 21 (1915): 418.

17. Paul Bradshaw, *The Search for the Origins of Christian Worship* (London: SPCK, 1992), 69.

18. Zulueta, "Preface to 'The Eucharistic Triduum,'" x.

19. Distinguishing between spiritual and sacramental Communion, H. V. Gill asserts that the presence of Christ in sacramental Communion must have an effect, so long as the reception is licit. Spiritual communion depends entirely upon the dispositions of the devotee and requires an act of faith in the Real Presence, the intention to receive sacramentally, and even an act (prayer) of thanksgiving as if one *had* received sacramentally. The graces that derive from a spiritual Communion are "great." Gill, "Spiritual Communion," 517.

20. Thomas Franklin O'Meara, interview with the author, Notre Dame, Indiana, July 1995.

21. *ET*, 75.

22. Francis A. Purcell, "Frequent Communion in Parishes," *EPUL* 30 (1924): 304.

23. "Bishop of the Blessed Sacrament," *EPUL* 21 (1915): 442.

24. Charles R. Morris. *American Catholic: The Saints and Sinners Who Built America's Most Powerful Church* (New York: Times Books / Random House, 1997), 49–50.

25. Morris, *American Catholic*, 49.

26. Morris, *American Catholic*, 52.

27. Orsi, *Madonna of 115th Street*, xv.

28. Morris, *American Catholic*, 44, unnumbered footnote.

29. Patrick J. Corish, *The Irish Catholic Experience: A Historical Survey* (Wilmington, Delaware: Michael Glazier, 1985), 133.

30. Sean J. Connolly, *Priests and People in Pre-famine Ireland, 1780–1845* (New York: St. Martin's, 1982), 186.

31. Mary Ann Clawson, "Fraternal Organizations," *Encyclopedia of American Social History*, 1993 ed.

32. Francis J. Cassilly, "The Frequent Communion Guild," *EPUL* 18 (1912): 45.

33. Sacerdos, "Frequent Communion," *EPUL* 25 (1919): 171.

34. Patrick O'Connor, "The Silver Jubilee of Frequent Communion," *Ecclesiastical Review* (December 1930): 561–69, cited in Frances Joanna Hastings, "Pope Pius X and Frequent Communion" (Sacred Science dissertation, St. Bonaventure University, St. Bonaventure, New York, 1951), 40.

35. Cassilly, "The Frequent Communion Guild," 44.

36. Cassilly," "The Frequent Communion Guild," 43.

37. F. George Dineen, "Frequent Communion Promoted by Organization," *The Queen's Work* 6, no. 3 (March 1917): 120.

38. Cassilly, "The Frequent Communion Guild," 46.

39. Cassilly, "The Frequent Communion Guild," 46.

40. Dineen, "Frequent Communion Promoted by Organization," 121.

41. Dineen, "Frequent Communion Promoted by Organization," 120.

42. For an overview of the sodality movement in the United States, see William D. Dinges, "An Army of Youth: The Sodality Movement and the Practice of Apostolic Mission," *U.S. Catholic Historian* 19, no. 3 (2001): 35–50.

43. Dineen, "Frequent Communion Promoted by Organization," 120.

44. Elizabeth Brady, "The Guard of Honor," *Queen's Work* 4, no. 3 (March 1916): 121–28.

45. Cassilly, "The Frequent Communion Guild," 46; Dineen, "Frequent Communion Promoted by Organization," 122.

46. Tentler, *History of the Catholic Archdiocese of Detroit*, 168.

47. Dineen, "Frequent Communion Promoted by Organization," 121.

48. "The Knights of the Blessed Sacrament," *EPUL* 23 (1917): 38. *Advertised* is used loosely, for the notice occurs in article format.

49. "Knights of the Blessed Sacrament," 38.

50. "The Association of the Knights of the Blessed Sacrament," *Ssac* (1917): 74.

51. "The Association of the Knights," *Ssac* (1917): 74.

52. "Knights of the Blessed Sacrament," 38.

53. "Director's Notes and Report: Knights of the Blessed Sacrament," *EPUL* 28 (1922): 185.

54. "Director's Notes and Report: Knights," 185.

55. F. A. Purcell, "Frequent Communion in Parishes," *EPUL* 30 (1924): 304.

56. Purcell, "Frequent Communion in Parishes," 304.

57. "Wanted: You!" *Ssac* (1921): 575.

58. *Ssac* reported that, after two months of existence, 9,620 Masses, 7,305 Communions, and 4,580 hours of Adoration had been offered. "Eucharistic Peace Crusade," *Ssac* (1921): 727.

59. The following articles boost similar organizations: "Pious Union for the Communion of Children," *EPUL* 18 (1912): 149–55, reported on the activity of the Holy Father in establishing an "Association Primaria" for the increase of frequent Communion among children; the article included the statutes. "The League of Little Communicants: to Christian Educators," *Ssac* (1917): 96–97, urged simultaneous training for first and frequent Communion, and articulated the notion that clubs were excellent at sustaining desired behaviors. Like Cassilly's group, this one ranked its members by frequency of reception of Communion and provided badges and the like. The concept seemed to bear repetition a generation later. John Vismara of Detroit urged the formation of "Holy Communion Clubs" for children; the impetus to this idea was not only encouraging frequent Communion, but maintaining the levels of reception through the summer months. His beguiling name for these clubs is "Gangs for Christ." John Vismara, "Holy Communion Clubs," *Ecclesiastical Review* 107 (1942): 382–87.

60. "The Eucharistic Peace Crusade: The Children's Part," *Ssac* (1921): 698.

61. Dineen, "Frequent Communion Promoted by Organization," 121.

62. "Multiplying Organizations," *Queen's Work* 7, no. 1 (July 1917): 30.

63. Herman J. Tholen, *The Knights of Columbus: Their First Fifty Years in Kansas* (N.p.: Kansas State Council, 1950), 87.

64. Roger Baudier Sr. and Millard F. Everett, *Anchor and Fleur-de-Lis: Knights of Columbus in Louisiana, 1902–1962* (New Orleans: Louisiana State Council, Knights of Columbus, 1965), 72.

65. Richard C. J. Laskin to Arthur Riley, 20 September 1953, autograph card, transcribed by Arthur Riley, Knights of Columbus Supreme Council Archives, New Haven, Connecticut. The San Salvador Council also lodged a claim to have originated the Communion breakfast nearly two years earlier.

66. Louis McCauley, to Arthur Riley, 5 July 1951, autograph card, transcribed by Arthur Riley, Knights of Columbus Supreme Council Archives, New Haven, Connecticut.

67. Baudier and Everett, *Anchor and Fleur-de-Lis*, 73.

68. Tholen, *Knights of Columbus*, 88.

69. Editorials, "Communion Breakfast Season," *Tablet*, 2 March 1929, 60–61, and "Here and There," *Columbia*, May 1929, 3.

70. Arthur Riley, autograph card, apparently quoting a report from the Oklahoma State Council of the Knights, Knights of Columbus Supreme Council Archives, New Haven, Connecticut.

71. Baudier and Everett, *Anchor and Fleur-de-Lis*, 72.

72. Supreme Council Proceedings, 1933, p. 72, Knights of Columbus Supreme Council Archives, New Haven, Connecticut.

73. Supreme Council Proceedings, 1941, p. 121, Knights of Columbus Supreme Council Archives, New Haven, Connecticut.

74. Edward Mooney, Sermon, Supreme Council Proceedings, 1941, p. 149, Knights of Columbus Supreme Council Archives, New Haven, Connecticut.

75. Thomas M. Schwertner, "The Eucharistic Congress and the Holy Name Society," *EPUL* 32 (1926): 110–16; and, on the continuing relevance of the original end of the Holy Name Society, the eradication of blasphemy, J. R. Newell, "Need of the Holy Name Society," *EPUL* 24 (1918): 41–49.

76. Nawn, "The People's Eucharistic League," 42.

## Chapter Six

# Competition among Pieties

The international Eucharistic movement aimed to reconfigure the piety of the entire Church toward the Eucharist, and more frequent Communion advanced this purpose. But other excellent pious practices could not be demeaned.[1] Rather, these devotional emphases were first used by the movement to invite their partisans into the Eucharistic movement and then were massaged into shapes that pointed to and even exalted the Eucharist. Correspondingly, both *EPUL* and *Ssac* remained comprehensive in their reporting, but what they reported was, if possible, cast in a Eucharistic light. Two significant devotions that were so reshaped—devotion to the Blessed Mother and to the Sacred Heart of Jesus—illustrate the process.

Marian devotions, more than any other, could have impeded the exaltation of the Eucharist. These devotions, bolstered by such doctrinal developments as the solemn declarations of both the Immaculate Conception (1854) and the Assumption (1950) as dogmas, dominated the life of the Church for a century.[2] "Indeed, so great was this revival that leaders of the Church call the years between 1850 and 1950 the Marian Age."[3] Seven European apparitions of Mary galvanized the world of the faithful during this century and Marian congresses formed an interesting counterpoint to the Eucharistic congresses.[4]

Historians such as Barbara Corrado Pope who investigate the Marian revival see it as magnitudinous, but Chinnici asserts that the Eucharistic movement claims pride of place in the competition for devotional activities.[5] Thus the tools may not yet be at hand to compare this revival with that of the Eucharist. Such mass movements, studied intensely and contextualized only with the standard historiography of Catholicism, usually a "great men" historiography, may have been large and vital, but comparisons among movements can be made only with great caution. If the issue is to be judged by the outcome, the Eucharistic movement and campaigns for frequent Communion may claim a greater vitality and influence than even the Marian devotional campaigns.

Historical and sociological perspectives on the history of devotions in the Roman Catholic Church since the Reformation consider this the fundamental pattern of their development: An individual or small cadre creates or revivifies a piety. The institutional Church admits, perhaps reluctantly, devotions into its repertoire, only after years of gradually increasing popularity, and then not only condones the devotions but embraces them and promotes them with vigor. This pattern certainly pertains to the advent of frequent Communion, which began in the lay-organized Eucharistic movement and was finally adopted and magnified by Pius X twenty-four years after the first Eucharistic congress. In the process, the popular devotions might require molding for the sake of doctrinal clarity, if not orthodoxy, and they are then assigned proper places in the taxonomy of devotions according to formal theological principles. Since the Reformation, the need to harness these popular devotions has stemmed from the struggles with the persisting devastations of the institutional Church. Indeed, institutional dynamics do work this way—change begins at the margins, and if the change is palatable and beneficial, ultimately, to the institution, and if the change resonates with cultural and psychological trends, it triumphs. During the Reformation and the Enlightenment, the normal social and bourgeois reaction to the stressful situation was to strive to control. This was abetted by defensiveness, by organization, and by uniformity. These devotional developments are not at all insulated from general historical trends. As the fruits of the Industrial Revolution were quantification, organization, centralization, and even nationalization, so too were devotions more quantified, organized, centralized under bureaucratic management, and replaced or reconfigured along national, rather than local, lines.[6]

Ann Taves, Thomas Kselman, and Barbara Corrado Pope provide some historical and sociological insights to help understand the Eucharistic movement. Taves, analyzing the devotional literature of nineteenth-century Catholicism in the United States, asserts that the rich devotionalism of the era was deliberately brought under the control of the clergy. She mitigates the thesis of Marie-Hélèn Froeschlé-Chopard and William A. Christian that divides pre- and post-Tridentine Catholicism preeminently along the lines of the individual's direct access to the transcendent. "Under the older system, the individual had direct access, they [Froeschlé-Chopard and Christian] argue, to graces and favors through divine intermediaries, while under the new system all graces and favors were mediated through the clergy."[7] In contrast to the European examples, the situation in America did not dichotomize direct access from clerical mediation, but rather established a taxonomy of means of access. Taves continues:

Rather than eliminating the possibility of obtaining graces and favors through divine intermediaries [through direct personal contact with them], the emphasis on the priest and the sacraments simply attempted to subordinate practices associated with relics, saints, and shrines to practices such as confession and communion.

Thus, relative to the older, pre-Tridentine forms of devotion, ultramontane devotionalism not only centralized and standardized practice, but also subordinated devotions to Mary and the saints to devotion to Jesus in the Blessed Sacrament. Saints were downplayed relative to Jesus and Mary; Mary was subordinated, at least in theory, to Jesus; and the sacramentals were subordinated, again at least in theory, to the sacraments.[8]

Applying the same template in a more particular instance, Kselman sees the French Church, desparate during the cultural upheavals consequent to the French Revolution, co-opting the primitive traditions of local pilgrimages to the revitalization of its own political and religious influence.[9] At times, these pilgrimages were regarded by the ecclesiastical authorities as pure superstition. Writing of the French Church's attitude toward pilgrimages, Barbara Corrado Pope writes, "By 1873 the official attitude had changed, and the church had moved to tie these potentially subversive impulses to the sacramental system."[10] She explains that the effect of Pius IX's reign was "to enhance the power of the papacy and successfully to exert its right to spiritual primacy."[11] While a host of causes, both of the secular and ecclesial realms, spurred this increase in papal prestige, Corrado Pope claims that it was creation of an ordered universe of pieties finally that gave the pope a large measure of control over the faithful.

> The culmination of Pius's efforts to win allegiance of the laity was the successful promotion of a certain kind of piety. Pius and his immediate successors advocated new or renewed devotions that emphasized the affective rather than the rational or ethical aspects of faith. That is, they chose to direct rather than to condemn or ignore emotional and potentially subversive religious impulses in order to maintain and increase Catholic influence. The adoration of the Eucharist, the Sacred Heart of Jesus, and Mary were emotional cults fully supported by the papacy.[12]

Theological rationales for these rearrangements of pieties little interest these scholars; the sociological paradigm considers the complexities of devotional developments more as schemes for power.

If these sociological and historical perspectives have worth, then the triumph of the Eucharistic movement seems inescapable. The summary thesis states that since the Council of Trent the Church moved consistently toward ever-increasing clerical and official control over the religious practices of the faithful. Consonant with this trend, the sacrament of the Eucharist, frequently received in Holy Communion, offered three paramount advantages.

First, its administration was strictly reserved to the clergy. This cohered, too, with the general pattern of American Catholic Church history in the nineteenth century, itself consistent with patterns of development in the Church in Europe since the Middle Ages.

> By defining those rites that the clergy alone could perform as the only regular means of grace, the medieval theologians limited the laity's means of access to the holy, at least in theory, and thus enhanced the power of the clergy. Veneration of the Blessed Sacrament tacitly affirmed this set of presuppositions and thus helped to enhance the distinction between laity and clergy.[13]

As devotional books evolved in the nineteenth century in the United States, more and more prominent were those prayers that centered upon universal pieties, as opposed to those that were particularly local, and upon the sacraments. Marian and Sacred Heart and Blessed Sacrament devotions all increased.[14]

In terms of administration, the unique sacrament was matrimony, in which the couple themselves were the ministers, but without the priest-witness, the sacrament was not binding. Still, the sacramental ritual itself implied that the very active priest was the agent. The bishop administered ordination and confirmation. The priest—with the exceptional emergency baptism by a layperson—imparted the rest of the sacraments. As stock in the sacraments rose through the nineteenth century, the clergy acquired power through more effective, if not exclusive, access to the sacred. Through the centuries, only the priest himself was permitted ever to distribute Communion; the exception was that a layperson could consume the reserved Sacrament if it was in danger of desecration.

Second, the Mass was the regular, even daily, public worship of the Church. Its repetition, not to mention the panoply with which it was celebrated, reinforced the social prestige of the minister. The power to consecrate the Eucharist was, moreover, derived from the bishop, and the prevalent ecclesiology of the nineteenth century saw the bishop's power as derived from the pope's.

Third, the power of the priest to celebrate the Mass, popularly regarded and ritually conveyed through ordination as a personal power, was an awesome and ultimate power—a reiteration of the mysteries of the Incarnation and Passion on the altar.

Theologically, the Eucharist made present to the faithful the Passion that accomplished no less than the redemption of the universe. Ritually, the profundity of this "incarnation" was conveyed by the pervasive sense of awe in the Mass, as well as in the range of Eucharistic devotions such as Benediction, Forty Hours, and the Feast of Corpus Christi. Thus, insofar as the issue was power, the Eucharist was the grand prize; theologically, it was ultimate. Suppose that the Eucharistic movement succeeded in thoroughly convincing the faithful of the validity of the Church's sacramental theology, and further grant that Rodney Stark's rational-choice theory of religion is valid and applicable to this intramural contest among devotions. Here is a journalistic epitome of Stark's theory:

> People act rationally in choosing their religion. If they are believers, they make constant cost-benefit analysis, consciously or unconsciously, about what form of religion to practice. Religious beliefs and practices make up the product that is on sale in the market. . . . In a free-market religious economy there is a healthy abundance of choice (religious pluralism), which leads naturally to vigorous competition and efficient supply.[15]

In light of these eminently plausible suppositions, it follows that the Eucharist, and the frequent appropriation of it in Holy Communion, would achieve pride of place. The benefits of receiving Holy Communion hugely outweigh the costs.

Other devotions depended upon the Eucharist, theologically, by virtue of the meaning of the Eucharist as the Real Presence of Christ. These other devotions were countenanced by the Eucharistic movement as invitations to enter into the life of the Church, or as particular and personal guarantors of the commitment of the faithful. Also, they provided "healthy competition" that encouraged "efficient supply."

See how this theological dependence became clear as the Eucharistic movement creatively appropriated Mary: An alliance between devotion to Mary and the Eucharist was epitomized in the epithet of the Blessed Mother, approved officially by Pope Pius X, "Our Lady of the Blessed Sacrament."[16] This title originated in the thought of Saint Pierre-Julien Eymard, who prescribed this ejaculation to the Blessed Sacrament Fathers: "Our Lady of the Most Blessed Sacrament, mother and model of adorers, pray for us who have recourse to thee."[17] Lintelo explained that the honorific followed from the identity of the body of Jesus, born of Mary, and the Real Presence in the Eucharist. The title intended to "honor that intimate union which subsists between Jesus and Mary."[18] In short, this title of Mary was a prayerful expression of the mystery of the Incarnation, and it thus confirmed the humanity of Jesus.

The title found its ultimacy in the Eucharist. Indeed, the theological significance of Mary paled in comparison to this Eucharistic envelope. "When saying 'Our Lady of the Blessed Sacrament,' we hail her as the perfect model for fulfilling our duties towards the Eucharist, and we ask her to obtain for us the grace to perform them less imperfectly."[19] Lintelo established a clear sense of the priority both of redemption and of the role of Jesus in that "God wills that the more we study the greatness of Mary, the more clearly we perceive her close connection with all the mysteries of our redemption."[20] The redemption of humanity included the Theotokos; despite her "office as Mediatrix" of the graces of redemption, the Eucharist was key. Lintelo continued, "In that capacity [as Mediatrix] she is entrusted with the disposal of the Eucharist, the most abundant source of all graces, the most efficacious means of salvation. In her love for souls she devotes herself to making them know and love Jesus in the Blessed Sacrament, and bringing them to draw more copiously from the fountain of living water."[21] In a more popular and pietistic linkage between Mary and the Eucharist, she was depicted as the virtual minister of Holy Communion. Lois Donovan wrote, in a poem entitled, "Communion,"

> This morning, when Our Blessed Mother led
> Her Little Son to me, and laid His hand in mine,
> "Take thou thy Lord and keep Him safe," she said;
> "As much as He is mine, so He is thine."[22]

In the same vein of naive religiosity, Mary became, ultimately, a model of the frequent communicant, especially in speculations upon her life between the Ascension and her Assumption.

> Mary lived for more than ten years after the ascension of her Divine Son. How was her soul mainly occupied during that period? . . . The answer cannot be doubtful: she lived upon the Eucharist and by the Eucharist; for, as the Holy Spirit testifies, this was the distinctive feature of the primitive Church: "They were persevering . . . in the communication of the breaking of the bread."[23]

Mary became, in the hands of the Eucharistic movement, a model of all communicants. Of course, the scriptural evidence was quite tenuous, and the apocryphal literature did not support such conclusions. The notion is rooted in the logic that, because Mary adored her Son perfectly, she modeled the adoration that the recipient of Communion should practice. No question arose about Mary's sacramental reception of the Communion; it was asserted: "Mary is the most perfect example of the devout communicant, since she was the most perfect adorer of her Divine Son, and appreciate[d] more than any angel or saint the infinite love and the wonderful beauties of the Holy Eucharist."[24]

The Marian devotion of the Dominican rosary was unquestionably an eminent pious exercise among American Catholics in the beginning of the twentieth century. Its nature was to provide the devotee with a substantial and sensory presence in its beads.[25] The Blessed Sacrament Fathers and the Eucharistic movement attempted to transform the rosary into a meditation upon the Real Presence of Jesus in the Sacrament of the Altar. This was not, however, a violation of the essences of the devotion. For "the rosary has always been evolving in a lively way. It is not one text but many; actually, multiple versions embedded in a constellation of texts that described, interpreted, and marketed forms of the devotion to users who collectively shaped and selected the ultimate version of choice."[26]

Both *EPUL* and *Ssac* acknowledged implicitly that Marian devotion was one of the chief competitors with the Eucharistic movement in the United States. In a sense, articles on this devotion simply addressed the continual interests of the readership of the magazines; the laity were devotees of the rosary. This gratification of the readerships of *EPUL* and the *Ssac* was, however, accompanied by the shaping of this devotion and its very real demotion relative to the Eucharist.

Even a precursor of the liturgical movement, such as Father Herbert Thurston, SJ, writing in 1900, reported that the rosary was "the most widely spread and most highly prized of all our modern popular devotions."[27] Taves's analysis of Catholic devotional books in the mid-1800s discovered that the rosary superseded all other devotions as a topic.[28]

The Dominican rosary, the most popular form, is Marian in two aspects, its origin and its text.[29] So far as Catholics were aware in the 1890s, it had been conferred upon Saint Dominic by an apparition of the Blessed Virgin herself, and its purpose was to aid in the conversion of the Albigensian heretics.[30] The stuff of the devotion was the prayer, the Hail Mary (Ave Maria), recited in the vernacular 150 times. This prayer consists of two sections. The first is a direct quotation of two passages from the Gospel of Luke—the words of the greeting of Mary by the angel Gabriel in announcing the Incarnation (Luke 1:28) and the words of her cousin Elizabeth at the Visitation (Luke 1:42); the second is a request for the intercession of Mary for the praying sinner, especially at the hour of death. In popular piety, each Hail Mary was "homage" to the Mother of God.[31] The rosary was more than a prayer, for it constituted the "chief daily proof of filial loyalty to the Mother of God."[32] Because it was usable in public or in private, the rosary did not oblige devotees to reveal their faith to the world.

A rough gauge of the Marian character of the beads in the popular mind can be deduced from an analysis of publications about the rosary. Mary was an indubitable theme in nine publications about the rosary; Jesus, in three.[33]

The meditative aspect of the devotion, however, centered upon the life of Christ. While the Aves were being said, the faithful were to recall episodes from the life of Jesus, divided into themes of sorrow, joy, and glory. "With these best of vocal prayers mental prayer may be joined; for, while the beads glide through our fingers and the *Hail Marys* fall from our lips, our minds and hearts may be quietly turned towards one of the joyful, sorrowful, or glorious mysteries of Our Lord's life, such as every prayer-book explains them to us."[34] The devotion, in the ideal, was contrapuntal—echoing the greetings of Gabriel and Elizabeth and calling upon Mary to succor the sinner in the treble clef, and meditating upon the life of Jesus in the bass. But the rhetoric in the articles that aim to revivify the elements of the rosary that referred to Jesus Christ implied that the reader would be surprised at the supposed emphasis upon the Redeemer in these mysteries. "'Yes,' the author continued, 'for in each of these scenes Our Lord is the principal figure, as He must needs be, even when His Blessed Mother is beside Him.'"[35] In other words, the Christian core had been displaced in the actual praying of the beads. Correcting this, *EPUL* proclaimed the rosary as the "epitome of the entire human life of Christ."[36]

Jesus was the sun whose gravity could bring the rosary into the orbit of the Eucharistic movement. The conceptual structures of this movement, however, radiated outward from the central notion of the Real Presence. Logically this connected with the nature of the Mass as the unbloody but real sacrifice, making the bloody sacrifice, the Cross, present. Indeed, some Eucharistic enthusiasts judged that the Real Presence–Mass complex, particularly because it transcended historicity and physicality and made the presence of Jesus real to the individual communicant, was in some sense superior to the historical Passion.[37] "As of the Incarnation, the Eucharist is the extension of the Passion. It extends it in every sense, not only in duration and immensity, but also in depth and intensity. It abases the Savior in annihilations more profound than those of Calvary. It delivers Him still more helpless, as it were, to the injurious treatment of sinners."[38] Because the Passion, in a word, redeemed the universe, the entirety of the life of Jesus as reported in the Gospels centered upon the Cross and took all of its meaning from the atoning death of the Savior. Allegorical methods of meditating upon the Mass favored this collapsing of biblical narrative, sacramental action, and soteriological consummation. "At the breaking of the Host, the Church allows us to contemplate on the Cross the Body that was torn under the stripes of flagellation, under the points of the nails and the thorns. . . . Again, she [the Church] desires to represent at the same time the breaking of the bread that Christ Himself made at the Last Supper."[39] These allegorical meditations were provided to the lay readership of *Ssac* not for use during Mass, but rather for use during the Adoration, the hour of prayer before the reserved Blessed Sacrament.

Theological equivalences were, like those in algebra, reversible. Thus, since the Eucharistic Presence equaled the Passion, and since the life of Christ culminated in the Passion, the entire life of Jesus was "Eucharistic." "In his 'Meditations on the Life of the Sacred Heart in the Blessed Eucharist,' Father Borgo, SJ, has beautifully brought out the similarities of love and sacrifice, of humility and obedience, of beatitude and grace, in the dual life of the Sacred Heart during Its three and thirty years on earth and since then on the Christian altar."[40] That Jesus taught and healed shrank into irrelevancy. Communion meant appropriation of redemption, but the physicality of the theology of the Real Presence expressed this, too, in very physical terms. Receiving Communion was literally eating the Body of Christ, but salvation was establishing utmost intimacy with God in Communion. These equivalences, before the advent of frequent Communion, reached an emotional watershed in the iconic spirituality of the "Prisoner of the Tabernacle."[41]

Within this context and to accomplish the program of the Eucharistic movement, the rosary was to be reshaped so that it centered in Christ, not just theoretically, but as actually prayed. The movement went much further than reemphasizing that meditations upon the fifteen episodes of the life of Christ accompanied the mantric recitation of the Aves; it subordinated these meditations upon Christ's life to the Blessed Sacrament and even to Communion. Father Albert Tesnière, SSS, in his "Les mystères du rosaire proposés pour l'adoration du Tres Saint Sacrament," presented "under each of the fifteen mysteries a fourfold meditation in relation to the Eucharistic life of Christ."[42] In an article in *EPUL*, O'B thus obliquely gave some of the credit to this French doctor of theology for his own much more suggestive and telegraphic modification of the rosary so that it satisfied the requirement for the Adoration performed by the members of the PEL. Here is a sampling of the scheme; between the joyful and glorious mysteries of the life of Christ, O'B expounded upon the sorrowful:

1. *The Agony in the Garden*—The first unworthy Communion of the Traitor Apostle. *Fruit*—Hour's adoration.
2. *The Scourging at the Pillar*—The desertion of the Apostles, a foreshadow of indifference and neglect towards the Blessed Sacrament. *Fruit*—Spread of Eucharistic devotion.
3. *The Crowning with Thorns*—The insults and profanations committed towards Jesus in the Blessed Sacrament. *Fruit*—Reparation.
4. *The Carrying of the Cross*—Unworthy Communions. *Fruit*—Eucharistic sermons.
5. *The Crucifixion*—Sacrilegious Mass. *Fruit*—Preparation for Mass.[43]

That this suggestion appears in *EPUL*, the magazine for priests, does not vitiate its illustrating the common strategy of reconfiguring devotions for the sake of strengthening liturgical and sacramental elements of Catholic piety.

Marian piety was yoked to the Christological, and the Christological was subordinated to the Eucharistic. As an editor of *Ssac* wrote, "The dominant thought of each of these various festivals [in June] may easily be correlated with Eucharistic aspiration, since the Blessed Sacrament epitomizes all the mysteries of Jesus and Mary."[44]

Events of the life of Jesus, as highlighted and encoded in the rosary, did not appear in their redemptive-history significance, but in their sacramental significance with respect to the greatest of all sacraments, the Eucharist.

> One of the great spiritual writers of France declared that his mind and heart were so impressed with the marvelous depth of the beauty, greatness, and love of Our Divine Lord in the Blessed Eucharist that wherever he might read in the Holy Scriptures, he readily found therein a reference to the Blessed Sacrament, either directly or in figure. It is quite true that the inspired book is full of this stupendous Mystery of Love.[45]

Holy Communion applied redemption to the individual. Insofar as the priest was imbued with the sense of the orderly interconnections among doctrines of salvation and Communion, doctrinal and devotional perversions did not arise.

In addition to changing the meaning of the rosary, the campaign modified, or at least attempted to modify, its verbal actualization. The standard rosary simply repeated the Aves in succession within their decades, and between each ten beads the Lord's Prayer and a Glory Be were prayed. Eucharistic periodicals, however, either reported or suggested various changes. The simplest alteration, suggested for a public Holy Hour by a priest in Iowa, was to make the rosary "Eucharistic" by reciting the aspiration, "O Sacrament, Most Holy! O Sacrament, Divine! All praise and all thanksgiving be every moment thine!" after each Ave.[46]

A radical alteration of the rosary needed an impressive foundational story to achieve credibility, and so one was attributed to Saint Pascal Baylon, who said the Dominican rosary twenty times a day and who is the patron saint of Eucharistic congresses. The story claimed the new method—or an entirely new devotion, still reliant upon the beads—had been explained during an apparition of both the Blessed Virgin and Our Lord to Saint Pascal.[47] These visitors had prescribed, so the story goes, a shifting of the prayers marked by the beads, an astonishing reconfiguration of the texts: First, in place of the Ave, Pascal was instructed to say, "Ave, benignissime Jesu! Hail, sweetest Jesus!"[48] Second, where previously the Lord's Prayer had been said, the Ave was to be recited—so it would be spoken now 18 times, rather than 150. The Credo was retained on the crucifix. This account of the newly named prayer, the "Chaplet of the Blessed Sacrament," did not specify new subjects for meditation.

Two methods, then, characterized the co-opting of the rosary, both as devotion and as physical object, for the Eucharistic movement. One method was to insist upon the reestablishment of a prayerful and meditative connection between Mary and Christ. This method was largely educational. The second method was to "rewrite" the devotion so that its *lex orandi* cohered with systematic theology, either by inserting Christic and Eucharistic aspirations or by replacing the matter of the recitation with other verbal prayers.

These several strategies of the Eucharistic movement to build upon Marian devotion to further its own agenda—coining a new epithet for Mary, pious imaginings about her receiving Communion and, in fact, distributing it, and reconfiguring the prayers of the rosary—reached an extreme in a book of Arthur M. Viau, *The Virgin in the Holy Eucharist*. The thesis of this work is that Mary and all the saints, by virtue of the doctrine of the Mystical Body of Christ, are present in the Eucharistic species. Viau explained, "So when we receive Holy Communion, not only Jesus is there as in heaven but also Mary and all the Saints."[49] Viau admits that this is a new doctrine, but he argues that new doctrines are admitted, in principle, in the then-recent writings of Pope Pius XII and that this doctrine will be especially helpful in ecumenical relations because the doctrine derives from Viau's reading of the book of Revelation![50] For the layperson, the devotional upshot of this doctrine is the use of the rosary as a thanksgiving after Communion. "Therefore if Mary is so close to us we should say Hello to her, which means say the Rosary."[51] This book bore neither *imprimatur* nor *nihil obstat*, and in pencil on the front cover of the volume I examined, from the library of Mary Immaculate Seminary in Northampton, Pennsylvania, was written, "contains dangerous doctrine."

The other prominent devotion at the turn of the nineteenth century was devotion to the Sacred Heart. One Bishop Verville, painting freely and perhaps wishfully, posited a sequence of devotional emphases—namely, Marian devotion followed by Eucharistic devotion, although his turn of phrase hybridized the Eucharistic with Sacred Heart devotion. He said at Angers in 1901, "The nineteenth century has been the century of the Blessed Virgin—the twentieth century [will be] that of the Eucharistic Heart [of Christ]."[52] The Sacred Heart devotion had received its greatest boost from Saint Margaret-Mary Alacoque in France during the reign of Louis XIV. The devotion is "deeply implicated in the history of modern France," because it served as an emblem first and nostalgically for the grandeur of France during the Sun King's rule, then for the conservative and religious forces during the French Revolution, then for the aspirations of France to regain its prestige in the aftermath of the Franco-Prussian war, and, finally, for perduring resistance to secularized government.[53] In fact, the construction of the Basilica of the Sacred Heart on Montmartre in Paris, itself conceived as an act of reparation for France's secularization, kept the Sacred Heart prominent in France. This did not happen spontaneously. "The devotion of the Sacre-Coeur in nineteenth-century France represents a campaign of cultural politics of breathtaking skill and sophistication."[54]

That devotion to the Sacred Heart was a hallmark of the Jesuits, a most vital and influential order, also pointed to the popularity of the devotion.[55] So great was this devotion that the term *Sacred Heart* was used as synonymous for the historical Jesus, as the quotation from O'B, above, indicated. In ranking important elements of devotional history of Catholicism since Trent, J. M. Derély, though he was the promoter of the Eucharistic crusade in France and perhaps because he was a Jesuit, ranked the revelations of the Sacred Heart to Saint Margaret-Mary Alacoque first and the return to frequent Communion second.[56] Presumably the revelations were more important because the devotions to which they gave rise were more prevalent and because the emblem of the devotion was so enmeshed in French political history. Circulation figures for the *Messenger of the Sacred Heart* and the extent of its publication in so many languages and lands confirm the breadth of this devotion.

For us, the key difference between the popular Marian rosary and membership in the Apostleship of Prayer was that this latter devotion included among its several pious practices frequent—that is, monthly—reception of Holy Communion. In particular, this monthly reception of Holy Communion was systematized into a "novena" of Communions, which was ascribed to the special revelation of Jesus to Saint Margaret-Mary. Jesus said, in what was packaged and publicized as the Twelfth Promise of the Sacred Heart,

> I promise you [Margaret-Mary] that, in the excessive mercy of my Heart, my all-powerful love will grant to all who communicate on the First Friday of the month for nine consecutive months, the grace of final repentance; they shall not die in my displeasure nor without the sacraments; my divine Heart shall be their safe refuge in their last moments.[57]

More broadly and to the point of this study, the raison d'être of the devotion to the Sacred Heart was in the Eucharist. Holy Communion was to be received specifically as an act of reparation.[58]

Reparation was the dominant pietistic impulse of the devotion, even as the Incarnation was its dogmatic impulse in that the heart of a human being represents the physical humanity. Reparation was predicated upon the notion that Jesus, as the Blessed Sacrament and by virtue of the Real Presence, was worthy at the very least of the frequent and pious attention and gratitude of all the faithful. All the irreverent—nonbelievers, Protestants, tepid Catholics—could benefit from reparation. Even as the Roman Catholic faithful failed to show proper etiquette or, worse, ignored Jesus on the altar by absenting themselves from Mass or, incalculably worse, wounded Jesus by receiving Holy Communion unworthily, unfaithfully, or sacrilegiously, reparation was due by those yet faithful adherents to the Sacred Heart devotion. Atheists, rationalists and positivists, and some Protestants scoffed at the doctrine of the Real Presence or, worse, blasphemed or, incalculably worst, desecrated the Host. Spiritually and effectively, and in imitation of the sacrificial death of Jesus, the devotees of the Sacred Heart offered themselves and their prayers and their Communions in compensation for neglect, abuse, and profanation of the Blessed Sacrament. Reparation was not Margaret-Mary's innovation. It was "widespread in seventeenth-century France. This attitude sprang from the emphasis of the Council of Trent on the Real Presence of Jesus Christ in the Blessed Sacrament and the actual desecration of Roman Catholic churches by the Huguenots during the wars of religion."[59] Reparation could take the form of a procession.

> Another procession in which the king [Francis I of France] participated as a penitent occurred in 1535 to make reparation for a Protestant poster that blasphemed the blessed sacrament of the altar, in which the blessed sacrament and every relic available was carried through the streets by priests and acolytes while people stood with lighted torches along the route of the procession.[60]

Reparation spirituality may be a milder form of "victim spirituality."[61] One highly dramatic revelation to Saint Margaret-Mary, as reported in a Eucharistic periodical, showed how reparation operated even in a local community and could forge links between the transgressor and the devout:

> One day, when Our Lord had shown Blessed Margaret Mary the bad treatment He had received in a soul who had communicated with affection to sin, seized with fear and sorrow, she cast herself at His feet, watered them with the tears she could not restrain, and said to Him: "My Lord and my God, if my life will be of any use to repair these injuries, although what Thou dost receive from me is a thousand times greater, yet behold me! I am Thy slave. Do with me whatever Thou pleasest." He replied: "Whenever I make known to thee the bad treatment I receive from that soul, I wish thee to prostrate at My feet after Communion and make honorable atonement to My Heart. Offer to the Father for the same end the bloody sacrifice of the Cross, along with thy own being, to pay homage to Mine and to repair the indignities I receive in this Heart." At these words, I [Margaret-Mary] suffered great pains.[62]

It seems that, given the doctrine of the Real Presence and the utter transcendence of the Godhead, voluntarily so circumscribed in the Blessed Sacrament and given the degree of gratitude and attention proportional to this mystery, reparation became an inexhaustible obligation.[63] The Third National

Eucharistic Congress in New York in 1904 resolved to combat "apparent irreverence" and "neglect of" the Blessed Sacrament by an educational initiative.[64] Reparation was so significant a part of the Eucharistic mission (i.e., parish retreat) as orchestrated by the Passionist, Father Vincent, that the closing of the mission was marked by a ritual gesture, the lighting of the "Lamp of Reparation and Supplication."[65]

The sacramental and frequent reception of the Body of Christ, though encouraged by devotion to the Sacred Heart, was also gingerly reshaped by it. Frequent Communion and the Sacred Heart danced together. For instance, Anna M. Gillin concluded her discussion of the Feast of the Presentation, saying, "And we ourselves shall be happy. We shall understand better and love more devotedly the Sacred Heart of Christ, whose infinite love conceived and made possible the Blessed Sacrament, and who longs to have all His creatures come to Him frequently."[66] Instances of such sentiments could be multiplied.

Devotion to the Sacred Heart was greatly fostered in the nineteenth century by papal policies, and throughout this century it expanded significantly beyond the piety of reparation that Margaret-Mary Alacoque received in her visions at Paray-le-Monial in 1673 to 1675.[67] The devotion was ultimately connected with and contributed to a new understanding of God as the God of Love, replacing a regnant "pastorale de la peur."[68] The devotion, in the obvious, natural, and nearly universal figure of the heart of the Savior, emphasized both the humanity of Jesus and the particular loving capacity of this ever human, ever divine, being.[69] An emphasis upon the rich doctrine of the Incarnation follows from this devotional emphasis. "Two distinct loves emanate from the two distinct natures in Christ, and the symbol of both loves, the human and divine, is the Sacred Heart of Jesus Christ, 'true God and true Man.'"[70] Insofar as the unspeakably immense love of Jesus was ignored, reparation was appropriate. But even this ignoring Him did not impede Jesus's love for disbelievers or the tepid; the acts of reparation by the faithful both solicited conversion of the lax and faithless, and satisfied justice with respect to the adoration that was Jesus's due. This satisfaction corresponded, in its puny way, with the satisfaction of justice that Jesus effected with his passion.

Jansenistic piety emphasized the need for the communicant to be worthy of the sacrament and was tantamount to terrorizing the faithful about eating and drinking damnation to themselves in unworthy reception. Jansenists opposed devotion to the Sacred Heart, especially because of the "benevolent cast of its anthropology and soteriology."[71] Because the Sacred Heart devotion invigorated a sense of the love of Jesus by its natural symbolism, it prepared the way for frequent Communion not only by requiring monthly Communions for the completion of the novena and meriting a successful death, but also in counteracting Jansenistic rigorism. Recall that *STS* explicitly mobilized frequent Communion to extinguish Jansenism; devotion to the Sacred Heart and frequent Communion were tightly allied.

The Eucharistic movement underscored the connection between communicating and the Sacred Heart first by capitalizing upon the devotion's requiring frequent Communion. Although the literature of the Eucharistic movement did not advert to it, genuine commitment to the Sacred Heart required monthly Communion, and this enhanced the prospects for the promotion of yet more frequent, even daily, Communion. Saint Margaret-Mary urged Communion in an action of reparation on first Fridays twelve times per year. Her purpose may have been greater reception of the sacrament.[72] Besides this practical connection, the Eucharistic movement proposed a simple linkage between the Sacred Heart and Communion: the love of God. The very institution of the Eucharist thus connected this redeeming love to the Sacred Heart in the writings of the Eucharistic movement.

> When the hour chosen from all eternity by the wisdom of the Father had come for its [the Eucharist's] institution, all the pent-up love of an eternity burst forth from the Adorable Heart of Jesus in that cry of his soul to his chosen apostles. . . . And then he instituted that Sacrament of Love which has been the center and the very life of the Church, ever since its establishment.[73]

In addition, the particular Eucharistic aspects of the Sacred Heart attracted the attention of the Eucharistic movement and these aspects were emphasized. For instance, Father Peter M. Bregenzer, CSsR, recalled that the apparitions of Jesus to Saint Margaret-Mary occurred while she was praying before the Blessed Sacrament, exposed for Adoration.[74] Saint Claude De la Colombière (d. 1682), the Jesuit counselor of Margaret-Mary and publicist of the devotion, elected by Jesus himself, expressed no need to worry about venial sins while approaching Holy Communion.[75] "Provided the habit of living in mortal sin has been given up, provided it is no longer loved but on the contrary feared, provided occasions of committing it are avoided, while a sincere desire of salvation and of leading a Christian life is felt, I affirm that no other conditions are required for frequent communion."[76] He also provided many maxims that promoted frequent Communion: "Are you imperfect? Communicate often to progress in perfection."[77] De la Colombière's sentiments were not, of course, unique, but the source of his fame was devotion to the Sacred Heart, and so he embodied the coherence of the two devotions. The Eucharistic movement appropriated this Jesuit to increase frequency of Communion.

In the United States, deliberative actions of the PEL urged education of the faithful about its own framework for devotions. At the close of its convention in 1904, two motions pertain to the Sacred Heart in particular.

13. *Resolved,* That priests enlighten their people as to the real object of the devotion of the Sacred Heart and instruct them to seek the love of the Sacred Heart of Christ in the very Sacrament of His Love [i.e., the Eucharist].

14. *Resolved,* That devotions to the Blessed Sacrament and the Sacred Heart are mutual aids, the one to the other; that there can be no true devotion to the Sacred Heart that does not tend to frequent reception of Holy Communion. [78]

To the Eucharistic movement, all pious practices ultimately led to the Blessed Sacrament, and the campaign for frequent Communion recognized that receiving the sacrament was the culmination of devotion.

One consequence of *STS* was even greater detaching of Communion from the Mass. For example, Father John F. O'Hara, CSC (d. 1960), eventually cardinal archbishop of Philadelphia, as prefect at the University of Notre Dame would hear confessions and communicate students at their initiative and on their schedules. Holy Communion, linked more closely to confession than Mass, was thus removed from immediate and conscious participation in the Eucharistic liturgy. In response to O'Hara, some priest colleagues formed an opposing group, the Eucharistic Union, which insisted upon Holy Communion immediately after the priest's sermon.[79] O'Hara posted at Notre Dame data about Communions received and publicized his efforts nationally. In school year 1920–1921, the average daily number of Communions was 486; in 1929–1930, 1,409.[80] While such tactics as O'Hara's may seem harmful to sacramental literacy in retrospect, Nathan Mitchell observes that the nature of the sacrament as a physical object, coupled with proper devotional practices, safeguards its power to refer to the Eucharistic liturgy, itself the action of the entire community.[81]

Leaving no situation unexploited, the Eucharistic movement in the United States included the actions of the Sacred Heart in its own foundational myth. On the occasion of the twenty-fifth anniversary of Camillus Maes's consecration as bishop of Covington, Father Emile Poirier, SSS, speculated on what motivated this Belgian immigrant to involve himself in PEL. Speaking of these numerous and burdensome efforts on behalf of the Eucharistic Reign of Christ, he explained, "The reason of it all is explained to us by the symbol that appears in his coat of arms: The Sacred Heart of Jesus."[82] Bishop Maes, in a sermon at a meeting of the PPL in New York some years before, had spoken of the Eucharistic movement in a similar idiom. Bishop Maes "spoke in praise of the work which the People's League is doing to foster this union of hearts with that Heart of Love."[83]

While the love of Jesus connected Communion and the Sacred Heart, some systemization of the relation between the devotions challenged the pens of the contributors to the Eucharistic periodicals. One approach was freely scriptural in relying upon the piercing of the "side" of Jesus in the Passion. To connect the Blessed Sacrament with the Sacred Heart, a scriptural heart, layers of parallels developed:

> The sacred presence of Jesus, however, in the Holy Eucharist is the very heart of life and sacrament of the Church and her channels of grace. Thus it is true that the pierced heart of Jesus is final proof of sacrifice and sacrament of His body and blood. . . . Verily, the Blessed Sacrament is the gift of love of the Sacred Heart of Jesus.[84]

Underlying this treatment, however, was the doctrine of the Real Presence, which signified a physiological identity between the sacrament, the physical body, and, hypostatically, the divine nature of Jesus. As a human body must have a heart, so, "the heart of Jesus *is in* the body and blood [on the altar] as real and actual as Jesus Himself."[85]

As was the case with the rosary, the Sacred Heart was linked to the Blessed Sacrament by devotional piety. Even before 1900, a connection was made in a prayer composed for a retreat that, though preached by a Passionist priest, was focused now not directly on the Passion, as was the custom of that order, but on the Eucharist. This prayer was called "An Act of Reparation to Jesus Christ in the Blessed Sacrament," and it was dominated by the impetus of the devotion to the Sacred Heart, reparation.

> I adore Thee, I bless Thee, I love Thee, O Sacred Heart of Jesus in the Most Holy Sacrament of the Altar, I offer Thee, through the Immaculate Heart of Thy Holy Mother, the Sacred Host reposing in our tabernacles, to atone for all the sacrileges, impieties, profanations, and other crimes, by which Thou, O most Loving Heart, art outraged throughout the Universe.[86]

It is no surprise, given the Marian ethos, that the prayer allowed the offering through Mary in her own Immaculate Heart. The language of the prayer expressed an extraordinarily highly developed sense of the priesthood of the assembly in that the prayer is an "offering" of the "Sacred Host" by the lay retreatants.

The Eucharistic movement also articulated the relations between the Sacred Heart and frequent Communion by means of an exacting scholastic analysis.[87] In the abstract, devotions have their own objects, either formal or material. The formal object is the "reason that moves us to have devotion."[88] The material object divides into the primary, which is always an integral person, and the secondary, which is a particular aspect of the person.[89] The primary material object of all devotion to Christ, and ultimately even of Marian devotion, is the person of Jesus. The Heart, by the commonplace and extended meanings of *heart*, betokens love; as a devotional focus and by virtue of its connection with reparation, it emphasizes the nature of Our Lord and the "ardent love for mankind" that humanity ceaselessly slights.[90]

Here is the essential link between the two devotions: The Most Blessed Sacrament as a center of devotion also has as its primary material object the person of Jesus Christ. Therefore what distinguishes the Blessed Sacrament devotion is its reference to the love of Jesus as particularly manifest in his remaining among the faithful in the Real Presence. Simply stated, the person and love of Jesus connect the two devotions. The devotions differ according to the rococo systematic theology of the early twentieth century in their "special material object" and in their "special formal object."[91] More to the point of distinguishing the two devotions, the Sacred Heart—given its history, rationale, and practices—emphasizes the suffering of Jesus and the ingratitude of the faithful who scorn Him. Devotion to the Blessed Sacrament, in contrast, if fully implemented, eliminates the need for Sacred Heart devotion because no crimes against the Blessed Sacrament would then require reparation, the very reason for the devotion.[92]

The strategy of the Eucharistic movement was to appropriate the immense devotion to the Sacred Heart for its own advance, and so it discovered and emphasized the connectedness of the two devotions. In other contexts and for other purposes, however, separating the two modes of piety had proved desirable. For example, one American devotional work of the late eighteenth century, published under the auspices of the then recently disbanded Jesuits, read, "SIXTH QUERY: *What is the Difference between the Devotion to the Sacred Heart, and that which is paid to the blessed Sacrament? A. 1. It is very great. They differ in their object, motive, and end.*"[93] The difference in object is simply that the devotion to the Sacred Heart centers upon the heart of Jesus. The heart is indeed quite graphic; here a psychoanalytical historian describes it: "Imagine, for example, the heart ripped from the body of a man, wrapped tightly with a circlet of thorns, pierced with a knife, and then displayed on the outside of that man's chest. Not a stylized 'Valentine' heart, mind you, but a real, physical heart, complete with aortic opening and asymmetrical shape."[94] Blessed Sacrament devotion centers in the Eucharist, and this includes the *whole* body of Jesus. This devotion seems therefore more concerned than Sacred Heart devotions with iterating the doctrine of the Real Presence. The difference in motive applies to the respective devotee's reactions to two separate aspects of Jesus: The motive of devotion to the Sacred Heart is to respond to the love of God, manifest in the sufferings of Jesus that are symbolized by the image of the Sacred Heart. The devotee of the Blessed Sacrament responds not so much to the love of Jesus but to the awesome dignity of the sacrament. With respect to the "ends" of the two devotions, the Sacred Heart emphasizes the injuries to Christ in the Blessed Sacrament, and these injuries naturally evoke the acts of reparation of the devotee. Focus upon the Blessed Sacrament itself would as much as possible disregard its "sacrilegious indignities."[95] This distancing of the two devotional media may also have been motivated by considerations of "franchise," for Jesuits especially promulgated devotion to the Sacred Heart.

The efforts to connect the Sacred Heart devotion to Eucharistic devotion culminate in the hybridizing of the devotions to the Blessed Sacrament and the Sacred Heart. This hybrid devotion packages elements of the two in a new way, so that it is not exactly itself "new," and it is manifested in the coining of a Christic title, the Eucharistic Heart of Jesus, in 1854 by the Bishop of Saint Claude.[96] It followed a predictable course of growing popularity through the nineteenth century, often intersected with the activities of the Eucharistic movement, and achieved prominence with its institutionalization as an archconfraternity with its own requisite magazine under the direction of the Redemptorists in 1903.[97] Opposition to this hybrid centered around its indistinguishability from devotion to the Sacred Heart and around its emblem, "the heart of Jesus surrounded by flames in the middle of the Sacred Host."[98]

Advantages of this devotion seem subtle, for "the devotion to the Eucharistic Heart of Jesus is not substantially different from the devotion to the Sacred Heart."[99] The distinction, according to Bregenzer, is that the Sacred Heart devotion focuses on "the entire love of Jesus, taking His Heart as the figurative seat of love," and it is broad in accepting events in the expression of love, "the passion and Death of the Saviour, the institution of the Eucharist, the source of Grace, our final Judge, etc."[100] The *Eucharistic* Heart, on the other hand, focuses upon the "love of the Heart of Jesus in the Eucharist, and especially the cause of the Real Presence, namely His supreme love in instituting the Blessed Sacrament, giving Himself thereby perpetually to us to be our Victim, our Food, and our Friend. The importance of this special love, this Eucharistic love cannot be overestimated."[101] Engaging in this devotion would lead to a great love for the Eucharist and the Real Presence; the devotion reminded the devotee that in the Real Presence subsisted the Sacred Heart, "burning with love for us without ceasing until the culmination of the ages."[102] Thus, the historicity of the life of Jesus paled in comparison to the availability of Jesus to the faithful today in the sacrament at that moment. The devotion, identically to that of the Sacred Heart, demanded "acts of love, adoration, praise, thanksgiving, reparation, petition, propitiation, etc., . . . [and the] highly indulgenced and approved vocal prayers in honor of the Eucharistic Heart. Add to this frequent Communion."[103] Because frequent Communion had become an agenda of the entire Church, thanks to Saint Pius

X, this afterthought was not particularly distinguishing; the vocal prayers of the devotion are what distinguished the devotion to the Eucharistic Heart.

Has, in fact, frequent Communion has been restored? Essentially, the restoration pertains to the laity, and the term *frequent* describes a relative condition. Further, greater frequency of reception logically implies a perceptible and numerical increase in the numbers of Communion hosts distributed— thus more Communions. Because Pius X is indisputably pivotal in the alleged restoration, let him assess its success.

According to the terms of *STS*, Holy Communion has not become sufficiently frequent because it is not yet received daily by the majority of the laity. The Sacred Congregation of the Council during Pius X's pontificate merely proscribed forbidding daily Communion: "Frequent and daily Communion, as a practice most earnestly desired by Christ our Lord and by the Catholic Church, should be open to all the faithful, of whatever rank and condition of life; so that no one who is in the state of grace, and who approaches the holy table with a right and devout intention . . . can be prohibited therefrom."[104] The Eucharistic decrees and actions that surround *STS*, however, left no doubt that the pope intended a positive campaign to encourage universal and daily recourse to the Lord's Table. The revolutionary "restoration" of frequent Holy Communion has been met, certainly, in the area of our focused investigation, among English-speaking citizens of the United States, where Communion is weekly among those who attend Sunday Mass. The more dramatic goal of daily Communion remains largely unmet. Furthermore, this book hopes to encourage investigations of Communion practices in other cultural spheres so that Pius's achievement can be properly assessed.

## A TAXONOMY OF PIETY

In the late nineteenth century, calls for more frequent reception of Communion slowly swelled within the Eucharistic movement. Such exhortations not only predated the movement, but echoed through the centuries since the days of Chrysostom and, in fact, have provided the standard evidence for the general desuetude of Holy Communion. The preeminent theological concern of post-Reformation Catholicism with respect to the Eucharist was an insistence upon the Real Presence. In the nineteenth century, receiving Communion signaled a rejection of liberalism and scientific positivism.[105] The Eucharistic movement arose from the admixture of politics, philosophy, and religion in France in the mid- to late nineteenth century. The dread reality of intimacy with God in the Blessed Sacrament necessitated an awareness of the gravity of receiving, and so, while the movement promoted greater reception of

Communion, its correlative mission was to educate the faithful about the significance of the action, in itself a profound participation in the Mass.[106]

The Eucharistic movement positioned the Blessed Sacrament at the apex of holy things and in the process carefully and vigorously tried to reconfigure multiple pieties. We have here investigated only two of these, the rosary and the Sacred Heart. The Eucharistic movement prayed, and its *lex orandi* conformed the universe of devotions to a sophisticated sacramental theology, a *lex credendi*. The movement harped upon the meaning of the Eucharist—that is, the functional equivalent with respect to salvation—even though it did not distinguish between "devotion" and "liturgy."

What is this sacramental theology? In short, the Eucharist is identical to the Passion, and hence to the salvation of the world; in those days, popularly and devotionally, the Passion hardly pointed to the Resurrection. Academic theology, too, virtually ignored this. F. X. Durrwell was largely responsible for correcting this overly narrow view of redemption; his point of departure was biblical.[107] He described the theological situation in the late 1950s:

> Not so long ago theologians used to study the Redemption without mentioning the Resurrection at all. The fact of Easter was made to yield its utmost value as a piece of apologetics; but no-one thought of examining it in itself as one of the inexhaustible mysteries of our salvation. . . . When the Resurrection was mentioned, it was not so much to give it any part in our salvation as to show it as Christ's personal triumph over his enemies, and a kind of glorious counterblast to the years of humiliation he had endured to redeem us.[108]

Indeed, Charles Davis tantalizingly connected the revitalization of a popular awareness of the Resurrection with recent liturgical reforms. "More than any other factor the liturgical revival is making ordinary Catholics aware of the Resurrection as a mystery of salvation. The consequences of this are so many that we can say that the present renewal in the Church is essentially a rediscovery of the Resurrection."[109] Anscar Vonier, OSB (d. 1938), a generation before Durrwell, had pointed to the connection between receiving Communion and a theology of redemption that was integrated with the Resurrection.

> Festiveness is the only temper which Christians may bring to the reception of that heavenly bread; they cannot be sad, they must rejoice with the angels in heaven when eating that divine manna. It is not known to the history of Christian spirituality that the faithful ever approached the Eucharistic table with other dispositions than those of gladness and triumph.[110]

Vonier's work first appeared in 1914, as the campaign for frequent Communion was fully active.

The overriding emphasis in the early twentieth century was that Jesus suffered. Such a devotion to the bleeding Sacred Heart emphasized the pain of the Crucifixion as well as the continuing pain of the Real Presence of Jesus in the Eucharistic species, reserved but ignored and desecrated. Of course, the pain followed from the saving love of Jesus for each person. Still, Jesus was the "Prisoner of the Tabernacle" in most popular devotion and insofar as Communion remained infrequent. In fact, Vonier conceded that this type of spirituality, with emphasis upon reparation to the indignities Christ "suffers" in the Eucharist, reserved, was licit, but he corrected that piety by reference to the glorification of Christ in heaven as a consequence of the Resurrection. "The sufferings of Christ may be said to haunt the mind of the Church. . . . But it is, of course, beyond all doubt that in Himself, in His self-subsisting personality at the right hand of the Almighty, Christ is infinitely far from the contact of evil, sadness and woe."[111]

It is the Resurrection that makes the Eucharist a "monument of that Death like unto which there is no other death," and therefore festive.[112]

Both salvation in history and in the Eucharist manifest the love of God; the Eucharist is particular among the sacraments in expressing this love of God because it connects explicitly with the Cross even by the words of institution. This being the case, only a taxonomy of devotions that makes Eucharist paramount accords with Christian dogma.

Did devotion to the Blessed Sacrament, manifest most liturgically and sacramentally in frequent Holy Communion, occur prior to the revitalization of the theology of salvation in the full Paschal Mystery? Alternatively, did a growth in awareness of soteriology promote devotion to the Real Presence and more Holy Communions? As a chicken-and-egg question, this may be insoluble.

Promoting the Blessed Sacrament as an object of devotion was probably not motivated by profoundly theological reasons. The first resolution of the first national priests' Eucharistic congress actually specified that the devotion was retained because it could be perceived as manly and also specifically in order to "control" Catholic men.

> 1. Devotion to the Most Blessed Sacrament is eminently calculated to foster strong, solid, and enlightened piety, to influence those who are capable of exercising influence upon others, to appeal powerfully to men. But to reach this class of persons, whom more than any others it is important to control, the dogma bearing upon this mystery should from time to time be clearly and strongly explained.[113]

This particular witness indicates that the Blessed Sacrament was at the time viewed as a solution to a pastoral difficulty: the relative lack of practice of the faith by males.

The pages of the periodicals of the Fathers of the Blessed Sacrament and the proceedings of the Eucharistic assemblies that the magazines report together exhibit the will to reconfigure devotions. All aspects of spirituality fell within the purview of the editors and leaders. A resolution from the third national Eucharistic congress (1904) laments the lack of proportion between theological realities and popular devotional practices.

> 5. *Resolved,* That to correct the apparent irreverence to, or at least the neglect of, the Blessed Sacrament which may be observed in some instances in our churches, the sense of the Eucharistic League is that, all devotions should be centered in the Real Presence, and that all priests are advised to reiterate their instructions to the people, that, however right and useful it may be and is to honor the images of Christ and His saints, as they relate to Him and to them, such honor should never be paid to them to the neglect of the worship due to God in the Sacrament of the Altar, where He is really present, Body, Blood, Soul, and Divinity.[114]

This ordering of devotions according to academic theology shares in the wider culture's organizing impulse in the wake of the Industrial Revolution.

Prominent historians of devotion, such as Taves and Orsi, perceive that the Church was following a course of consolidation of power and was motivated, perhaps unconsciously, by an impetus to control.[115] This thrust to control originated in the Counter-Reformation, and it is a commonplace of sociology that institutions that perceive themselves as embattled become much more rigorous.[116] More particularly to the United States, but more broadly in terms of the ambient culture, social historians concur that, from the end of the Civil War and through the 1920s, virtually all institutions were centralized at an astonishing rate, and this was largely facilitated by both the Civil War and World War I.[117] The Church partook of these trends: Romanizing the American Catholic church became a solution to bitter and contentious rivalries along ethnic lines, and to Romanize was to centralize. On the continent, a parade of political disasters throughout the 1800s had the pope become the "prisoner of the Vatican," but the loss of the Church's cultural and political influence encouraged its attention to devotional issues. As the origins of the international Eucharistic movement in France in the 1880s revealed, however, in most arenas a wall of separation between religious on the one hand and political and cultural events on the other was chimerical.

Theologically, however, the explicit motive of the Church in its Eucharistic movement was to align properly the devotional lives of the faithful and the theology of salvation. In so doing in the United States, the Church transformed itself from an extremely diverse amalgam, largely consisting of superstitious peasants, into well-assimilated American Roman Catholics.[118]

If Catholic devotions at the turn of the century were a smorgasbord, they constituted an organized buffet wherein appetizers and vegetables and desserts could all be chosen to suit one's palate, but wherein the one obligatory main course defined one's membership and ratified one's identity. The influence of neo-scholasticism made the choice of courses more exact and was of a piece with the final closing processions of the Eucharistic congresses, where the order of march literally presented, for the appreciation of the faithful, proximity to God in the ostensorium through the agency of the hierarchical Church.

An instance of such a taxonomy, convenient and relevant because it locates rosary and Sacred Heart devotions, and simple because it is intended for religious educators, climbs along two paths to its apex, the Blessed Sacrament. The taxonomy implies, first, psychological and spiritual growth in the practice of religion, and this growth parallels intellectual appreciation of the mysteries of the faith. As an educator, Xaverian Brother Julien (d. 1937) stressed both the age-appropriateness of certain devotions and the inestimable value of imbuing children with the sense of the transcendent early and continuously: "As childhood is attracted to childhood, so, for the very young, devotion to the Infant Jesus is very appealing; and the primary teacher can readily instill a solid love that is tender, compassionate, and will prove a groundwork for subsequent teachers."[119] The two pieties that must be inculcated earliest were private morning and evening prayers and frequent assistance at Mass.[120] Brother Julien's ladder of devotions then showed the rung of the Sacred Heart because this was so emphatic of the love of Jesus and of our redemption by the Cross. The next step was the inculcation of Holy Name devotions, which derived their value from two assets. First, commitment to avoiding blasphemy provided witness of the faith to the secular world and was hence evangelical. Second, because the devotions were social, membership in the society provided support in one's spiritual life. Next in the ladder of devotions, the rosary cultivated devotion to the Blessed Virgin Mary, who was "the tender part of our religion."[121] Unlike the Eucharistic periodicals, Brother Julien allowed the rosary to remain, as it were, Marian, and recommended that a battery of methods be marshaled to instill devotion to Mary. The very top of the ladder was the Blessed Sacrament; this was the source of the "light" of all the other devotions. The real point of these other devotions was to point to Jesus Christ in the Blessed Sacrament.

> Finally, in the matter of devotions, no matter how praiseworthy their immediate object may be, all, to be spiritually valuable, must eventually lead to the Author and center of all devotion—Jesus in the Blessed Sacrament. . . . In the spiritual order, we gaze upon the Light of lights with more profit when the darkness of

sin and imperfections has been gradually obliterated by the lesser lights of devotions having Jesus in the Blessed Sacrament at once their power and end.[122]

Brother Julien concluded the essay with the injunction to promote frequent Communion among the pupils, and he motivated this recommendation in the following words: "There [at the altar], devotion is culminated, for devotion is love; and the highest expression of love—the grandest act of devotion—is when God meets man, when Heart Divine says to heart human: 'Do this in commemoration of Me.'"[123] In context, the "doing" cannot be construed as the consecration of the bread and wine; rather, it means that, in the communicating, the faithful were uniting in the sacrifice of Jesus, and performing their own offerings. Mother Mary Loyola, a convert to Catholicism and a Sister of Loretto (d. 1930), depicted the dynamic of offering as a response to the saving love of God; to this, an offering of the totality of life would be insufficient, and so the soul's offering must expand its object. "I offer thee the virtues and merits of all the Angels and saints. I offer thee the heart of Mary most holy. . . . I offer thee thy own most sacred Heart."[124] The Eucharistic movement adjusted popular devotions so that their meanings became more theologically sophisticated and focused upon the economy of salvation through Christ's Passion.

## NOTES

1. R. Laurence Moore's book details the dovetailing of the commercial and spiritual, but since his analysis applies to unmitigated competition, not only between denominations but also between religion and leisure, it does not readily apply to this study. "In it [a situation of pluralism and noninvolvement by the state] religious institutions become consumer commodities. And . . . a good deal of religious activity comes to be dominated by the logic of market economies." R. Laurence Moore, *Selling God: American Religion in the Marketplace of Culture* (New York: Oxford, 1994), 7.

2. Barbara Corrado Pope, "Immaculate and Powerful: The Marian Revival in the Nineteenth Century," in *Immaculate and Powerful: The Female in Sacred Image and Social Reality*, edited by Margaret R. Miles (Boston: Beacon, 1985), 173.

3. Pope, "Marian Revival," 173.

4. Pope, "Marian Revival," 171.

5. Chinnici, "Eucharist," 146.

6. "This new form of devotion [modern and mass pilgrimages] was also an adaptation to an increasingly urban and industrial society. In the end it sapped the power of local French shrines and created a mass rather than 'folk' religious culture." Pope, "Marian Revival," 175. The penchant for quantifying which the Eucharistic

movement absorbed or augmented from the ambient culture is evident in the regular reporting of data on such things as numbers of Communions by Father John O'Hara, CSC, Prefect at the University of Notre Dame. R. Laurence Moore documents the interpenetration of the commercial and the spiritual in the United States, but his study largely limits itself to Protestant initiatives. "Beginning early in the nineteenth century, religious leaders contributed to a process that made the organization of spiritual affairs in America congruent with an individualistic market-driven economy." Moore, *Selling God*, 119. This commercialization of religion created an energized environment simultaneous with the Eucharistic movement, which was well aware of the danger of loss of members to Protestantism.

7. Taves, *Household*, 102.

8. Taves, *Household*, 102.

9. Before 1873, many clergymen had condemned pilgrimages, but after that year, "the official attitude changed, and the church moved to tie these potentially subversive impulses to the sacramental system." Pope, "Marian Revival," 174–75.

10. Pope, "Marian Revival," 175. Stephen Coubé noted that by the year 1900, pilgrimage usually culminated in a general Communion. "It is also customary now, for hundreds and thousands of men to approach the holy table in a body, on certain solemn occasions, and to kneel round the altar in immense numbers on pilgrimages." Since Communion was administered by the clergy, this perception corroborates the thesis of growing control of popular pieties by the officials of the Church. Stephen Coubé, *Discourses on Weekly Communion*, 129.

11. Pope, "Marian Revival," 182.

12. Pope, "Marian Revival," 182–83.

13. Taves, *Household*, 103.

14. Taves, *Household*, 111.

15. Toby Lester, "Oh, Gods!" *Atlantic Monthly* 289, no. 2 (February 2002): 43.

16. *ET*, 148; the title was described as "new" in Joseph V. Gerold, "The Third Annual Convention of the Diocese of Pittsburg [*sic*]," *EPUL* 12 (1906): 155.

17. *ET*, 148.

18. *ET*, 149.

19. *ET*, 150.

20. *ET*, 148.

21. *ET*, 150.

22. Lois Donovan, "Communion," *Ssac* 19 (1916): 423.

23. *ET*, 150.

24. Anna M. Gillin, "Dispositions for a Worthy Communion," *Ssac* (1916): 454.

25. Michael J. Carroll, *Catholic Cults and Devotions: A Psychological Inquiry* (Kingston, Ontario: McGill-Queen's, 1989), 5–16.

26. Anne Winston-Allen, *Stories of the Rose: The Making of the Rosary in the Middle Ages* (University Park: Pennsylvania State University Press, 1997), 8.

27. Herbert Thurston, "Our Popular Devotions, II: the Rosary," *Month* 96, no. 436 (October 1900): 403.

28. Taves, *Household*, 149.

29. The Dominican rosary is that which became most popular of various ways of praying the beads and is the only one discussed here. Other types of rosaries, often called chaplets, include the Bridgettine; those rosaries of Our Lady of Consolation, of the Immaculate Conception, and of the Immaculate Heart of Mary; and the Seraphic rosary. Carroll, *Catholic Cults and Devotions*, 197n4.

30. The narrative of this origin of the rosary is only documented nearly 250 years after the death of Saint Dominic. Carroll, *Catholic Cults and Devotions*, 11–12.

31. O'B [*sic*], "A Eucharistic Rosary," *EPUL* (1896): 218–19. Because the roll of members of the PEL listed at that time thirteen O'Briens and one O'Boylan, the identity of this author remains obscure. Likely candidates are Thomas O'Brien, William O'Brien Pardow, and Eliza O'Brien Lummis, all cited elsewhere in this book.

32. "October Thoughts about the Rosary," *Ssac* 14 (1911): 513.

33. Romig, *Guide to Catholic Literature*, 1: 993.

34. "October Thoughts," 514–15.

35. "October Thoughts," 515.

36. O'B, "A Eucharistic Rosary," 218.

37. This contrasts with a much more sophisticated and biblically based theology. See, for example, Josef Pieper, *In Search of the Sacred: Contributions to an Answer*, translated by Lothar Krauth (San Francisco: Ignatius, 1991), 128.

38. Albert Tesnière, "Communion in the Life of Jesus Christ," *EPUL* 24 (1918): 226–27.

39. Chauvin, "Ceremonies," 172.

40. O'B, "A Eucharistic Rosary," 217–18.

41. This was a commonplace of the era. Popular artistic realizations of this figure of speech are available in Catherine Rosenbaum, "Images-souvenirs de première Communion," in *La Première Communion: Quartre siècles d'histoire*, edited by Jean Delumeau (Paris: Desclée de Brouwer, 1987), 159–60.

42. O'B, "A Eucharistic Rosary," 218.

43. O'B, "A Eucharistic Rosary," 219–20.

44. "Archconfraternity of the Blessed Sacrament, or the People's Eucharistic League," *Ssac* 19 (1916): 426.

45. Gillin, "Dispositions for a Worthy Communion," 448.

46. Theodore Warning, "The People's Eucharistic League," *Ssac* 14 (1911): 526. The holy hour itself, as an important form of popular, paraliturgical devotion and precursor of the liturgical movement, deserves scholarly attention. Vincent Ferrer Kienberger described a holy hour according to two completely separate plans. One plan accords with the method of Eymard, which focused upon the Blessed Sacrament and used three modalities of prayer—adoration, thanksgiving, and petition. The other plan uses the rosary as its outline. "The Holy Hour," *EPUL* 24 (1918): 298–99.

47. The term *rosary* refers not only to the total method of the devotion, but also to the beads. Carroll, *Catholic Cults and Devotions*, 11.

48. "Saint Pascal's Rosary of the Blessed Sacrament," *Ssac* 14 (1911): 515; this article is attributed to the *Bulletin Eucharistique*.

49. Arthur M. Viau, *The Virgin in the Holy Eucharist*, 2 volumes (LaFargeville, New York: n.p., 1946), 17.

50. Viau, *The Virgin in the Holy Eucharist*, 10–16.

51. Viau, *The Virgin in the Holy Eucharist*, 18.

52. Peter M. Bregenzer, "Devotion to the Eucharistic Heart," *EPUL* 29 (1923): 163.

53. Raymond Jonas, *France and the Cult of the Sacred Heart: An Epic Tale for Modern Times* (Berkeley: University of California Press, 2000).

54. Jonas, *Cult of the Sacred Heart*, 5.

55. Robert Emmett Curran, *American Jesuit Spirituality: The Maryland Tradition, 1634–1900* (New York: Paulist, 1988), 18–19.

56. Derély, "Les décrets eucharistiques," 897.

57. Annice Callahan, "The Visions of Margaret Mary Alacoque from a Rahnerian Perspective," in *Modern Christian Spirituality: Methodological and Historical Essays*, edited by Bradley C. Hanson (Atlanta: Scholars, 1990), 186n9. Rahner implies that this great promise of the Sacred Heart does not contradict "experience or dogmatic principles," but he cautions that it must be preached very carefully so as not to occasion "sinning by thoughtlessness or presumption against the mercy of God." Karl Rahner, "Some Theses for a Theology of Devotion to the Sacred Heart," in *Theological Investigations*, vol. 3, *The Theology of the Spiritual Life*, translated by Karl-H. and Boniface Kruger (Baltimore: Helicon, 1967), 352.

58. James L. Connolly, "Benediction of the Blessed Sacrament: Its History and Present Status," *Ecclesiastical Review* 85 (November 1931): 460.

59. Callahan, "Visions of Margaret Mary Alacoque," 199.

60. Senn, *People's Work*, 244.

61. Paula M. Kane, "'She Offered Herself Up': The Victim Soul and Victim Spirituality in Catholicism," *Church History* 71, no. 1 (2002): 91–97.

62. "Subject of Adoration," *EPUL* 22 (1916): 104–5.

63. Rahner seems to isolate *reparation* from its particularly Eucharistic context in the modern development of the devotion to the Sacred Heart so that he can connect it with the pious contemplation of the suffering of the Lord, and, more broadly, with "*all* the works and acts done in his grace and love." Rahner, "Some Theses," 348–49.

64. James H. McGean, "Proceedings, Third Eucharistic Congress," *EPUL* 10 (1904): 551.

65. Vincent, "Eucharistic Mission," *EPUL* 5 (1899): 102.

66. Gillin, "Dispositions for a Worthy Communion," 454.

67. Callahan, "Visions of Margaret Mary Alacoque," 187.

68. "Care of the parish through fear." Gibson, *French Catholicism*, 241.

69. William O'Brien Pardow, "The Relation of Devotion to the Sacred Heart and to the Blessed Sacrament," *EPUL* 12 (1906): 127–28; Abbé Roland, "The Heart of Jesus in the Eucharist," *EPUL* 13 (1907): 144–53.

70. Vincent Ferrer Kienberger, "The Sacred Heart and the Holy Eucharist," *EPUL* 29 (1923): 177.

71. Curran, *American Jesuit Spirituality*, 19.

72. Callahan, "The Visions of Margaret Mary Alacoque," 191n16.

73. Raphael Fuhr, "The Holy Eucharist and Sacred Music," *EPUL* 27 (1921): 354.

74. Bregenzer, "Devotion," 167. Abbé Roland specifies that Margaret-Mary's eyes were fixed, rather, upon the tabernacle when Christ appeared. Roland, "Heart of Jesus in the Eucharist," 151. Included in the messages of Saint Margaret-Mary was the information that Jesus is particularly insulted when the Blessed Sacrament is exposed upon the altar. Joseph M. Keller, *The Sacred Heart. Anecdotes and Examples to Assist in Promoting the Devotion to the Sacred Heart* (New York: Benziger, 1899), 27.

75. Keller, *The Sacred Heart. Anecdotes and Examples*, 34.

76. Keller, *Sacred Heart*, 34.

77. "Maxims of the Ven. Father De la Colombière on Frequent Communion," *EPUL* 4 (1898): 139.

78. McGean, "Proceedings, Third Eucharistic Congress," 552–53. Similar motions can be quoted innumerably. The resolutions at the first national Eucharistic congress, held in Washington in 1895, did not specifically urge frequent Communion upon the laity; rather, they encouraged the reverend fathers to model the thanksgiving after Communion for the people and to prepare first communicants thoroughly. Walter Elliot, "Report of the Transactions of the Meeting," in *Eucharistic Conferences: The Papers Presented at the First American Eucharistic Congress, Washington, D.C., October, 1895* (New York: Catholic Book Exchange, 1896), 183–86.

79. Thomas T. McAvoy, *Father O'Hara of Notre Dame, the Cardinal Archbishop of Philadelphia* (Notre Dame, Indiana: University of Notre Dame Press, 1967), 79 and 92–93; the final chapter of this book delves into the issue of properly liturgical Holy Communion.

80. John O'Hara, "What Is Behind Notre Dame Football?" *Religious Bulletin*, 11 October 1930, n.p., PNDP 83-Re-1B, Archives of the University of Notre Dame, Notre Dame, Indiana.

81. Mitchell, *Cult and Controversy*, 255.

82. E. Poirier, "The Jubilee of Our Right Reverend Protector," *EPUL* 16 (1910): 162.

83. "The Peoples' Eucharistic League," 61.

84. Joseph Sellinger, "The Relation of the Sacred Heart of Jesus to the Blessed Sacrament," *EPUL* 27 (1921): 267.

85. Sellinger, "Relation of the Sacred Heart," 267.

86. Vincent, "Eucharistic Mission," 100.

87. Kienberger, "Sacred Heart," 177.

88. Pardow, "Relation of Devotion," 126; Kienberger used the same categories seventeen years later.

89. Rahner finds this "usual" dogmatic explanation of the nature of the Sacred Heart of Jesus both "linguistically" and "objectively" unhelpful. Rahner, "Some Theses," 336–37.

90. Pardow, "Relation of Devotion," 129.

91. Pardow, "Relation of Devotion," 131–32.

92. Pardow, "Relation of Devotion," 132.

93. *The Pious Guide to Prayer and Devotion* [1792], reprinted in Curran, *American Jesuit Spirituality*, 157; Curran gives no further bibliographic information about this manual in the archives at Georgetown University.

94. Michael P. Carroll, *Catholic Cults and Devotions*, 3; Karl Rahner emphasizes that the heart is very stylistic indeed so as to refer to its transcendent meaning. Rahner, "Some Theses," 333.

95. *The Pious Guide*, 157.

96. The bishop's name is not mentioned in the article, and the country of the diocese is also omitted. Bregenzer, "Devotion," 162.

97. Bregenzer, "Devotion," 164.

98. Bregenzer, "Devotion," 162–63.

99. Bregenzer, "Devotion," 164.

100. Bregenzer, "Devotion," 165.

101. Bregenzer, "Devotion," 165.

102. Bregenzer, "Devotion," 167.

103. Bregenzer, "Devotion," 167.

104. "On the Daily Reception of Communion," 13.

105. That frequent Communion coheres with the antimodernist thrust of the Vatican is evident in Leo XIII's *Mirae Caritatis*. His context is the assertion the Real Presence is indeed a miracle, and then he notes that many "prodigies" (*prodigia*) of the Blessed Sacrament occur to assure us of this fact. The miraculous, however, is a challenge to the rational and scientific: "It is plain that by this Sacrament faith is fed, in it the mind finds its nourishment, the objections of rationalists are brought to naught, and abundant light is thrown on the supernatural order." *MC*, 502.

106. The vast involvement of the laity in the Eucharistic movement was, according to Joseph P. Chinnici, momentous in their empowerment and hence as a preparation for Catholic social action; in the sacramental realm, this coheres with how the receiving of the sacrament actually allows the communicant to take a "more active ecclesiological role." Chinnici, "Eucharist," 150.

107. Bernard Sesboüé, "Salut," *Dictionnaire de spirituallité*.

108. Charles Davis, "Introduction," in *The Resurrection: A Biblical Study*, by Francis Xavier Durrwell, translated by Rosemary Sheed (New York: Sheed and Ward, 1960), xxiii.

109. Davis, "Introduction," xix.

110. Anscar Vonier, *The Victory of Christ*, in *The Collected Works of Abbot Vonier*, vol. 1: *The Incarnation and Redemption* (Westminster, Maryland: Newman, n.d.), 312.

111. Vonier, *Victory of Christ*, 210.

112. Vonier, *Victory of Christ*, 309.

113. Elliot, "Report of the Transactions," 183.

114. McGean, "Proceedings, Third Eucharistic Congress," 551.

115. "The devotional practices promoted during the mid-nineteenth century were thus promoted by the hierarchy to standardize practices within the church internationally; to relocate devotional practices in the parish church under the control of the priest; to distinguish Catholics from non-Catholics; and to rally the laity to the church

and its hierarchy in the face of perceived dangers from without." Taves, *Household*, 111. Similarly, Orsi's *Madonna of 115th Street* details densely how the officials of the Roman Catholic Church, who happened to be Irish, in New York City gained control over the *festa*.

116. Taves, *Household*, 94–95.

117. Stuart McConnell, "The Gilded Age," and Lynn Dumenil, "The Progressive Era through the 1920s," *Encyclopedia of American Social History*, 1993 ed.

118. My use of the word *superstitious* may derive more from the prejudices of the Irish American, Roman Catholic clerical elite in the nineteenth century than from the situation proper. Orsi reports this perspective, saying, "Right from the beginning, official Catholic observers criticized Italian religiosity for being exotic and pagan." He also details the assimilative sentiments with respect to the recent immigrants. Orsi, *Madonna of 115th Street*, xiv, 54ff.

119. Brother Julien [George A. Ryan], "Devotion and Devotions," *Catholic Educational Review* 4 (September 1912): 170.

120. Brother Julien, "Devotion and Devotions," 171–72.

121. Brother Julien, "Devotion and Devotions," 176.

122. Brother Julien, "Devotion and Devotions," 178.

123. Brother Julien, "Devotion and Devotions," 178.

124. Mother Mary Loyola [Elizabeth Giles], *Welcome Holy Communion: Before and After*, edited by Herbert Thurston (1904; reprint, London: Burns Oates & Washbourne, 1948), 11–12.

## Chapter Seven

# Theology, Liturgical and Systematic

Systematic theology for the duration of the Eucharistic and liturgical movements remained resolutely constant in its articulation of the sacramental theology of the Eucharist. Pope Leo XIII's encyclical *Aeterni Patris* (4 August 1879) had enthroned Thomas Aquinas in seminary education worldwide largely because Scholasticism was considered a powerful and faithful method for determining relationships among faith, nature, and culture.[1] What may have been so appealing to Leo were the nineteenth-century ahistorical readings of Aquinas. The theological mainstream exclusively concerned itself with the Real Presence of Jesus in the Eucharistic species, even as post-Reformation history and the devotional *lex orandi* determined otherwise.

In this environment, articulations of the doctrine of the Real Presence by members of the Eucharistic and liturgical movements did convey the universally professed and stalwartly guarded doctrine. Joseph Kramp summarized for a general readership the unquestionable doctrine of the Eucharist as the Real Presence:

> We all believe in the presence of our Lord Jesus Christ in the holy Eucharist. We all believe that He is present as God and as Man, with soul and body, truly, really, substantially, these words being taken in the meaning and sense which Catholic tradition and the Church's teaching apply to them. (We emphasize this, because the great reformers also speak in part of a true, real, and substantial presence.) We all believe that Christ as God and as Man is deserving of our adoration—as Man on account of the mysterious union of the divine and human natures in Him, which we call hypostatic.[2]

By repeating the "we all," Kramp created—or even presumed—a community of believers. This community was more than a stylistic flourish, but was

integral to Kramp's perception of the social nature of the Eucharist as the
Body of Christ. The Real Presence was, for Kramp, only a starting point for
his expansive understanding of the sacrament.

In his tightly woven essay, Kramp also suggested that the prevailing Eucharist doctrine in 1930 derived from those polemical dynamics that fueled
the Tridentine articulations of the doctrine of the Real Presence. Predating
those polemics were, of course, the disputes in the monastery at Corby in the
ninth century and involving Berengarius in the eleventh, to which he needed
not refer.

The Eucharistic movement tarried in a theological cusp until Pius X embraced the restoration of frequent Communion. Tiresome insistence upon
the theology of the Real Presence supported equally repetitive injunctions to
avail oneself of visits to the Blessed Sacrament, to excite one's religious affections by gazing upon the Blessed Sacrament exposed, and to witness one's
faith publicly by processing in honor of the Blessed Sacrament on the feast
of Corpus Christi.

The practice of a *liturgical* piety of the Eucharist emerged from the Eucharistic movement, as the programs from the Eucharistic congresses show. So
far as faith in Providence allows a separation between history and theology, a
properly theological reason for the gradual emergence of a Eucharistic piety
in the second half of the nineteenth century may be this: The very nature of all
the sacraments required their physicalness, and sacramental theology insisted
upon this point. The Eucharist, in its matter of bread and wine, conveyed
forcibly and nearly inescapably, despite innumerable ages of ritually enacted
denial, its "foodness." In the same vein, Nathan Mitchell concludes his discourse on the intrinsic physicalness of the Holy Eucharist and its ineluctable
natural symbolism thus: "The eucharistic food that remains after Mass ceases
to be a mere object; it becomes an action in its own right, inviting us to return to the table, to commit ourselves more deeply to one another."[3] As the
dominant image of God as judge was transformed through such devotions as
that of the Sacred Heart, God became a loving redeemer; simultaneously, the
distant and awesome God, gazed upon in his disguise of bread and displayed
in an ornate monstrance, evolved into a personal, accessible, even edible God,
Jesus in the Blessed Sacrament.

The founding of religious orders reveals how the one aspect of the Eucharist, the Real Presence, dominated piety in the early nineteenth century.
Between 1807 and 1858 in France alone were founded four orders of nuns
whose titles include the phrase "perpetual adoration," and a fifth, founded by
Saint Pierre-Julien Eymard, was radically committed to this work.[4] By the
promulgation of *STS*, religious were drafted into the campaign for frequent

Communion by their example.[5] Eymard's Blessed Sacrament Fathers originally promoted Eucharistic devotion and this emphasized adoration of the Real Presence, especially at ceremonies during which the reserved host was exposed to view.

> The cult of the exposition of the Blessed Sacrament is the need of our times; it is necessary to have this public protestation of the faith of the people in the divinity of Jesus Christ and in the truth of His sacramental presence. It is the best of all refutations to oppose to renegades, apostates, the impious and the indifferent. This cult is necessary to save society. Society is aging because it has no longer a center of truth and charity, but it will grow strong and full of vigor as soon as all its members gather around Life, around Jesus in the Eucharist. It is necessary to bring Him from His retreat to be placed anew at the head of Christian societies, that He may save and direct them.[6]

In the language of the day, devotion did not exclude receiving Holy Communion. As the Eucharistic movement gradually espoused more frequent Communion, the Blessed Sacrament Fathers were able to incorporate this piety into their program of devotions with holy enthusiasm, for "devotion" was then more broadly defined.

While it is beyond this book to review the immense literature of the Eucharistic congresses, even the quantity of papers devoted to the two topics—adoration and Communion—indicate growing interest in Communion and, hence, in the broadest sense, in the liturgy. Remember, though, that adoration did not exclude receiving Communion but often did lead to it, as Liguori's discursive prayers of the visits to the Blessed Sacrament emphasized.

At the first International Eucharistic Congress in Lille in 1881, seven speakers addressed the topic of adoration of the Blessed Sacrament; only two touched upon frequent Communion, and rather tangentially and spontaneously. The first, in the general evening session, Father Joseph Leman, urged frequent Communion and reverence for the Holy Name of Jesus in an address entitled, "The Reëstablishment of the Rights of Jesus Christ."[7] In fact, Communion stood subordinate to the goal of reverence for the name of Jesus, which in turn was subordinate to an institutional re-Christianization of the state in France. The rhetorical highlight of the congress was a dialogic prayer lead by Jesuit Charles Verbecke / Verbeke (d. 1889) during a spontaneous candlelit procession. The prayer itself was an act of reparation, generously recalling profanations and irreverences toward the Real Presence, but it did request that the faithful might "participate frequently in the Eucharist banquet; assist often at the sacrifice of Thy love."[8] Because of their diction and context, these phrases requested more frequent Communion in a veiled, almost coded way. Just eighteen years later, at Lourdes, six papers and three most influential sermons by Father Stephen Coubé examined and thereby promoted frequent—in his case, *weekly*—Communion.[9]

Often, Holy Communion seemed more a means to an end than an end itself; it was considered by the members of the Eucharistic movement a courageous statement of religious faith to the scoffing anticlericals and rationalists. Even more so than marching in a procession or going on a pilgrimage, Communion reception was an enacted personal commitment both to faith and to the Real Presence. As faith-filled and public, receiving signified a defiance of the rational and empirical.

Strictly apologetical texts of the late nineteenth century undervalue this testimonial and sacramental Communion. For example, Father Jean-Baptiste Berthier, MS (d. 1908), organized his entire discussion at the congress on the Eucharist around two headings: sacrament and sacrifice. In a rather juridical vein, Berthier addressed dispositions for Communion in nine pages, but in defining Eucharist, he wrote, "Holy Communion does not belong to the essence of the Sacrament, but is only the indispensable condition of its effects."[10] Berthier's ignoring of Communion actually more accorded with worship at his time than with what Trent had actually said about the Eucharist. Kramp saw three essential aspects of the Eucharist addressed by that normative council—namely, sacrifice, Communion, and Real Presence. Significantly, in contrast to Berthier, Kramp depicted Communion as integral to the Eucharist: "We all believe that we receive this very Christ in Communion as the food of our souls or, as we also say, sacramentally. We all believe that the Mass is a sacrifice; a sacrifice which at the same time is a mysterious making present of the great Sacrifice of Redemption on Calvary."[11] A tide of publicity in favor of frequent reception of Holy Communion and its presumed effectiveness had, by 1930, when Kramp was writing, instituted a way of praying that corrected the theology of the Eucharist.

The sober formulations of systematic theology could not have been openly disparaged by the liturgical movement, but the leading lights of the liturgical movement could observe that systematics had ossified. The standard theology had become insufficiently bracing for progressive liturgical thinkers and for the laity. As H. A. Reinhold wrote, "For hundreds of years we have lived in a self-imposed narrow patch of apologetic theology, watered by a thin trickle coming down to us from the dammed-up lake of individual mysticism, while the distant roar of the pure waters of sacramental, communal, and ecclesial mysticism seemed only to be heard by the saints."[12] Joseph Kramp, bridging the Eucharistic and liturgical movements, attempted to articulate a more inclusive and balanced theology of the Eucharist than that available from the strictly systematic theologians.[13] His methodology was integrally related to the liturgical reforms he proposed.

Through his ideals Kramp exemplified a method of advancing systematic Eucharistic theology beyond the apologetic—he self-consciously sought an accommodation, even a synthesis, of Thomistic and practically liturgical theology. His preface to *Eucharistia* expressed the hope that the book might "serve to point out the way to those others who are interested in present eucharistic questions and who recognize the necessity of uniting the eucharistic and the liturgical."[14] Kramp's influence among members of the American liturgical movement can be seen in several ways. Father William Busch (d. 1971) translated Kramp into English from German; Father Virgil Michel acknowledged his debt to Kramp; Michael Mathis, CSC (d. 1960), owned a copy of *Eucharistia*.[15] Kramp was well-reviewed in the journals of the Eucharistic movement, too. His preeminent interest in doing theology was the liturgy, and he applied a rich notion of *lex credendi* to keen insights about the *lex orandi*. Finally and advantageously, Kramp also addressed at some length the topic that has been the lens for inspecting the relationship between the liturgical movement and the Eucharistic movements—namely, whether Communion could continue to be administered disjunctively from the action of the Mass, and even apart from the Mass, or whether Communion should be received integrally in the Mass, "with" the priest.

The French liturgical scholar Bernard Botte (b. 1893) reminisced about how Communion had been distributed in his youth.

> As for communion, it was distributed before Mass, after Mass, or in the middle of Mass, but never at the moment indicated by the liturgy. The schedule was the determining factor: communion was distributed every fifteen minutes. When Mass began on the hour you were sure to see, as the clock struck a quarter past, a priest in a surplice come out of the sacristy, rush to the altar, and interrupt the celebrant in order to take a ciborium out of the tabernacle.[16]

This perduring issue had been resurrected within the history of the Eucharistic movement in van Caloen's speech during the Eucharistic Congress at Liège in 1883, and Lintelo and Beauduin sparred about it a generation after van Caloen.[17]

Kramp, writing nearly twenty years thereafter, formulated the topic in terms of the *reintegration* of Communion into the Mass. The question was the same, nonetheless, for all three generations, "What precisely should be the time and place for the distribution of Holy Communion?"[18] The texts themselves of the liturgy safeguarded against distortion into idiosyncratic or dangerous devotional practices.[19]

The Church and her liturgy tenaciously maintain the original sequence regarding the importance of the various phases of the Eucharist: sacrifice, sacrament, presence. The Sacrament must fit into and subordinate itself to the Sacrifice; and to the presence of Christ the homage is paid for which Sacrifice and Sacrament in the framework of the Divine Office leave room.[20]

This line of thought seems a particular application of the principles articulated by Romano Guardini.

This scholarly priest proposed that two spheres of prayer were proper and advantageous so long as they retained their correct relationship. Liturgical prayer was to be normative because it was public and official and hence theologically comprehensive. The supplement to liturgical prayer was private and devotional prayer, an arena in which the emotions were given play.[21] Liturgical prayer, to be dogmatically comprehensive, needed to be based upon thought rather than emotion:

In the end, therefore, prayer in common will be fruitful only in so far as it does not concentrate markedly, or at any rate exclusively, on particular portions of revealed truth, but embraces, as far as possible, the whole of Divine teaching. This is especially important where the people are concerned, because they easily tend to develop a partiality for particular mysteries of faith which for some reason have become dear to them.[22]

This postulation of a balance between modes of prayer could be proved or disproved by the experiences of worship and prayer consequent to the Second Vatican Council. In its own context, Guardini's point seems to have been to weaken opposition to the liturgical movement. Those who had invested in particular and vibrant and even lucrative devotions perceived these new, strictly liturgical notions as menaces.

Kramp summarized Guardini's principle succinctly. "The Church has in her liturgy a most logical and detailed conception and attitude, in which only at set periods account is taken of the popular Eucharistic piety of the faithful but without ever compromising her basic position in the least."[23] Both Kramp and Guardini agreed that the dynamic development of liturgy through the centuries had allowed for the absorption of popular devotions. But receiving Communion outside of Mass was a liturgical aberration against which Kramp complained. Note that Kramp diplomatically blamed only a popular mentality, even though some leaders of the Eucharistic movement would feel the sting of Kramp's irritation.

No connection between the Mass and Communion is recognized other than that the Mass affords the opportunity to communicate. But one can communicate at all times; it is possible even by an act of the soul, for adoration excels everything and unites everything into one. It is remarkable that the popular opinion obtains that the recitation of the Rosary during a Mass has more value than outside of Mass; while Communion is rather received before Mass than during it.[24]

Devotional Communion, or Communion-on-demand, was really an opposite of liturgical Communion, and it cohered, according to Kramp, with two of the interrelated deficiencies of, on the one hand, a fundamental distortion of Christology and soteriology, and, on the other, individualism, universally reviled as of a piece with liberalism, rationalism, and modernism.

The first level of theological distortion clearly related to the liturgy. Kramp, regarding the Eucharistic pieties of his day, discerned that devotional Communion and visual Eucharistic devotions reinforced each other. Here, Mass served merely to manufacture the matter containing the Real Presence. The Real Presence was then to be adored very often and received rarely. "Few consider the Mass as a Sacrifice or know how to make use of the Mass texts; the majority see in the Mass only the opportunity for renewing the presence of Christ among men, so that they may greet Him respectfully and receive Him into their souls."[25] The other aspects of the Mass—its sacrificial nature and the meaning of Communion—had become largely invisible to the laity, though they both abide in the normative documents from the Council of Trent.[26] Nothing less than ritual disintegration had occurred: reception of Communion, bracketed by set forms of preparation and thanksgiving, executed in private, occurred at any time.[27] Worship that did not embody the reality of "fellowship" in Christ was, according to Kramp, unworthy and lacking in "liturgical sense."[28]

From this way of praying followed a second and profound theological distortion. Because the faithful individually or even individualistically "received the divine Guest, and in their preparation and thanksgiving stretched the contrasts to the farthest possible limits: God came to man, the Creator to the sinful creature, etc."[29] The "God" who came to man was Christ, the Real Presence in the Eucharist. Because Communion was disjunct from the Mass, it was a static *thing*. Still, as the utterly transcendent God, both Communion and Christ lost their proper and traditionally understood roles in salvation. Really, the reasoning process appears extremely simple:

> Christ is God and is present as God in the Eucharist, and consequently I pay God all the homage which I show Christ. The idea of Christ as the Mediator between God and us is not put into practice. . . . In the present-day Catholic consciousness Christ does not stand on our side, as it were, facing God (as our Mediator): He stands on the side of God opposite to us (and the mediators of our prayer life are the Saints).[30]

Overemphasizing the Real Presence in the Eucharist tended toward robbing Christ of his humanity—of course, this was through ritual practice and thus through the law of praying, not through seismic shifts in theological thought. In his monograph *Eucharistia*, Kramp pursued the consequences of this distancing from and distortion of Jesus. Emphasis upon the Incarnation as a focus of worship reduced the role of the Father. The Church always discouraged this slighting of the Father in prayer. "Worship of God the Father has to a large extent become worship of the eucharistic God-man. This is undoubtedly a somewhat narrow and one-sided devotional attitude."[31] Does it not also challenge the doctrine of the Trinity?

In his day, Kramp found lacking three interrelated elements of the Eucharist. Its sacrificial nature stood unacknowledged by the laity, generally; the nature of the sacrifice required, for efficacy, its appropriation by the individual in Communion; in order to appropriate the sacrifice, the communicant needed to unite with Jesus. Communion as a devotion—that is, as disconnected from the Mass—was not merely a violation of primeval practices. Such Communions jeopardized salvation itself. Kramp expressed this quite hyperbolically: "Communion before Mass taken entirely by itself appears—even if not considered as such theoretically—as worship of self rather than worship of God; the first care is for the *ego* (in the Communion separated from the sacrifice), and then only for God (in the Mass, which is rather attended as a thanksgiving after Communion than actively participated in)."[32] Devotional Communion abetted individualism in its most egregious manifestation, self-idolatry. Kramp analyzed this phenomenon along two lines: First, it was a theological failing; it denied the texts of the liturgy that served to guarantee probity, and it dehumanized Christ and his role as the mediator in salvation. Second, devotional Communion cultivated a psychological flaw.

Properly liturgical Communion would, according to Kramp, combat these consequences. The texts of the liturgy mandated Communion *with* the priest *during* the Mass. This performance of Holy Communion, Kramp maintained, symbolically enacted (i.e., so the communicant would experience) and effected (i.e., the action of Christ in the sacrament) union with Christ and God.[33] "The Church's true attitude is not only: unto Christ!, but rather unto an all-embracing fellowship in Christ, and in and with Christ unto God."[34] Union with Christ, not only symbolically evident but also corroborated by patristic literature and freshened by the nineteenth-century theologians J. A. Möhler, J. B. Franzelin, and M. J. Scheeben, would destroy individualism, for this union would establish a Mystical Body.[35] In so doing, proper Communion would restore the social fabric so shredded by the revolutions of the nineteenth century. It is important to recall that this social program was the impetus for both the Eucharistic and liturgical movements. Kramp summarized the Mystical (and sacramental) Body of the Redeemer in this way: "Christ does not live only as a person, but also as the Church, as a unitary organism. . . . Christ lives in the Eucharist and so there is no more appropriate expression for our union with Him and with one another than the communion of the Eucharist."[36]

Besides addressing the malign individualism both of the industrialized age and of sacramental custom, properly liturgical Communion would defuse the problem of routinization that was only occasionally and proleptically mentioned in the propaganda for frequent Communion. Of course, Kramp did not challenge the papally sanctioned campaigns, but he did imply that frequent and daily Communion-on-demand would lead to a dulling of religious zeal.

Those who, like Lintelo, had wanted Communion at any and all hours were Kramp's obvious target. Perhaps Kramp was seeking to cast the liturgical movement as a corrective to the campaign for frequent Communion, itself a major part of the Eucharistic movement. Was integrating Communion into the Mass tantamount to allowing the Mass itself to become the proximate preparation for communicating? Recall that Godts and his partisans had wanted to guarantee the dignity of Holy Communion by keeping it rare or, more accurately, by letting it become frequent only if the traditional preparations for it were strictly observed. Godts had not only feared sacrilegious Communions but also, and more to the point of his debate with Lintelo, casual Communions, as casual Communions would erode the doctrine of the Real Presence.

Kramp poetically expressed how liturgically correct and integral Communion would prevent this erosion of the doctrine of the Real Presence. Frequent Communion "in its proper setting can in nowise lead to a dulling of the religious life because it is entwined in an active unity, that reflects the highest and profoundest life in God and for God."[37] Because Communion should be recognizable as profoundly social, its integration into the action of the Mass would reveal and enact its social nature. Holy Communion would connect the communicant to Jesus and to salvation in him, as well as to other believers—that is, to the Church, the Mystical Body of Jesus. "Thus Communion is the way and life in Christ to the Father; it is food and drink for our organic supernatural life as children of God; in short, it is the bond of union with God, with Christ, with all members it is common fellowship in origin, essence, and effect."[38] Union with Christ in liturgical Communion would prevent the complacency of "frequent, even daily" Communion. Complacency was, in a simple model used by Godts, exactly that element of daily Communion that would have most threatened the Real Presence.

Although Kramp did not explicitly mention the form and shape of other liturgical modifications that aimed at combating individualism, it seems that vocal participation in the text of the Mass, as in the *missa recitativa*, was one. Kramp alluded to elements of worship that enacted a community idea and that were opposed by the old-fashioned devotees of individualistic prayer during Mass. Note that the very idea of the Mystical Body implied changes in the way Mass was celebrated. Kramp observed that "many [communicants] look upon the community idea as burdensome and annoying, because it prevents the undisturbed following of one's purely personal impulses to adoration."[39] To eschew individualism, to enter into community, to connect with the officiating priest and with the action of the Mass and with the church at prayer and ultimately, with Jesus in the Eucharist would drive the individualistically and falsely pious faithful into "the quiet corners of the church."[40]

In addition to bridging the Eucharistic and liturgical movements, Joseph Kramp benefited from a tide of more and more use of Communion by the laity in his formulating a practical liturgical theology of Communion and, by extension from that, the Eucharist. In addition to this tide, sacramental theology coordinated with increasing use of Communion prepared the way for Kramp with its own explorations of the act of Communion and the meaning of sacrifice. He was able, therefore, to take for granted the Real Presence and to emphasize Communion and sacrifice, the two other pillars of Eucharistic theology from Trent.

One intentional thrust of the Eucharistic movement was to combat individualism; frequent Communion resulted from the movement. The campaigns for frequent Communion revivified the ancient notion that the fruit of Communion was union with Christ, and the success of the campaigns permitted each communicant the experience of this union, sacramentally. This union found beautifully compelling and communal expression in the Pauline image of the Body of Christ. In other words, the sacramental Real Presence (Body of Christ) overlapped with the Mystical Body. These two metaphors reveal a thrust against individualism in two vital movements of the Church in the early twentieth century. Kramp's writings not only anticipate the fuller articulation of the theology of the Body of Christ by Pius XII in *Mystici Corporis* (29 June 1943), but they also provide a ritually based impetus toward the ecclesial reception of the encyclical. This impetus is liturgical Communion. Virgil Michel's notes for a laymen's retreat at Saint John's in 1937 embody this sentiment while reflecting on the utter inadequacy of fifteen minutes for the individualistic thanksgiving after Communion. He says that the true meaning of thanksgiving is "not for 15 minutes, but for a whole day, a week. Hence real thanks more than a prayer. Christ's strength for living out continually."[41]

# NOTES

1. Gerald A. McCool, *Catholic Theology in the Nineteenth Century: The Quest for a Unitary Method* (New York: Crossroad / Seabury, 1977), 228–34.

2. Kramp, "Religio-Psychological Attitude," 514.

3. Mitchell, *Cult and Controversy*, 345.

4. Schwertner, *Eucharistic Renaissance*, 12ff.

5. Both *STS* (article 14) and *QMM* (article 93) require that they each be read aloud in the vernacular annually within all religious houses.

6. Schwertner, *Eucharistic Renaissance*, 15.

7. Schwertner, *Eucharistic Renaissance*, 86.

8. Schwertner, *Eucharistic Renaissance*, 89.

9. "There was a special warmth in the third part of this sermon [by Bishop Billiere of Tarbes] which was fanned into a living flame in the three sermons delivered by Father Coubé on weekly, and, if possible, daily Communion." Schwertner, *Eucharistic Renaissance*, 134.

10. Jean-Baptiste Berthier, *A Compendium of Theology*, 4 volumes, translated by Sydney A. Raemers (Saint Louis: Herder, 1931), 2: 74.

11. Kramp, "Religio-Psychological Attitude," 514.

12. Reinhold, *Dynamics of Liturgy*, 34.

13. Kramp quoted Guardini's *The Spirit of the Liturgy* with respect to this coalescing of the two movements. "The eucharistic movement will not yield the fulness of its blessing until it is merged with the liturgical movement." Joseph Kramp, *Eucharistia*, translated by William Busch, foreword by Austin Dowling (Saint Paul: E. M. Lohmann, 1929), 103.

14. Kramp, *Eucharistia*, 14.

15. In the foreword to *My Sacrifice and Yours*, Michel admits that his pamphlet derives from sermons he gave in New York City in the summer of 1926. He continues, "Anyone seeking a more detailed explanation of the subject here treated, can profitably refer to two books that have recently appeared in this country: Kramp-Miller, *The Sacrifice of the New Law* (Herder Co.), and Kramp-Busch, *Eucharistia* (Lohmann Co.)." Virgil Michel, *My Sacrifice and Yours*, Popular Liturgical Library, series 1, no. 3 (Collegeville, Minnesota: Liturgical Press, 1927), iii.

16. Bernard Botte, *From Silence to Participation: An Insider's View of Liturgical Renewal*, translated by John Sullivan (Washington: Pastoral Press, 1988), 2–3, cited in Frank C. Senn, *The Stewardship of the Mysteries* (New York: Paulist Press, 1999), 128–29.

17. Frank Senn asserts, without documentation, that Communion was being received in the proper liturgical moment by 1915. Senn, *Stewardship of the Mysteries*, 129.

18. In a position paper in 1943, Bishop Gröber of Freiburg, Germany, complained about several issues advocated by liturgical reformers, including the reception of Holy Communion during the Mass. According to Anthony Ruff, Gröber's objection was simple: such led to an "unnecessary lengthening of the service." Anthony Ruff,

*Sacred Music and Liturgical Reform: Treasures and Transformations* (Chicago: Hillenbrand, 2007), 239.

19. Guardini explained that this surety within the liturgy comes from its refinement through time and through the community of the Church. Romano Guardini, *The Spirit of the Liturgy*, trans. Ada Lane (New York: Sheed and Ward, 1953), 120ff.

20. Kramp, "Religio-Psychological Attitude," 521.

21. Guardini, *Spirit of the Liturgy*, 123.

22. Guardini, *Spirit of the Liturgy*, 128.

23. Kramp, "Religio-Psychological Attitude," 518.

24. Kramp, "Religio-Psychological Attitude," 516.

25. Kramp, "Religio-Psychological Attitude," 515.

26. Kramp perceived that this practice followed from undue emphasis upon the Real Presence during the Counter-Reformation. In other words, the emphases of Trent would have been ritually reflected in very few Communions and much visual piety. Kramp, "Religio-Psychological Attitude," 514–15.

27. Kramp, "Religio-Psychological Attitude," 517.

28. Kramp, "Religio-Psychological Attitude," 520–21.

29. Kramp, "Religio-Psychological Attitude," 516.

30. Kramp, "Religio-Psychological Attitude," 517.

31. Kramp, *Eucharistia*, 15.

32. Kramp, "Religio-Psychological Attitude," 519.

33. Such a notion is not new. Its harbingers in the nineteenth century include Pius IX, who in *Nostis et Nobiscum–Fontes* (5 December 1849) "stressed the unifying power of Holy Communion. He called the Eucharist the symbol of that single body of which Christ is the head, to which he wished men, as members, to be united with a most intimate union of faith, hope, and charity." Stadler, *Historical Synopsis and Commentary*, 34.

34. Kramp, "Religio-Psychological Attitude," 520.

35. Kenneth R. Himes, "Eucharist and Justice: Assessing the Legacy of Virgil Michel," *Worship* (May 1988): 201.

36. Kramp, "Religio-Psychological Attitude," 519. The concept of the Mystical Body of Christ dates, of course, to the Pauline corpus, and Kramp observed, "We all believe in the vivifying presence of Christ in His Church, which has been called His mystical body." Kramp, "Religio-Psychological Attitude," 514. "The connections between Paul's ecclesiological metaphor *par excellence* and sacramental reception of the body of Christ may merit a detailed scholarly treatment. Certainly both the theological re-emergence of the Mystical Body and its practice in frequent Communion occurred synchronously. At the root of the [liturgical] movement was an appreciation of the Church as the Mystical Body of Christ, a notion long obscured, and especially so since the days of anti-Protestant polemics. Today, the term 'Mystical Body of Christ' is a household word among American Catholics, but this was not always so. A survey and complete bibliography of thought on the Mystical Body for the years 1890–1940, showed only eight articles in the more important English, Irish, and American periodicals before 1926 when *Orate Fratres* was founded. Rodger van Allen, *The Commonweal and American Catholicism* (Philadelphia: Fortress Press,

1974), 81; Paul B. Marx, *Virgil Michel and the Liturgical Movement* (Collegeville, Minnesota: Liturgical Press, 1957), 82ff.

37. Kramp, "Religio-Psychological Attitude," 520.

38. Kramp, "Religio-Psychological Attitude," 519; Pope Leo XIII cited both Cyprian and Augustine along the lines of the unifying power of Communion, and then cited, similarly, the Council of Trent. *MC*, 504.

39. Kramp, "Religio-Psychological Attitude," 517.

40. Kramp, "Religio-Psychological Attitude," 517.

41. Virgil Michel, typewritten document for laymen's retreat, 1937, 6, Virgil George Michel, 1890–1938, Papers, 1923–1938, SJA Manuscript Collection (Z 22-36), Saint John's Abbey Archives, Collegeville, Minnesota.

# Bibliography

## PRIMARY SOURCES

### Published Materials

### Catholic Church

Council of Trent. *Canons and Decrees of the Council of Trent: Original Text with English Translation.* Translated by H. J. Schroeder. Saint Louis: B. Herder, 1941.

Pope Leo XIII. *Mirae Caritatis. Acta Sanctae Sedis* 34 (1902, pages 641–54). In *The Papal Encyclicals: 1878–1903*, edited by Claudia Carlen, 499–507. Raleigh, North Carolina: Consortium / McGrath, 1981.

Pope Pius XII. *Christus Dominus. Acta Apostolicae Sanctae* 45 (1953, pages 15–24). In *The Apostolic Constitution "Christus Dominus": Text, Translation, and Commentary, with Short Annotations on the Motu Proprio "Sacram Communionem,"* translated by John Ford, edited by James Ruddy, 390. Catholic University of America Canon Law Studies, no. 390. Washington, D.C.: Catholic University Press, 1957.

———. *Mediator Dei. Acta Apostolicae Sanctae* 39 (1947, pages 521–95). In *The Papal Encyclicals: 1939–1958*, edited by Claudia Carlen. Raleigh, North Carolina: Consortium / McGrath, 1981.

———. *Mystici Corporis Christi. Acta Apostolicae Sanctae* 35 (1943, pages 193–248). In *The Papal Encyclicals: 1939–1958*, edited by Claudia Carlen, 37–63. Raleigh, North Carolina: Consortium / McGrath, 1981.

———. *Sacram Communionem. Acta Apostolicae Sanctae* 49 (1957, pages 177–78). In *The Apostolic Constitution "Christus Dominus": Text, Translation, and Commentary, with Short Annotations on the Motu Proprio "Sacram Communionem,"* translated by John Ford, edited by James Ruddy. Catholic University of America Canon Law Studies, no. 390. Washington, D.C.: Catholic University Press, 1957.

Sacred Congregation of Bishops and Regulars. *Quemadmodum. Acta Sanctae Sedis* 23 (pages 505–8). In *The Decree "Quemadmodum," with Explanations*, translated by A. Sabetti. Baltimore: John Murphy, 1892. Reprint in Dacian Dee, *The Manifestation of Conscience*, 91–93. Catholic University of America Canon Law Studies, no. 410. Washington, D.C.: Catholic University Press, 1960.

Sacred Congregation of Indulgences. "Yearly Triduum of Prayer for the Purpose of Promoting Frequent Communion." In *The Eucharistic Triduum: An Aid to Priests in Preaching Frequent and Daily Communion According to the Decrees of H.H. Pius X*, by Jules Lintelo, translated by F. M. de Zulueta, 16–19. London: R. & T. Washbourne, 1909.

Sacred Congregation of the Council. *Cum Ad Aures*. In *The Decree on Daily Communion: A Historical Sketch and Commentary*, by Juan Bautista Ferreres, translated by H. Jimenez, 154–59. London: Sands, 1909.

———. *Sacra Tridentina Synodus*. *Acta Sanctae Sedis* 38 (1905, pages 400–6). In *The New Liturgy: A Documentation, 1903–1965*, edited by R. Kevin Seasoltz, 11–15. New York: Herder & Herder, 1966.

Sacred Congregation of the Sacraments. *Quam Singulari*. *Acta Apostolicae Sedis* 2 (1910, pages 577–83). In *The New Liturgy: A Documentation, 1903–1965*, edited by R. Kevin Seasoltz, 17–22. New York: Herder & Herder, 1966.

Second Provincial Council of Baltimore. "Pastoral Letter, Issued by the Second Provincial Council of Baltimore, October 27, 1833." In *The Pastoral Letters of the United States Catholic Bishops*, edited by Hugh J. Nolan, 67–81. Washington, D.C.: National Conference of Catholic Bishops / United States Catholic Conference, 1983.

Second Vatican Council. *The Documents of Vatican II*. Edited by Walter M. Abbott and Joseph Gallagher. Introduction by Lawrence Shehan. New York: Guild Press / America Press Association, 1966.

United States Conference of Catholic Bishops. "Happy Are Those Who Are Called to His Supper." Washington: USCCB, 2006.

## François-Xavier Godts

*L'apôtre moderne du T.S. Sacrement: S. Alphonse, docteur de l'église*. Bruxelles: Larose, 1905.

*Deuxième réponse au R. P. Lintelo*. Bruxelles: Albert Dewit, 1905.

*Exagérations historiques et théologiques concernant la Communion quotidienne*. Roulers: Jules de Meester, 1904.

*Réponse au R. P. Couët*. Bruxelles: Albert Dewit, 1905.

*Réponse aux lettres à un prêtre à propos d'une polémique sur la Communion fréquente par le Père Jules Lintelo de la compagnie de Jésus*. [Bruxelles: Albert De Wit,] 1905.

## Jules Lintelo

*The Eucharistic Triduum: An Aid to Priests in Preaching Frequent and Daily Communion According to the Decrees of H.H. Pius X*. Translated by F. M. de Zulueta. London: R. & T. Washbourne, 1909.

*Lettres à un prêtre à propos d'une polemique sur la Communion fréquente.* Second and revised edition. Tournai: H. & L. Casterman, 1905.

"The Preacher's and Confessor's Influence in Promoting Frequent Communion," *Emmanuel* 13 (1907): 190–97.

"Rapport intimes entre la Communion fréquente et la vie liturgique: deux aspects du mouvement eucharistique." *Cours et conférence deux semaines liturgiques,* 2:263–71. Louvain: Mont César, 1914.

## Individual Works

Antoni, Stefano. *Why Do So Many Vain Fears Keep You from Frequent and Daily Communion?* New York: Sentinel, 1923.

Bastien, Petrus [Pierre]. *De frequenti quotidianaque communione ad normam decreti "Sacra tridentina synodus."* Rome: Desclée, Lefebvre et Socii, 1907.

Baudier, Roger, Sr., and Millard F. Everett. *Anchor and Fleur-de-Lis: Knights of Columbus in Louisiana, 1902–1962.* New Orleans: Louisiana State Council, Knights of Columbus, 1965.

Brother Julien [George A. Ryan]. "Devotion and Devotions." *Catholic Educational Review* 4 (1912): 170.

Clarke, Richard Frederick. "Roman Catholics in America." In *Through Other Eyes: Some Impressions of American Catholicism by Foreign Visitors from 1777 to the Present,* edited by Dan Herr and Joel Wells, 75–88. Westminster, Maryland: Newman, 1965.

Coubé, Stephen. *The Great Supper of God; or Discourses on Weekly Communion.* Translated by Ida Griffiss. Edited by F. X. Brady. New York: Benziger, 1901.

Dalgairns, John Bernard. *The Devotion to the Heart of Jesus with an Introduction on the History of Jansenism.* Philadelphia: H. L. Kilner, 1854.

Donovan, Cornelius Francis. *The Story of the Twenty-Eighth International Eucharistic Congress, Held at Chicago, Illinois, United States of America, from June 20–24, 1926.* Chicago: Eucharistic Congress Committee, 1927.

Durrwell, François-Xavier. *The Resurrection: A Biblical Study.* Translated by Rosemary Sheed. Introduction by Charles Davis. New York: Sheed and Ward, 1960.

Elliot, Walter. "Report of the Transactions of the Meeting." In *Eucharistic Conferences: The Papers Presented at the First American Eucharistic Congress, Washington, D.C., October, 1895,* 180–86. New York: Catholic Book Exchange, 1896.

Ferreres, Juan Bautista. *The Decree on Daily Communion: A Historical Sketch and Commentary.* Translated by H. Jimenez. London: Sands, 1909.

Foley, Jeremiah F. "How to Promote Devotion to the Blessed Sacrament Among the People." In *Eucharistic Conferences: The Papers Presented at the First American Eucharistic Congress, Washington, D.C., October, 1895,* 89–114. New York: Catholic Book Exchange, 1896.

Frassinetti, Giuseppe. *The New Parish Priest's Practical Manual.* Second edition. Translated by William Hutch. New York: Burns and Oates / Catholic Publications Society, 1885.

Gennari, Casimir. "Approbation of the Author's Eucharistic Tracts from His Eminence Cardinal Gennari, on Behalf of His Holiness Pius X." In *The Eucharistic Triduum: An Aid to Priests in Preaching Frequent and Daily Communion According to the Decrees of H.H. Pius X*, by Jules Lintelo. Translated by F. M. de Zulueta. London: R. & T. Washbourne, 1909.

———. "De la Communion fréquente et du décret 'Quemadmodum.'" In *Directoire canonique a l'usage des congrégations a voeux simples*, by Pierre Bastien, 394–421. Translated by Pierre Bastien. Maredsous: Maredsous, 1904.

———. *Consultazioni morali-canonishe-liturgiche su casi e materie svariate che specialmente riguardano i tempi nostri*. 2nd edition. Rome: Monitore Ecclesiastico, 1902.

———. "Rescript on the Prayer for the Pious Custom of Daily Communion," *Emmanuel* 11 (1905): 205.

Guardini, Romano. *The Spirit of the Liturgy*. Translated by Ada Lane. New York: Sheed and Ward, 1953.

Keller, Joseph. *The Sacred Heart: Anecdotes and Examples to Assist in Promoting the Devotion to the Sacred Heart*. New York: Benziger, 1899.

Kramp, Joseph. *Eucharistia*. Translated by William Busch. Foreword by Austin Dowling. Saint Paul: E. M. Lohmann, 1929.

———. "A Religio-Psychological Attitude toward the Eucharist." *Orate Fratres* 4 (1930): 514–21.

———. "Why Frequent Communion Is Declining." *Fortnightly Review* 29 (1922): 381.

Liguori, Alphonsus de. *Theologia moralis: editio nova*. Edited by Leonard Gaudé. Graz, Austria: Akademische Druck-U. Verlagsanstalt, 1954.

———. *Visits to the Blessed Sacrament and to the Blessed Virgin*. In *The Holy Eucharist*, vol. 4 of *The Complete Works of Saint Alphonsus de Liguori, Doctor of the Church . . . Holy Redeemer*, edited by Eugene Grimm. Brooklyn: Redemptorist Fathers, n.d.; third revised reprint, 1934.

Loyola, Mary [Elizabeth Giles]. *Welcome: Holy Communion, Before and After*. Edited by Herbert Thurston. London: Burns, Oates & Washbourne, 1948.

Michel, Virgil. *My Sacrifice and Yours*. Popular Liturgical Library, series 1, no. 3. Collegeville, Minnesota: Liturgical Press, 1927.

———. "Frequent Communion and Social Regeneration." *Orate Fratres* 10, no. 5 (1936): 198–202.

[Parton, James.] "Our Roman Catholic Brethren." *The Atlantic Monthly* 21, no. 126 (1868): 433, 434, 436.

Reinhold, Hans Anscar. *The Dynamics of Liturgy*. Foreword by Edward G. Murray. New York: Macmillan, 1961.

———. "Frequent Communion, Accessible and Integrated." In *St. Pius X and Social Worship, 1903–1953*, 65–71. Elsberry, Missouri: Liturgical Conference, 1953.

Respighi, Pietro. "Instruction Given to the Members of the Priests' Eucharistic League, for the Propagation of the Pious Practice of Daily Communion, and Approved by Pius X." In *The Eucharistic Triduum: An Aid to Priests in Preaching Frequent and Daily Communion According to the Decrees of H.H. Pius X*, 20–26, by Jules Lintelo. Translated by F. M. de Zulueta. London: R. & T. Washbourne, 1909.

Seton, Elizabeth Bayley. *Elizabeth Seton: Selected Writings*. Edited by Ellin Kelly and Annabelle Melville. New York: Paulist, 1987.

Springer, Emil. *Haben wir Priester noch Vorurteile gegen die häufige und tägliche Kommunion der Gläubigen?* Paderborn: Bonifacius, 1910.

Taylor, Thomas N. "The Priests' Communion League for the Promotion of Daily Communion." In *Report of the Nineteenth Eucharistic Congress, Held at Westminster from 9th to 13th September, 1908*, 266–275. London: Sands, 1909.

Tholen, Herman J. *The Knights of Columbus: Their First Fifty Years in Kansas*. N.p.: Kansas State Council, 1950.

Viau, Arthur M. *The Virgin in the Holy Eucharist*. 2 volumes. LaFargeville, New York: n.p., 1946.

Vonier, Anscar. *The Collected Works of Abbot Vonier*. Vol. 1, *The Incarnation and Redemption*. Foreword by Bruno Fehrenbacher. Westminster, Maryland: Newman, n.d.

Zulueta, Francis M. de. "Translator's Preface." In *The Eucharistic Triduum: An Aid to Priests in Preaching Frequent and Daily Communion According to the Decrees of H.H. Pius X*, by Jules Lintelo, vii–xxv. London: R. & T. Washbourne, 1909.

## American Ecclesiastical Review / Ecclesiastical Review

Brinkmeyer, Henry. "The Establishment of a Eucharistic Monthly," n.s. 1, 11, no. 5 (November 1894): 352–54.

Bush, E. A. "Means of Propagating the League," n.s. 1, 11, no. 5 (November 1894): 349–52.

Connolly, James L. "Benediction of the Blessed Sacrament: Its History and Present Status," 85 (November 1931): 449–63.

Heuser, Joseph. "The Holy Father's Wish Regarding Daily Communion," 35 (1906): 60–67.

Maes, Camillus P. "The First Convention of the Eucharistic League in the United States," n.s. 1, 11, no. 5 (November 1894): 338–42.

[Mundwiler], Fintan. "History and Present Status of the Eucharistic League in the United States," n.s. 1, 11 (November, 1894): 329–32.

O'Connor, Patrick. "The Silver Jubilee of Frequent Communion," 83 (December 1930): 561–69.

Vismara, John. "Holy Communion Clubs," 107 (1942): 382–87.

## Columbia

"Here and There," May 1929, 3.

## Emmanuel: Official Monthly of the Priests' Eucharistic League

Note: Unsigned articles are in reverse chronological order.

"In Memoriam—Archbishop Schrembs, National Protector of the Priests' Eucharistic League," 51 (1945): 341–43.

"Fifty Years of Eucharistic Service," 51 (1945): 1–4.

"Editor's Notes," 32 (1926): 278–79.

"History and Present Status of the PEL in the United States," 32 (1926): 245–49.

"The Priests' Eucharistic League—Its Nature and Purpose," 32 (1926): 236.

"Director's Notes and Report: Knights of the Blessed Sacrament," 28 (1922): 185.

"The Third Eucharistic Diocesan Congress of Rome," 27 (1921): 257–65.

"Philadelphia Regional Convention," 26 (1920): 241–46.

"A Retrospect of the Eucharistic Convention," 25 (1919): 410.

"Bishop Maes and the Eucharistic League," 23 (1917): 213–18.

"The Knights of the Blessed Sacrament," 23 (1917): 38–39.

"Subject of Adoration: The Sacred Heart and Eucharistic Reparation," 22 (1916): 97–105.

"Bishop of the Blessed Sacrament," 21 (1915): 442.

"Pious Union for the Communion of Children," 18 (1912): 149–55.

"How to Erect New Centres of the People's Eucharistic League," 17 (1911): 200–8.

"The Priests' Communion League, Read at the Eucharistic Meeting of Metz," 13 (1907): 279–88.

"The Decree on Daily Communion," 12 (1906): 149–52.

"Supplement to the May Number of 'Emmanuel,' . . . Statutes of the Association of the Priests' Eucharistic League," 8 (1902): I–VIII.

"The People's Eucharistic League: Philadelphia Report," 6 (1900): 40–41.

"Second Report of the People's Eucharistic League," 4 (1898): 203–6.

"Maxims of the Ven. Father De la Colombière on Frequent Communion," 4 (1898): 137–39.

"The People's Eucharistic League," 4 (1898): 56–62.

"The Story of the Eucharistic Movement in the United States," 2 (1896): 49–52.

"*Statuta associationis sacerdotum adoratorum seu aggregationis sacerdotalis congregationi ssmi sacramenti a R. P. Eymard institutæ*," 1 (1895): 5–9.


Note: Signed and pseudonymous articles are alphabetized by signature.

Bachman, E. M. "Frequent and Daily Communion, Read Before the Eucharistic Congress of Pittsburgh, October 15, 1907," 14 (1908): 1–11.

Bregenzer, Peter M. "The Devotion to the Eucharistic Heart," 29 (1923): 161–68.

Cassilly, Francis J. "The Frequent Communion Guild," 18 (1912): 43–48.

Curran, Charles F. "Sermon Plans for the Weekly Adoration Hour," 43 (1937): 246–50.

French, James. "The Hours' Adoration," 15 (1909): 1–10.

Fuhr, Raphael. "The Holy Eucharist and Sacred Music," 27 (1921): 353–65.

Gerold, Joseph V. "The Third Annual Convention of the Diocese of Pittsburg [*sic*]," 12 (1906): 154–57.

Kienberger, Vincent Ferrer. "The Sacred Heart and the Holy Eucharist," 29 (1923): 175–79.

——. "The Holy Hour," 24 (1918): 394–99.

Kirlin, Joseph L. J. "The Priests' Eucharistic League—Its Nature and Purpose," 32 (1926): 235–39.

Lavelle, M. J., and Eliza O'Brien Lummis. "The People's Eucharistic League," 6 (1900): 34–40.

Lemieux, Hector. "Life or Death," special centenary edition (October 1956): 499–505.

MacCarthy, Joseph. "Is Frequent Communion Necessary for Salvation?" 21 (1915): 418–25.

Maes, Camillus. "*Salvete, adoratores*," 1 (1895): 1–3.

Maler, Bede. "The Jubilee-Convention of the Priests' Eucharistic League in the US: 1894–1919," 25 (1919): 244–54.

McGean, James H. "Proceedings of the Third Eucharistic Congress under the Auspices of the Most Rev. John M. Farley, D.D., Archbishop of New York," 10 (1904): 535–53.

McN, J. A. "A Plea for Daily Communion," 15 (1909): 86–93.

Nawn, John Henry. "The People's Eucharistic League," 31 (1925): 42–48.

Newell, J. R. "Need of the Holy Name Society," 24 (1918): 41–49.

O'B. "A Eucharistic Rosary," 2 (1896): 217–20.

O'Brien, Thomas. "Eucharistic Confraternities and the People's Eucharistic League," 11 (1905): 125–35.

O.S.B. "Organization of the Eucharistic Movement: A Proposition Submitted to the Eucharistic Convention of Philadelphia, 1899," 5 (1899): 220–25.

Pardow, William O'Brien. "The Relation of Devotion to the Sacred Heart and to the Blessed Sacrament," 12 (1906): 125–41.

Poirier, Emile. "The Jubilee of Our Right Reverend Protector," 16 (1910): 161–63.

Poletti, Carlo M. "Eucharistic Congress of the Priests' Eucharistic League in Rome," 19 (1913): 84–85.

Purcell, F. A. "Frequent Communion in Parishes," 30 (1924): 302–6.

Roland, Abbé. "The Heart of Jesus in the Eucharist," 13 (1907): 144–53.

Sacerdos. "Frequent Communion," 25 (1919): 164–74.

Schlathoelter, L. F. "Frequent Communion is Necessary for Salvation," 21 (1915): 369–74.

Schwertner, Thomas. "The Eucharistic Congress and the Holy Name Society," 32 (1926): 110–16.

Sellinger, Joseph. "The Relation of the Sacred Heart of Jesus to the Blessed Sacrament," 27 (1921): 266–68.

Tesnière, Albert. "Communion in the Life of Jesus Christ," 24 (1918): 220–29.

———. "Commentary on the Rescript [on the Prayer for the Pious Custom of Daily Communion]," 11 (1905): 204–7.

———. "Commentary on the Prayer for the Spread of Daily Communion," 11 (1905): 199–202.

V.F.K. "A Retrospect of the Eucharistic Convention [at Notre Dame, Indiana]," 25 (1919): 401–11.

Vincent. "Eucharistic Mission," 5 (1899): 97–103.

### Fortnightly Review

Burnett, Sarah C. "A Timely Pamphlet on Daily Communion," 22 (1915): 558–62.
Kramp, Joseph. "Why Frequent Communion Is Declining," 29 (1922): 381–83, 399–401.

### Month

Thurston, Herbert. "Our Popular Devotions II: The Rosary," 96 (October 1900): 403.

### The Queen's Work

Brady, Elizabeth. "The Guard of Honor," 4, no. 3 (1916): 121–28.
Dineen, F. George. "Frequent Communion Promoted by Organization," 6, no. 3 (1917): 120–23.
——. "Multiplying Organizations," 7, no. 1 (1917): 30.

### Sentinel of the Blessed Sacrament

Note: Unsigned articles are in reverse chronological order.

"Eucharistic Peace Crusade," 24 (1921): 727–28.
"The Eucharistic Peace Crusade—the Children's Part," 24 (1921): 697–98.
"Wanted—You!" 24 (1921): 573–75.
"International Gregorian Congress," 23 (1920): 332–33.
"The League of Little Communicants: to Christian Educators," 20 (1917): 96–98.
"The Association of the Knights of the Blessed Sacrament," 20 (1917): 73–74.
"General Index," 20 (1917): 3.
"Archconfraternity of the Blessed Sacrament, or the People's Eucharistic League," 19 (1916): 499–502.
"A Practical Suggestion for Sodalities," 19 (1916): 496–97.
"Archconfraternity of the Blessed Sacrament, or the People's Eucharistic League," 19 (1916): 425–30.
"In Memoriam [Miss Eliza O'Brien Lummis]," 19 (1916): 150.
"Saint Pascal's Rosary of the Blessed Sacrament," 14 (1911): 516.
"October Thoughts about the Rosary," 14 (1911): 3.
"Spiritual Communion," 14 (1911): 74–75.

Note: Signed and pseudonymous articles are alphabetized by signature.

A.J.V. [*sic*]. "Archconfraternity of the Blessed Sacrament, or People's Eucharistic League: What It Is and How to Join It," 24 (1921): 369–72.
Chauvin, A. Joseph. "Subject of Adoration: The Liturgy of the Mass—Its Ceremonies," 21 (1918): 171–74, 244–47.
——. "Subject of Adoration: The Liturgy of the Mass—The Prayers," 21 (1918): 58–61, 113–17.

Donovan, Lois. "Communion," 19 (1916): 423.

Gillin, Anna M. "Dispositions for a Worthy Communion," 19 (1916): 447–54.

Poirier, Emile. "Eucharistic Periodicals and Publications," 21 (1918): 461–64.

Tesnière, Albert. "Commentary on the Decree of the Sacred Congregation of the Council, December 20, 1905, On Daily Communion: A Statement," 9 (1906): 259–63.

Warning, Theodore. "The People's Eucharistic League," 14 (1911): 526.


## Tablet

"Communion Breakfast Season," March 1929, 60–61.


## Unpublished Materials

"Cave, III-V: Eucharistic Projects for Men (1851–1856)," Typewritten Document. Blessed Sacrament Fathers' Provincial Archives, Cleveland (Highland Heights), Ohio.

Diekmann, Godfrey. Collegeville, Minnesota, note to the author, Notre Dame, Indiana, 20 May 1995.

Jurcik, Peter. Conversation with the author, La Salle University, Philadelphia, Summer 1995.

Knights of Columbus Supreme Council. Proceedings, 1933, p. 72. Knights of Columbus Supreme Council Archives, New Haven, Connecticut.

Laskin, Richard C. J., to Arthur Riley, 20 September 1953. Autograph card. Knights of Columbus Supreme Council Archives, New Haven, Connecticut.

Maler, Bede (1876–1937). Personal Records and Papers, Box 16, 1894–1903. Priests Eucharistic League–Correspondence, 1894–1903. Press Book 6. Saint Meinrad Archabbey Archives, Saint Meinrad, Indiana.

McCauley, Louis, to Arthur Riley, 5 July 1951. Autograph card. Knights of Columbus Supreme Council Archives, New Haven, Connecticut.

Michel, Virgil George (1890–1938). Papers, 1923–1938. SJA Manuscript Collection (Z 22–36). Saint John's Abbey Archives, Collegeville, Minnesota.

Mooney, Edward. Sermon. Supreme Council Proceedings 1941, p. 149, Knights of Columbus Supreme Council Archives, New Haven, Connecticut.

Newman, M. Demetria (d. 2008). "Some Interesting Memories of Sr. M. Demetria Newman, Regarding A[ltar] B[read]," typewritten document, transcription. Altar Bread / Oral History. Benedictine Sisters of Perpetual Adoration Archives, Clyde, Missouri.

O'Hara, John F. "What is Behind Notre Dame Football?" *Religious Bulletin* (11 October 1930), PNDP 83-Re-1B. University of Notre Dame Archives, Notre Dame, Indiana.

O'Meara, Thomas Franklin. Interview by author, Notre Dame, Indiana, July 1995.

Wagner, Vincent, to Father Petre, 3 June 1897. In Maler, Bede (1876–1937). Personal Records and Papers, Box 16, 1894–1903. Priests Eucharistic League–Correspondence, 1894–1903. Press Book 6. Saint Meinrad Archabbey Archives, Saint Meinrad, Indiana.

## SECONDARY SOURCES

Anglin, Thomas Francis. *The Eucharistic Fast: An Historical Synopsis and Commentary*. Canon Law Studies, no. 124. Washington, D.C.: Catholic University Press, 1941.

Aubert, Roger. "Pius X, a Conservative Reform Pope." In *The Church in the Industrial Age, History of the Church*, edited by Hubert Jedin and John Dolan, vol. 9, 381–93. Translated by Margit Resch. New York: Crossroad, 1981.

Avella, Steven M. "*'Cara America'*: Sources and Images of American Catholic Devotion to St. Pius X." Typewritten manuscript.

Baldovin, John. Review of *The Precommunion Rites*, vol. 5 in *A History of the Liturgy of St. John Chrysostom*, by Robert F. Taft. *Worship* (2002): 287–88.

Barzini, Luigi. *The Italians*. New York: Atheneum, 1964.

Beguiriztáin, Justo. *The Eucharistic Apostolate of St. Ignatius of Loyola*. Translated by John H. Collins. 1955.

Berthier, Jean-Baptiste. *A Compendium of Theology*. 4 volumes. Translated by Sydney A. Raemers. Saint Louis: Herder, 1931.

Bohl, Herbert. *Kommunionempfang der Gläubigen: Probleme seiner Integration in die Eucharistiefeier, eine liturgiewissenschaftliche Untersuchung*. Disputationes Theologicae 9. Frankfurt-am-Main: Peter D. Lang, 1980.

Bradshaw, Paul. "Difficulties in Doing Liturgical Theology." *Pacifica* 11 (1998): 185–92.

———. *The Search for the Origins of Christian Worship*. London: SPCK, 1992.

Browe, Peter. *Die häufige Kommunion in Mittelalter*. Münster: Regensbergsche, 1938.

Callahan, Annice. "The Visions of Margaret Mary Alacoque from a Rahnerian Perspective." In *Modern Christian Spirituality: Methodological and Historical Essays*, edited by Bradley C. Hanson, 183–200. American Academy of Religion Studies in Religion, vol. 62, ed. Lawrence S. Cunningham. Atlanta: Scholars, 1990.

Carroll, Michael P. *Catholic Cults and Devotions: A Psychological Inquiry*. Kingston: McGill-Queen's, 1989.

Chadbourne, Richard M. *Charles-Augustin Sainte-Beuve*. Boston: Twayne, 1977.

Chinnici, Joseph P. "The Eucharist, Symbol of the Church." In *Living Stones: The History and Structure of Catholic Spiritual Life in the United States*, 146–56. The Bicentennial History of the Catholic Church in the United States. New York: Macmillan, 1989.

Connolly, Sean J. *Priests and People in Pre-famine Ireland, 1780–1845*. New York: St. Martin's, 1982.

Corish, Patrick J. *The Irish Catholic Experience: A Historical Survey*. Wilmington, Delaware: Michael Glazier, 1985.

Crichton, J[ames]. D[unlop]. *Lights in Darkness: Forerunners of the Liturgical Movement*. Collegeville, Minnesota: Liturgical Press, 1996.

Curran, Robert Emmett. *American Jesuit Spirituality: The Maryland Tradition, 1634–1900*. New York: Paulist, 1988.

Davidson, James D. "The Catholic Church in the United States: 1950 to the Present." In *The Church Confronts Modernity: Catholicism Since 1950 in the United States, Ireland, and Quebec*, edited by Leslie Woodcock Tentler, 177–207. Washington, D.C.: Catholic University Press, 2007.

Davis, Charles. Introduction to *The Resurrection: A Biblical Study*, by François-Xavier Durrwell, xiii–xx. New York: Sheed and Ward, 1960.

Derély, J. M. "Les décrets eucharistiques du bienheureux Pie X." *Nouvelle revue theologique* 9 (1951): 896–911, 1033–47.

Dinet, Dominique. "Le jansénisme et les origines de la déchritianisation au XVIIIᵉ siècle. L'exemple des pays de l'Yonne." In *Du jansénisme à la laïcité: Le jansénisme et les origines de la déchristianisation*, 1–34. Les entretiens d'Auxerre, edited by Léo Hamon. Paris: Éditions de la maison des sciences de l'homme, 1983.

Dinges, William D. "'An Army of Youth': The Sodality Movement and the Practice of Apostolic Mission." *U.S. Catholic Historian* 19, no. 3 (2001): 35–50.

Dolan, Jay P. *Catholic Revivalism: The American Experience, 1830–1900*. Notre Dame, Indiana: Notre Dame University Press, 1978.

———. *The Immigrant Church: New York's Irish and German Catholics, 1815–1865*. Foreword by Martin E. Marty. Baltimore: Johns Hopkins University Press, 1977. Reprint, Notre Dame, Indiana: Notre Dame University Press, 1983.

Duffy, Eamon. *The Stripping of the Altars: Traditional Religion in England, c. 1400–c. 1580*. New Haven: Yale University Press, 1992.

Dumoutet, Édouard. *Le désir de voir l'hostie et les origines de la dévotion au Saint-Sacrement*. Paris: Gabriel Beauchesne, 1926.

Ellis, John Tracy. *American Catholicism*. Second revised edition. Chicago: University of Chicago Press, 1969.

Favazza, Joseph. "Forum: The Fragile Future of Reconciliation." *Worship* 71, no. 3 (1997): 236–44.

Fernessole, Pierre. *Pie X: Essai historique*. Paris: P. Lethielleux, 1953.

Foley, Edward. *From Age to Age: How Christians Have Celebrated Eucharist*. Chicago: Liturgy Training Publications, 1991.

Gaupin, Linda Lee. "First Eucharist and the Shape of Catechesis Since 'Quam Singulari.'" PhD dissertation, Catholic University, Washington, D.C., 1985.

Gibson, Ralph. *A Social History of French Catholicism, 1789–1914*. New York: Routledge, 1989.

Gill, H. V. "Spiritual Communion." *Irish Monthly* 71 (December 1943): 514–19.

Gleason, Philip. *Contending With Modernity: Catholic Higher Education in the Twentieth Century*. New York: Oxford University Press, 1995.

Gleason, Elizabeth G. Review of *The Lateran in 1600: Christian Concord in Counter-Reformation Rome*, by Jack Freiberg. *Church History* 66 (1997): 199.

Haliczer, Stephen. *Sexuality in the Confessional: A Sacrament Profaned*. Studies in the History of Sexuality. New York: Oxford, 1996.

Hamon, Léo. "Avant-propos." In *Du jansénisme à la laïcité: Le jansénisme et les origines de la déchristianisation*, 5–7. Les entretiens d'Auxerre, edited by Léo Hamon. Paris: Éditions de la maison des sciences de l'homme, 1983.

Haquin, André. "Le mouvement eucharistique et les décrets de S. Pie X." In *Dom Lambert Beauduin et le renouveau liturgique*, 30–60. Recherches et synthèses, section d'histoire 1. Preface by Olivier Rousseau. Gembloux: J. Duculot, 1970.

Hardon, John A. "Historical Antecedents of St. Pius X's Decree on Frequent Communion." *Theological Studies* 16 (December 1955): 493–532.

Hastings, Frances Joanne. "Pope Pius X and Frequent Communion." MA thesis, St. Bonaventure University, St. Bonaventure, New York, 1951.

Himes, Kenneth R. "Eucharist and Justice: Assessing the Legacy of Virgil Michel." *Worship* 62 (May 1988): 201–24.

Hogan, Edmund H. "Jansenism and Frequent Communion—A Consideration of the Bremond Thesis." *Irish Theological Quarterly* 53 (1987): 144–50.

Hughes, [Helen] Kathleen. *The Monk's Tale: A Biography of Godfrey Diekmann, O.S.B.* Introduction by Frederick R. McManus. Collegeville, Minnesota: Liturgical Press, 1991.

Jedin, Hubert. *A History of the Council of Trent.* Translated by Ernest Graf. London: Thomas Nelson, 1957.

Jonas, Raymond. *France and the Cult of the Sacred Heart: An Epic Tale for Modern Times.* Berkeley: University of California Press, 2000.

Jones, Frederick M. *Alphonsus de Liguori: The Saint of Bourbon Naples, 1696–1787.* Westminster, Maryland: Christian Classics, 1992.

Jones, Thomas Patrick. *The Development of the Office of Prefect of Religion at the University of Notre Dame from 1842 to 1952.* Washington, D.C.: Catholic University Press, 1960.

Jungmann, Josef A. "The Overall Historical Picture: The Defeat of Teutonic Arianism and the Revolution in Religious Culture in the Early Middle Ages." In *Pastoral Liturgy*, 1–101. New York: Herder and Herder, 1962.

Kane, Paula M. "'She Offered Herself Up': The Victim Soul and Victim Spirituality in Catholicism," *Church History* 71, no. 1 (2002): 91–97.

Kilmartin, Edward J. *The Eucharist in the Primitive Church.* Englewood Cliffs, New Jersey: Prentice-Hall, 1965.

Kleber, Albert. *History of St. Meinrad Archabbey.* St. Meinrad, Indiana: Grail, 1954.

Knox, Ronald Arbuthnot. *Enthusiasm: A Chapter in the History of Religion, with Special Reference to the XVII and XVIII Centuries.* New York: Galaxy / Oxford, 1961.

Komonchak, Joseph A. "Modernity and the Construction of Roman Catholicism," typewritten document provided to the author in 1996. Published version appeared in *Cristianesimo nella Storia* 18 (1997).

Kossman, E. H. *The Low Countries, 1780–1940.* Oxford History of Modern Europe. Oxford: Clarendon, 1978.

Kurtz, Lester R. *The Politics of Heresy: The Modernist Crisis in Roman Catholicism.* Berkeley: University of California Press, 1986.

Lebrun, Richard. Review of *Jansenism: Catholic Resistance to Authority from the Reformation to the French Revolution,* by William Doyle. *H-Net* and *H-Catholic,* January 2002. http://h-net.org/reviews/showrev.cgi?path=55251012840980.

Lester, Toby. "Oh, Gods!" *Atlantic Monthly* 289, no. 2 (February 2002): 37–45.

Marshall, Donald H. "Frequent and Daily Communion in the Catholic Church of Spain in the Sixteenth and Seventeenth Centuries." PhD diss., Harvard University, 1952.

Marx, Paul B. *Virgil Michel and the Liturgical Movement.* Collegeville, Minnesota: Liturgical Press, 1957.

McAvoy, Thomas Timothy. *Father O'Hara of Notre Dame, the Cardinal Archbishop of Philadelphia.* Notre Dame, Indiana: Notre Dame University Press, 1967.

McCool, Gerald A. *Catholic Theology in the Nineteenth Century: The Quest for a Unitary Method.* New York: Crossroad / Seabury, 1977.

McGrail, Peter. *First Communion: Ritual, Church and Popular Religious Identity.* Hampshire, England: Ashgate, 2007.

McGuinness, Margaret M. "Is It Wrong to Chew the Hosts: Changing Catholic Etiquette and the Eucharist, 1920–1970." *American Catholic Studies* 11 (1999): 29–48.

———. "'Let Us Go to the Altar': American Catholics and the Eucharist, 1926–1976." In *Habits of Devotion: Catholic Religious Practice in Twentieth-Century America,* edited by James M. O'Toole, 187–235. Ithaca, New York: Cornell University Press, 2004.

McManners, John. "Jansenism and Politics in the Eighteenth Century." In *Church, Society, and Politics: Papers Read at the Thirteenth Summer Meeting and the Fourteenth Winter Meeting of the Ecclesiastical History Society,* edited by Derek Baker, 253–273. Studies in Church History 12. Oxford: Basil Blackwell, 1975.

Meulemeester, Maurice de. *Le réverénd père François-Xavier Godts, rédemptoriste.* Louvain: S. Alphonse, 1929.

Mitchell, Nathan. *Cult and Controversy: The Worship of the Eucharist Outside Mass.* New York: Pueblo, 1982.

Moore, R. Laurence. *Selling God: American Religion in the Marketplace of Culture.* New York: Oxford University Press, 1994.

Morris, Charles R. *American Catholic: The Saints and Sinners Who Built America's Most Powerful Church.* New York: Times Books / Random House, 1997.

Nieri, Antonio. "Esperiense e riforme liturgiche." In *Le radici venete di San Pio X,* edited by Silvio Tramontin, 46–71. Brescia: Morcelliana, 1987.

*1924: Pages of Time: A Nostalgia News Report.* Goodlettsville, Tennesee: Interactive, n.d.

Nissen, Peter J. A. "Mobilizing the Catholic Masses through the Eucharist: The Practice of Communion from the Mid-19th Century to the Second Vatican Counsel." Translated by D. Mader. In *Bread of Heaven: Customs and Practices Surrounding Holy Communion,* edited by Charles Caspers, Gerard Lukken, and Gerard Rouwhorst, 145–64. Essays in the History of Liturgy and Culture / Liturgia condenda, 3. Kampen, The Netherlands: Kok Pharos, 1995.

O'Connell, Denis J. *A New Idea in the Life of Father Hecker.* Freiburg im Breisgau: Herder, 1897. Reprinted in Gerald P. Fogarty, *The Vatican and the Americanist Crisis: Denis J. O'Connell, American Agent in Rome, 1885–1903.* Miscellanea Historiae Pontificiae 36. Roma: Università Gregoriana, 1974; page numbers refer to this 1974 edition.

O'Malley, John W. *The First Jesuits.* Cambridge: Harvard University Press, 1993.

Orsi, Robert. *The Madonna of 115th Street: Faith and Community in Italian Harlem, 1880–1950.* New Haven: Yale University Press, 1985.

O'Toole, James. "Empty Confessionals: Where Have All the Sinners Gone?" *Commonweal* 23 (February 2001): 10–12.

——. "In the Court of Conscience: American Catholics and Confession, 1900–1975." In *Habits of Devotion: Catholic Religious Practice in Twentieth-Century America,* edited by James M. O'Toole, 131–86. Ithaca, New York: Cornell University Press, 2004.

Pelletier, Annette M. "Catechesis and Conquest: Communion?" *Worship* 80, no. 6 (2006): 500–11.

Pérouas, L. "La Pastorale liturgique au XVII$^e$ siècle." *Mélanges de science religieuse* 33 (1966): 42.

Pieper, Josef. *In Search of the Sacred: Contributions to an Answer.* Translated by Lothar Krauth. San Francisco: Ignatius, 1991.

Pope, Barbara Corrado. "Immaculate and Powerful: The Marian Revival in the Nineteenth Century." In *Immaculate and Powerful: The Female in Sacred Image and Social Reality,* edited by Clarissa W. Atkinson, Constance H. Buchanan, and Margaret R. Miles, 173–200. Boston: Beacon, 1985.

Quitslund, Sonya A. *Beauduin: A Prophet Vindicated.* New York: Newman, 1973.

Rahner, Karl. "'Behold this Heart!': Preliminaries to a Theology of Devotion to the Sacred Heart." In *Theological Investigations,* vol. 3, *The Theology of the Spiritual Life,* 321–30. Translated by Karl-H. and Boniface Kruger. Baltimore: Helicon, 1967.

——. "The Meaning of Frequent Confession of Devotion." In *Theological Investigations,* vol. 3, *The Theology of the Spiritual Life,* 177–89. Translated by Karl-H. and Boniface Kruger. Baltimore: Helicon, 1967.

——. "Some Theses for a Theology of Devotion to the Sacred Heart." In *Theological Investigations,* vol. 3, *The Theology of the Spiritual Life,* 331–52. Translated by Karl-H. and Boniface Kruger. Baltimore: Helicon, 1967.

Romig, Walter. *The Guide to Catholic Literature.* 8 volumes. Detroit: Walter Romig, 1940–1968.

Rosenbaum, Catherine. "Images-souvenirs de première Communion." In *La Première Communion: Quatre siècles d'histoire,* edited by Jean Delumeau, 133–69. Paris: Desclée de Brouwer, 1987.

Ruff, Anthony. *Sacred Music and Liturgical Reform: Treasures and Transformations.* Chicago: Hillenbrand, 2007.

Scannell, Thomas B. "The History of Daily Communion." In *Report of the Nineteenth Eucharistic Congress, Held at Westminster from 9th to 13th September 1908,* 214–27. London: Sands, 1909.

Schmidt, Joseph F. *Everything Is Grace: The Life and Way of Thérèse of Lisieux.* Ijamsville, Maryland: Word Among Us, 2007.

Schultz, Carrie T. "Do This in Memory of Me: American Catholicism and First Communion Customs in the Era of Quam Singulari." *American Catholic Studies* 115, no. 2 (2004): 45–66.

Schwertner, Thomas M. *The Eucharistic Renaissance, or the International Eucharistic Congresses.* New York: Macmillan, 1926.

Senn, Frank C. "The Frequency of Celebration and Reception of Communion in Protestantism." *Proceedings of the North American Academy of Liturgy* (1990): 98–118.

———. *The People's Work: A Social History of the Liturgy*. Minneapolis: Fortress, 2006.

———. *Stewardship of the Mysteries*. New York: Paulist, 1999.

Severin, Jules. *Vie du Père Lintelo de la compagnie de Jésus, apôtre de la Communion quotidienne, membre du bureau des congrès Eucharistiques*. Bruxelles: Librairie de l'action catholique, 1921.

Slater, Thomas. *A Short History of Moral Theology*. New York: Benziger, 1909.

Stadler, Joseph Nicholas. *Frequent Holy Communion: A Historical Synopsis and Commentary*. Catholic University of American Canon Law Studies, no. 263. Washington, D.C.: Catholic University Press, 1947.

Taft, Robert. "The Frequency of Eucharist throughout History." In *Beyond East and West: Problems in Liturgical Understanding*, 61–80. Washington, D.C.: Pastoral, 1984.

———. "Receiving Communion: A Forgotten Symbol?" In *Beyond East and West: Problems in Liturgical Understanding*, 101–10. Washington, D.C.: Pastoral, 1983.

Taves, Ann. *The Household of Faith: Roman Catholic Devotions in Mid-Nineteenth-Century America*. Notre Dame Studies in American Catholic History. Notre Dame, Indiana: Notre Dame University Press, 1986.

Tentler, Leslie Woodcock. *Seasons of Grace: A History of the Catholic Archdiocese of Detroit*. Foreword by Edmund Cardinal Szoka. Detroit: Wayne State University Press, 1990.

van Allen, Rodger. *The Commonweal and American Catholicism*. Philadelphia: Fortress, 1974.

Willging, Eugene P., and Herta Hatzfeld. *Catholic Serials of the Nineteenth Century in the United States: A Descriptive Bibliography and Union List*. 15 vols. Washington: Catholic University Press, 1968.

Winston-Allen, Anne. *Stories of the Rose: The Making of the Rosary in the Middle Ages*. University Park: Pennsylvania State University Press, 1997.

Wissel, Joseph. *The Redemptorist on the American Missions, The American Catholic Tradition*. Edited by Jay P. Dolan, Paul Messbarger, and Michael Novak. Third revised edition. 1920. Reprint, New York: Arno, 1978.

Woywod, Stanislaus. *The New Canon Law: A Commentary and Summary of the New Code of Canon Law*. Preface by Philip Bernardini. Third edition, revised. New York: Joseph F. Wagner, 1918.

Wright, Wendy M. *Heart Speaks to Heart: The Salesian Tradition*. Traditions of Christian Spirituality. London: Darton, Longman, and Todd, 2004.

## Dictionaries, Directories, and Encyclopedias

*Britannica Online*, 1994–1998.

Escholier, Marc Marie. "Jansen, Cornelius Otto," Encyclopaedia Britannica Online.

*The Catholic Encyclopedia*. New York: Robert Appleton, 1907.
Wynne, John J. "Apostleship of Prayer."

*Dictionnaire de spiritualité, ascétique et mystique, doctrine et histoire*. Paris: G. Beauchesne et ses fils, 1932–1995.
Duhr, Joseph. "Communion fréquente."
Sesboüé, Bernard. "Salut."

*Dictionnaire de théologie catholique*. Paris: Letouzy et Ané, 1929.
Dublanchy, E. "Communion eucharistique (fréquente)."

*Encyclopedia of American Social History*. New York: Scribner, 1993.
Clawson, Mary Ann. "Fraternal Organizations."
Dumenil, Lynn. "The Progressive Era through the 1920s."
McConnell, Stuart. "The Gilded Age."

Muller, Richard A. *Dictionary of Latin and Greek Theological Terms, Drawn Principally from Protestant Scholastic Theology*. Grand Rapids, Michigan: Baker Book House, 1985.

*New Catholic Encyclopedia*. New York: McGraw-Hill, 1967.
Barnes, A. "Duvergier de Hauranne, Jean."
Cognet, L. J. "Jansenism."
Connell, F. J. "Equiprobablism," and "Rigorism."
Herron, J. "Sunday and Holiday Observance."
Ledré, Charles. "Pius X, Pope, Saint."
Lehner, F. C. "Molina, Anthony de."
Matteucci, B. "Jansenistic Piety."
Mayeur, J. M. "Leo XIII."
Sause, B. "Council, Congregation of the."
Sheerin, F. L. "Molina, Luis de."
Sherzer, W. J. "Sunday."
Vereecke, L. "Saint Alphonsus Liguori."

*N. W. Ayer & Son's American Newspaper Annual and Directory*. Philadelphia: N. W. Ayer, 1924.

*Official Catholic Directory for the Year of Our Lord 1922*. New York: P. J. Kenedy, 1922.

Stelten, Leo F. *Dictionary of Ecclesiastical Latin: with an Appendix of Latin Expressions Defined and Clarified*. Peabody, Massachusetts: Hendrickson, 1995.

# About the Author

Brother **Joseph Dougherty**, FSC, teaches in the Department of Religion at La Salle University in Philadelphia, Pennsylvania. He has advanced degrees in English literature (from the University of Virginia) and theology (from Notre Dame University, with specialization in liturgy). He is a member of the American Society of Church History, the Catholic Academy of Liturgy, the College Theology Society, and the North American Academy of Liturgy. He has served on the advisory board of the Philadelphia Liturgical Institute, an ecumenical enterprise that began at the Episcopal Cathedral. He received the habit of the Brothers of the Christian Schools (de la Salle Brothers), an international teaching order of the Catholic Church, in 1982.

Breinigsville, PA USA
08 April 2010
235474BV00002BB/1/P